St. Helena Library
1492 Library Lane
St. Helena, CA 94574
(707) 963-5244

RETIREMENT AND ITS DISCONTENTS

RETIREMENT AND ITS DISCONTENTS

Why We Won't Stop Working, Even If We Can

Michelle Pannor Silver

Columbia University Press
New York

COLUMBIA
UNIVERSITY
PRESS

Columbia University Press gratefully acknowledges the generous support
for this book provided by Publisher's Circle member Stephen Case.

Columbia University Press
Publishers Since 1893
New York   Chichester, West Sussex
cup.columbia.edu
Copyright © 2018 Michelle Pannor Silver

Library of Congress Cataloging-in-Publication Data
Names: Silver, Michelle Pannor, author.
Title: Retirement and its discontents : why we won't stop working,
even if we can / Michelle Pannor Silver.
Description: New York : Columbia University Press, [2018] |
Includes bibliographical references and index.
Identifiers: LCCN 2018000805 (print) | LCCN 2018012239 (e-book) |
ISBN 9780231547925 (e-book) | ISBN 9780231188562
(cloth : acid-free paper)
Subjects: LCSH: Retirement—Social aspects. |
Retirement—Psychological aspects.
Classification: LCC HQ1062 (e-book) |
LCC HQ1062 .S5375 2018 (print) | DDC 306.6/8—dc23
LC record available at https://lccn.loc.gov/2018000805

Columbia University Press books are printed on permanent
and durable acid-free paper.
Printed in the United States of America

Cover design: Lisa Hamm
Cover image: Shutterstock

Retirement

re·tire·ment

ri-ˈtī(ə)rmənt/

noun

1.

the period of one's life after leaving one's job, profession, career, or life's work permanently, usually because of age.

2.

the action or fact of ceasing to play a sport competitively.

3.

a pension or other income on which a retired person lives.

4.

the act of withdrawal of something from service or use (such as removal of military force, according to plan).

5.

seclusion.

Contents

Preface

For many people, retirement is a much-awaited and enjoyable time in life. This book is not about those people. Some people retire because of personal health issues or to attend to caregiving obligations, and some suffer serious health issues shortly after they retire. Other people struggle in retirement because of financial obligations or a lack of retirement savings. This book is also not about those people.

This book is about retirees who struggle with feelings of discontentment in their retirement because their personal and work identities are intertwined. Every retiree I interviewed dealt with one of life's biggest challenges in a different way, depending on many factors, including their expectations about retirement and aging, how they prioritized work throughout their adult lives, how they dealt with earlier transitions in life, and what their work had meant to them. In many cases, the qualities that made them successful in their preretirement work were closely linked to the ways they experienced retirement.

This book is named for Sigmund Freud's *Civilization and Its Discontents*, which focuses on the contrast between an individual's quest for freedom and societal norms that restrict primitive instincts. While *Civilization and Its Discontents* is about a generalizable discontentment that emerges from social norms that limit our possibilities for satisfaction, *Retirement and Its Discontents* is about the ways that the social construct of retirement can stymie potential workforce contributions. The discontentment associated with retirement presented in this book is not a sentiment that can be generalized. Yet we can ask: if even these highly privileged individuals suffered, how can others who also identify closely with their work identity, but who have fewer economic resources, less status, or potential support, be expected to make a seamless transition to retirement? The experiences shared through this book illustrate how retirement can lead to what Émile Durkheim termed "anomie"—a situation whereby relatively no moral guidance is provided. In retirement, some individuals lose their source and sense of identity.

On a personal note, I am not and never have been retired. My journey into studying retirement began when I closed the doors to my father's practice for the last time almost twenty years ago. After struggling with dementia in his late 70s, there came a point at which my father could no longer see patients. As I shredded decades of files, I lamented the loss of a career that had been meaningful to his patients and a core source of my father's identity for more than half a century. He had no retirement party, and to this day, I'm not really sure if he ever completely realized what had transpired. Because of the dementia, my father was unable to fully comprehend his retirement. His emphasis on the importance of work and his retirement inspired my interest in the study of retirement.

For some people, retirement is a boring or sad topic, associated with endings. For me, retirement is a concept that has been an endless source of interest. Retirement is an important transition that stirs up questions about how we set priorities, create structure, and find meaning in life. For many people, retirement is supposed to be the ultimate goal and reward after a lifetime of work. Yet for some, it can be incredibly disappointing, frustrating, intimidating, and even more overwhelming than starting a career.

Shortly after my father's practice closed, I started working on my doctoral dissertation. I developed econometric models of retirement transitions to examine the relationship between pre-retirement occupations and several measures of health outcomes. I became interested along the way in the variation among definitions of *retirement* found across different research studies. Some researchers define being retired as having no working hours after years of paid employment, whereas others allow for the possibility of a partial retirement and others rely on self-reported measures, which may or may not include people who continue to work in some capacity. This led me to ask many questions: How did respondents define retirement? Why did they consider themselves retired? What was being retired like? What were their perceptions of retirement? How did the type of work they did affect the way they experienced retirement?

I secured my first opportunity to examine perceptions about retirement after receiving a grant to study a group of women who self-identified as being "retired." Among this diverse group of women, there was a subset who self-identified as retired homemakers who would defy just about any economist's definition of retirement because many had never worked for pay in their life. I began my journey into researching retirement perceptions with this group of retirees, but they are the last group I discuss in this book. I feature these retirees last because they are the biggest anomaly when compared with any of the other groups of people I interviewed. Unlike the others, these homemakers received no financial compensation and rarely received recognition for their work. Their experiences, however, make a valuable contribution to society and to our understanding of what it means to retire. They also enable us to examine how earlier life opportunities can influence a person's reaction to the potential challenges retirement can pose.

My next opportunity to examine perceptions of retirement came when I was fortuitously connected with the head of a faculty development committee from one of the largest departments of medicine in North America who had been tasked with figuring out how to negotiate the retirement transitions for an important group of doctors. Over the course of several years, I was invited to participate in committee meetings, new-faculty orientations, training sessions, and even retirement parties. Although my initial work was focused on working academic physicians' perceptions about retirement, it fostered connections with the retired doctors who I then interviewed for this book.

One day, while presenting my research on retirement from academic medicine, a gentleman from the audience approached me to ask why I hadn't talked with chief executive officers (CEOs) about their retirement transitions. Admittedly, I first thought the question was odd. In my mind, wealthy senior executives exemplified media portrayals of the happy retiree and I was concerned that he had missed the point of my talk. I was also entirely unsure of how in the world I would locate and convince retired CEOs to agree to an interview. But once he identified himself as a retired CEO and explained how several of the concerns I articulated had resonated with him, I was on my way to developing the study that forms the basis for chapter 3.

I also interviewed professors, a group close to my heart given my own professional interests. In many ways, the retirement experiences and perceptions shared by the professors I interviewed surprised me the most. I likely was so entrenched in trying to establish my career that I had failed to consider what things might be like on the other end of what sometimes feels like a long and dark academic tunnel. For the most part, their experiences contrasted with those of the busy CEOs who were constantly moving up and changing jobs, or the doctors who were dealing with life-and-death situations. Many of the professors, however, held a similar distaste for retirement, and these individuals shed new light on what it means to hold on tightly to our work identity.

Then, the university campus where I work hosted the Pan American Games. These games attracted world-class athletes and coaches, leaving the campus with a vibrant athletic facility that remains among the best in the world. Through various encounters at this athletic facility, I observed some very young people refer to themselves as "retired." I found the world of athletic retirement fascinating and tried to understand how their work as athletes influenced their perceptions of retirement. Learning about how they dealt with the transition dispelled some of my own assumptions about the relationship among the mind, body, and aging.

As more of us spend longer in retirement, in part because of increases in life expectancy that have occurred over the past century, the implications of work and retirement take on greater significance. This book reveals a set of retirement experiences. It emphasizes a fundamental tension between the freedom and autonomy associated with retirement and the need to maintain structure, a sense of social connectedness, and personal fulfillment. These experiences encourage us to examine and question our assumptions about the relationships that exist among work identity, age, and retirement. I hope this book inspires readers to question the social construct of retirement and to create a retirement strategy that avoids some of the discontentment shared through this book.

RETIREMENT AND ITS DISCONTENTS

1

Introduction

Work can be more than a way to earn a living. It can be an intellectual pursuit, a creative outlet, a connection to society, and a central component of who we are. For some people, work is deeply intertwined with personal identity; for others, work is simply a means to an end. Different people have different orientations to work and, similarly, people have different orientations to retirement.

Retirement is both a deeply personal decision and an important social phenomenon. Frequently, retirement indicates that a person has stopped working because he or she has reached a specific age. It is often associated with freedom and leisure. Although retirement is primarily thought of as a time to enjoy life without the burdens of work, some people can feel burdened by a life without work. For these people, retirement can feel deeply constraining and limiting. Retirement's freedom can create challenges for people whose life's work was closely associated with their sense of self-worth.

In *Civilization and Its Discontents*, Sigmund Freud articulated the contrast between an individual's quest for freedom and societal norms that restrict these primitive instincts.[1] He argued that social norms, rules, or laws that state, for instance, that we should not commit adultery or inflict physical harm on others, limit our possibilities for satisfaction and contentment. Yet, as a society, we agree to live within specific boundaries and to follow certain norms to help maintain order.

According to Robert Atchley, retirement is "an event, a process, a role or status, or a phase of life."[2] It is a socially expected phase of life and also is known as an autonomous phase, a time to enjoy the fruits of our labor, with few rules to follow. Thus, retirement is a social construct created through social institutions and social exchanges. It is not an innate or natural occurrence, and in many ways, it is an ambiguous concept. But a fundamental tension exists between the autonomy, flexibility, and lack of boundaries associated with retirement and our instincts to maintain structure, a sense of social connectedness, and personal fulfillment. Retirement has been socially constructed in a way that can give rise to feelings of great discontentment as it stymies some possible paths in favor of others.

In 1966, baby boomers were named *Time* magazine's "Man of the Year." They have redefined social norms at each stage of their lives and, as they approach traditional retirement age, it is no wonder that the meaning, timing, and purpose of retirement also are undergoing significant shifts. Since the oldest baby boomers turned 65 in 2011, around 10,000 people in the United States alone cross over the threshold of traditional retirement age each day.[3] Today, nearly 15 percent of the population in North America and 20 percent of the population in countries such as Japan, Germany, and Italy are over the age of 65.[4] Consider that two centuries ago, less than 2 percent of the population was over 65 years old. The National Institute of Aging estimates that people living in economically developed countries have added approximately three months to their life span for each year that transpired during the past century![5]

This shift necessitates a change not only in the way we think about pension systems but also in our assumptions about age, work, and retirement. For people who are lucky enough to be living in the time and place of the fortunate generation, retirement can be a lifestyle option.[6] But retirement also can be a time of deep uncertainty and a source of discontentment.

This book questions the lure, appeal, and enticement of a generalized retirement that is defined as "no longer working" and asks: What becomes of those whose departure from their life's work means losing a core and fundamental component of their personal identity? What are the repercussions of this burden?

The heart of this book is a series of chapters that feature stories of people who retired from five different types of work: doctors, chief executive officers (CEOs), elite athletes, professors, and homemakers. These individuals shared a loyalty to and passion for their life's work and experienced a sense of discontentment with the reality of retirement. They all faced a range of different life experiences, but each similarly struggled with managing their own expectations that retirement was tied to age and had to be carried out through full withdrawal from the labor force.

The discontentment associated with retirement is not a sentiment that can be generalized. The narratives shared in this book are not meant to explain broad population trends. Financial strain, health problems, and caregiving obligations cause significant hardship for many people in their retirement. This book does not focus on these important challenges, nor does it focus on the many people working in physically demanding jobs or those who are in poor health, for whom retirement cannot come soon enough. Instead, this book focuses on the retirement stories and perceptions about the retirement of people who always found work to be an important source of identity and fulfillment. Then they arrived at an arbitrary point in their lives where they felt obligated, or forced in some cases, to exit the labor force; in other words, they encountered and succumbed to a socially imposed expiration date.

Retirement and Its Discontents is about the larger structural problems that society must grapple with as individuals confront the mismatch between an idealized retirement and the reality of giving up identity, income, and status. The point of sharing these stories is not to say that their experiences are universal. Instead, I share them so that we can learn from their experiences to better understand how to avoid the traps they fall into. I hope that this book inspires readers to consider more deeply what is embedded in the social construct of retirement and to question our ageist assumptions about age, work, and retirement.

I begin this chapter with "A Brief History of Retirement," drawing attention to the fact that widespread retirement at 65 was only tenable when a relatively small proportion of the population lived much beyond this age. Next, I turn to the growing tendency for people to "Work Anytime, Anywhere," particularly those of us in professional roles who feel the omnipresence of our work. This concept highlights the point that for some people, separating work from other aspects of life can be difficult. As more of us approach the traditional retirement age, we experience "The Proliferation of Retirement," bringing us to a point at which retirement is expected, and yet we have no idea what to expect. Then I suggest that retirement, when understood as "Having an Expiration Date," runs counter to social interests while also creating great feelings of discontent for those individuals who succumb to out-of-date notions of retirement. At the end of this chapter, I introduce the key ideas shared in the chapters that follow, highlighting stories of people from each of the five different types of work backgrounds.

A BRIEF HISTORY OF RETIREMENT

Tracing its origins to the sixteenth century, retirement once described the retreat of armies.[7] Retirement has since been associated with withdrawing, fleeing from engagement, and receding from companionship in a desire to detach. These conceptualizations of retirement were later reflected in disengagement theory, which suggested that with age came a mutual withdrawal between older people and society.[8] Then the receipt of a pension signaled that a person was "retired."

In the late nineteenth and early twentieth centuries, economically developed countries began instituting social pension systems to provide continuing income to workers at a certain age.[9] Otto von Bismarck is often credited with introducing this iteration of retirement. In a speech delivered when he was 74 years old, von Bismarck proposed financial support for older Prussian workers when they became disabled or ill, and, in 1889, Germany became the first nation to institute a public pension system for workers when they turned 70 (well above the average length of time a worker was expected to live). In 1916, this age was lowered to 65 (still well above the life expectancy at the time). Most of Europe and Scandinavia developed similar public pension systems for older workers (also initiated at an age above life expectancy). In 1935, the United States followed suit and instituted Social Security for workers at age 65.[10] Canada's first universal pension, entitled Old Age Security, was instituted in 1952 for people 70 years old and over. Each public pension system provided financial compensation for eligible workers (by and large men who had accrued an amount of time working that was equivalent to most of their adult life), set to begin at an age that less than half of the population lived to enjoy.

These early public pension systems for older workers served two primary purposes. First, they addressed concerns about later-life poverty by providing financially for eligible workers who survived past the average life expectancy.[11] Second, early social insurance distribution systems essentially removed from desirable positions older workers who were deemed too old to be useful, to make room for younger workers who were assumed to be more capable, better able to handle physical labor, and in need of salaries to support growing families.[12]

If we look at workforce participation rates among men 65 years and older before the 1930s, rates exceeded 50 percent. Since the times when most economically developed countries instituted public pension systems, the workforce participation rate of men or women over the age of 65 has yet to exceed 50 percent.[13]

James Birren has described retirement as "an example of society's use of age as an arbitrary index."[14] Over time and in periods of high unemployment, employers, unions, and governments have needed ways to reduce the size of the workforce. And, as Atchley has explained, one solution was to mandate or incentivize retirement at a specific age.[15] For many decades, mandatory retirement was imposed at a specific chronological age. Mandatory retirement was lauded as helpful to older workers because for many it was linked with a degree of financial security. Additionally, it was helpful to younger workers, who were able to move more readily into the workforce or into higher positions. Although it reduced some of the uncertainties associated with old age, mandatory retirement essentially created a precedent for moving people out of paid employment automatically at a set age, with no consideration for their skills, ability, personal interests, workplace performance, experience, or institutional knowledge.

In thinking about the historical context of retirement, it's worth considering how attitudes about aging itself have changed. Western culture has not always had the lack of reverence for elders that marks many modern workplaces. It was not unusual in the late 1700s for young adults to try to make themselves appear older, powdering their wigs and wearing clothes styled to imitate the sloping shoulders of older adults. But by the 1800s, aging came to be perceived as more like an incurable disease that must be avoided, ignored, and forestalled. After the Industrial Revolution, as many countries were establishing pension systems, the status of older people declined further. As countries modernized, older adults were often stereotyped as less productive workers and were assumed to have little to offer in terms of useful information to teach the younger generations.[16]

As Lynn McDonald and Peter Donahue have explained, just when we think we have "a sound grasp of retirement, the picture shifts: new economic conditions arise, followed by related policy debates and changing individual preferences that require new explanations."[17] Since the turn of the twentieth century and into the twenty-first, mandatory retirement has been abolished in many types of work and regions of the world. And on the whole, its abolishment has been celebrated. Subsets of workers in fields such as aviation or the justice system, however, still face a mandatory retirement in North America. Throughout Europe, Asia, and South America, public servants as well as people employed across the private sector continue to face mandatory retirement. Even the Roman Catholic Church imposes a mandatory retirement age for priests, bishops, and archbishops (although cardinals and the pope are recused).

WORK ANYTIME, ANYWHERE

A true conflict exists between the history of retirement systems that issued a pension upon complete work stoppage (for the few who lived long enough to make it to retirement) and contemporary work culture. Today, the boundaries between the physical space and time defined as work and leisure are blurred, with greatly expanded options for when, where, and how to work. Many work spaces are designed to feel like home and even include spaces to relax, socialize, or engage in recreational activities. Technological advancements have made it possible for many of us to work any-time, anywhere. Work can be ubiquitous. For some people, clocking in or out is a foreign concept. A term has emerged—*blended work*—for the modern ability to leverage technology so that work need not be constrained by time or place.[18]

Regardless of whether or not people undertake blended work, they often select into their line of work because it suits their interests and disposition. The operative words here are "select into" because the process of going into a certain line of work involves selection bias. And much as people will often say that they "fell into" their work, society does not sort people into occupations randomly. Of course, not everyone is lucky enough or able to find work that meets their personal interests, let alone to feel passionate about their work. For many people, work is simply a way to meet financial needs. Yet, for some people, particularly for those who enter a profession, work is a way of life.[19] Professionals tend to work anytime, anywhere, which means they tend to think about it all the time, everywhere.

Another feature of professions is that they define conditions for acceptance and promotion. Being in a profession often requires earning certifications or credentials and complying with codes of conduct. Professions tend to require prolonged training in order to develop skills and mastery. To excel in a profession requires dedica-tion and a good fit between the demands of the profession and a person's ability and willingness to meet those work demands. Over time, professionals develop a receptivity to cues about levels of appropriate engagement with work relative to personal spheres of life—often, those levels of engagement are as much as possible, as often as possible.

Institutions, work settings, and organizational structures inform perceptions about boundaries between work and life out-side of work.[20] Those who remain in their profession over a long period of time tend to acclimate to their work in ways that meld with their core sense of who they are. We say that individuals have found their "calling" to describe a particularly good professional fit and to suggest that a person's work-related interest is being fulfilled.

Work can be a meaningful way of distinguishing people. In some social circles, describing our work is the operative response to cocktail party introductions. Identification with a professional group can effectively distinguish people, helping us create meaning and establish a sense of who we are. Identity theory suggests that self-categorization is an important component of social structure: the roles with which we identify, enhance our understanding of society as a whole.[21] Although much of social identity theory focuses on how people see themselves as members of a group in relation to other groups, an important component of this theory posits that people form a social identification when they have a strong sense of individuality that is linked with belonging to a specific socially constructed group.[22] Thus, when people describe their work, they are presenting a shorthand, a shared social identity understood in contrast to other shared social identities.[23]

In cases when work and personal identity are strongly bound, one must dig deep to uncover ways to apply the skills that led to professional success in order to find contentment as a retiree. Role identity theorists have focused on the match between individual behavior and the meanings people associate with that role, also emphasizing the importance of considering how people perceive their roles in the larger context of their life—that is, outside their group proper.[24]

For those who situate their core identity in ways that are inseparable from their work, stopping or altering this commitment to work through retirement can be difficult. The stronger the work identity, the more complicated the transition to retirement.

David Ekerdt has articulated the way in which retirement has come to be recognized as a separate stage of life, now featured on our cultural map. This stage of life reflects people's long-standing ways of living and tolerates retirement so long as it "honors an active life."[25] In describing the *busy ethic*, Ekerdt addressed the tensions that arise when a society values a strong work ethic and views productivity as paramount, yet simultaneously endorses a later stage of life that encourages a leisure-filled lifestyle.[26]

The *busy ethic* not only legitimates the pursuit of leisure in retirement but also demonstrates how retirement can be morally managed by providing a continuous framework for those who subscribe to the utility of keeping busy. For people who have always had their work on their mind, retirement can be an amorphous concept. Ekerdt's seminal research has demonstrated that the social foundations of retirement have altered in substantial ways over time, with implications for our social interactions and for personal well-being.[27]

THE PROLIFERATION OF RETIREMENT

Reaching retirement has been likened to having a car.[28] At first, all cars were considered luxuries. Now they are seen as basics—expected, although varying in options, models, and add-ons. As we live longer and are healthier and wealthier than previous generations, what it means to be "retired" must be amended.

In the past forty years, in economically developed countries, the gap between life expectancy and average age at retirement has widened dramatically, but in quite the opposite direction from earlier times.[29] In the 1970s, the average retirement age was close to the average life expectancy—around age 67 for men. Since then, the average man has come to spend upward of ten years living in retirement.[30] As figure 1.1 illustrates, the average retirement age has not moved in sync with life expectancy.

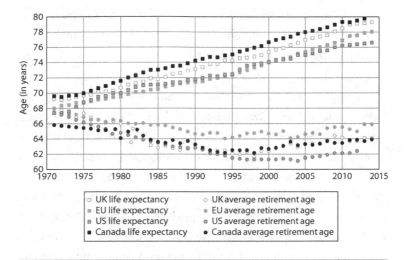

FIGURE 1.1 Life Expectancy and Average Retirement Age for Men in Canada, the European Union, the United Kingdom, and the United States (1970–2014)

Note: All life expectancy data came from the World Bank Group, looking at the variable "Life Expectancy at Birth, Male (Years)" (2016a). Average retirement age data (defined as the average effective age at which older workers withdraw from the labor force) came from the Organisation for Economic Co-operation and Development (2015).

As life expectancy has increased, more people are spending more time in retirement. To put it simply: the number of people who now live past traditional retirement age has more than tripled in the past half-century.[31] In current times, almost everyone can expect to reach retirement. And yet no one really knows what to expect in retirement.

Peter Laslett coined the term the "third age" to describe the phase of life that is marked by the end of an adulthood spent pursuing paid work and characterized by freedom, leisure activities, learning opportunities, and social engagement.[32] Retirees have become a key demographic market for consumer products, featured handsomely in advertisements that airbrush images of older adults so that they shine and glimmer, thriving in their "golden years" and enjoying the leisure activities associated with retirement. And although the discontentment associated with retirement is not a sentiment that can be generalized, it is one that has been ignored, glossed over, and obfuscated.

As Stephen Katz has articulated in his book *Cultural Aging: Life Course, Lifestyle, and Senior Worlds*, positive images that defy traditional negative stereotypes also downplay the harsh realities that can be associated with ending our life's work too soon, losing a sense of purpose, or having too much available time.[33] Media portrayals of gleeful retirees happily enjoying a new consumer product that brings vitality to their leisure activities, coupled with pension systems, which imply that the end of a productive life is marked by a specific age, can erode our possibilities for satisfaction and contentment. Perhaps most important, retirement can undermine the social good by underestimating the true value of highly skilled older adults.

HAVING AN EXPIRATION DATE

The confluence of historical precedent and social norms that link retirement with a specific age can play a large role in how people think about retirement timing. Age of pension eligibility remains highly influential in determining when many people retire. While pension systems can offer relief for those who need to or can't wait to retire, they can also effectively push others to retire earlier than they might be ready to, in many cases going against the best interests of individuals as well as society. These conditions have contributed to a suboptimal dependency ratio whereby a subset of workers is cast out despite having tremendous skills and many years left to contribute. This outcome ought to serve as a wakeup call for us to question ageist assumptions about age, work, and productivity that are perpetuated by employers, outmoded social norms, and age-graded financial incentives associated with public and private pension schemes.

Most of us live in "graying" societies, where lowered fertility rates and longer life spans have become the norm. More people are entering into the age of eligibility for retirement than are entering the workforce and beginning to pay into pension systems. As retirement becomes an increasingly long phase of life, many governments around the world are now struggling to find ways to keep mature adults in the workforce for as long as possible.[34]

Yet evidence suggests that, to this day, some employers continue to view older workers as having lower levels of productivity, out-of-date skill sets, and less utility than younger workers.[35] When these sorts of ageist assumptions fester, they create working conditions that range from uncomfortable to intolerable. An environment in which workers are pushed to feel that they have reached their prime, are overstaying their welcome, or have surpassed an arbitrary expiry date has negative implications at both the individual and societal level. At the individual level, workers may experience a noxious sense that they have become a burden or a relic. At the societal level, employers can end up phlegmatically disregarding workers based on their age and in turn inducing early retirement.

Concerns should arise when age *alone* dictates when a person retires. That is to say, age is predictive of next birthday, but it is not a good predictor of one's competence. After age 65, factors such as chronic medical conditions, cognitive functioning, and physical mobility become more helpful as indicators of work performance. And belying expiration date assumptions, evidence suggests that older adults are actually better than younger adults at making use of strategies that maximize work efficiency.[36]

When work is a source of social connection, stimulation, and purpose, retirement can lead to feeling isolated and excluded.

Instead of relishing self-actualization or a sense of accomplishment at the end of one's career, a strong preretirement work identity can delay or inhibit the ability to feel content in retirement. This disparity between idealized retirement and the reality of giving up identity, income, and status is itself difficult, leaving retirees to wonder: *these are the golden years?*

All this is borne out through the narratives shared in this book. The people I interviewed had work lives that were—and are—difficult to disentangle from their personal identities. By applying narrative gerontology in this book, I highlight the value of interviewing people to better understand their life experiences, relationships, and life transitions. This approach allows each story to unfold uniquely, revealing the deeply personal relationships among work, personal identity, aging, and retirement.[37]

Retirement can be experienced differently based on prior life experiences. When and where a person retires matters as much as the chronological point along the life course when retirement first occurs. Along these lines of thinking, I created an interview guide informed by the life course theoretical perspective.[38] One particularly noteworthy aspect of retirement I focused on was the retirement party. Joel Savishinsky has discussed the retirement ceremony as a ritual or rite of passage that, like others, marks accomplishments and helps people transition from one stage in life to the next.[39] But later-life ceremonies in industrial societies tend to lack connections to clear expectations. I questioned each participant about their retirement party in an attempt to better understand the meaning they associated with retirement. In doing so, I learned about another level of discontent, as participants largely viewed their parties as supposed markers of the end of their productive life.

The people whose narratives are shared in this book spent significant portions of their lives focused on the work they considered to be their "calling." Their work roles were autonomous, demanding, and required perseverance. In other ways, they differed—they were born and worked in a range of different countries, had different types of family dynamics, held distinct preretirement identities, and retired at different ages. In spite of these distinctions, each described a connection to their life's work that complicated their adjustment to retirement. In the following section, I summarize the next six chapters.

Chapter 2: Renegade Retirement and the Greedy Institution

THE DOCTORS

> To retire is to become a renegade. . . . You give your life to become a doctor. Leaving is like abandoning ship, cheating on your wife, and losing your shell.
>
> —*Emil, retired gastrointestinal surgeon*

Medicine is a "greedy institution" that allows little room for doctors to pursue other spheres of interest; this reality can pose important challenges in planning for and adjusting to retirement. Doctors are carefully selected into medicine and are acculturated through lengthy training and a demanding work culture. Retired doctors grapple with the consequences of scant financial planning and with a surfeit of time no longer consumed with work. They can feel like renegades: retiring can feel like deserting their life's work. Their stories show how strong personal connections with work had a price, including low engagement in family commitments and other spheres of interest. Eventually, the key characteristic that made them great doctors—their total commitment—was also a key barrier to finding contentment in retirement.

Chapter 3: Refined Retirement and Fulfillment Employment

THE CHIEF EXECUTIVE OFFICERS

> My heart still flutters sometimes, thinking about when I was in charge.
>
> —*Bob, retired CEO of a health-care consulting firm*

Media representations and advertisements foster images of wealthy retirees playing golf, enjoying the fruits of their labor on cruises, and spending money in various other ways. Although the retirement identity of many CEOs I interviewed included leisure activities, their new identity also emphasized productivity and continued engagement in work. This chapter introduces the concept of being "fulfillment employed," a term that describes the desire to contribute to society by continuing to work for pay in retirement despite having the financial means to stop working. The stories shared in this chapter describe the unique ways in which these CEOs' work identity influenced their transition to retirement, situated within a larger theoretical framework that questions what it means to be successful and productive.

Chapter 4: Early Retirement and Resilience

THE ELITE ATHLETES

> It's really scary, because you lose your sense of purpose. What's interesting about retiring is . . . all of a sudden my name is still the same, but I am not a gymnast anymore. . . . I remember it being really weird the first few months when you meet people and they ask you, "What are you doing?" And you're like,

"Nothing, I am not doing anything right now." Even when I was 7 years old, I was constantly working, you know?

—*Alison, retired Olympic gymnast*

In sports, everything can change in the blink of an eye. Elite athletes can go from being the best in the world to suddenly being out of the game. This chapter introduces a set of elite athletes who traveled the world representing their countries in their sport. They all had participated in the Olympic Games, but only a few continued in a related line of work. At a young age, these athletes retired from their sport and returned to the "normal" world, but they felt like foreigners in their bodies and minds. Their ability to focus on an adrenaline-fueled goal served them well as Olympians, but it created discontent as they struggled to find a new purpose in life as retired athletes.

Chapter 5: Late Retirement and Working in Place

THE PROFESSORS

Retirement is a hard one to get your head around. Tenure means a job for life . . . looking back, I could have made so much more money if I had channeled my energy elsewhere. . . . But, after all these years, the idea of leaving—it is really hard.

—*David, retired professor of health sciences*

In academia, the boundaries between work and nonwork are particularly blurred. Academics are expected to be the best in their field and to maintain a steady focus on their work. Yet, the ways they compete and perform differ vastly from most other types of professions. My interviews with academics illustrated an inherent resistance to retirement, even as these retirees also demonstrated that retirement could be a continuation of prior routines. Some academics retired because of a mandatory retirement age, yet they continued to work at their university doing similar but "unwaged" work. Others retired because of untenable departmental dynamics or having been lured by financial incentives associated with age-related pensions. Although each had different reasons for retiring, they could not abandon their work interests and remained in a virtually unchanged work environment, despite title changes to "emeritus" or "retired." Building on the concept of "aging in place," which refers to living at home or in a familiar setting rather than relocating to a health-care environment in later life, I suggest that these academics were "working in place." For them, retirement represented not a departure but a continuation of their life's work.

Chapter 6: Undefined Retirement and the Retirement Mystique

THE HOMEMAKERS

> I think I identify with being retired because my husband is. His work has always been important. I worked around him . . . I made things work. . . . I'm enjoying things now. Many of our friends are retired, and there are lots of social activities available to me now.
>
> —*Betty, retired homemaker*

The homemakers I interviewed self-identified as retired, despite the fact that they did not make a traditional transition out of a paid workforce. They based their retirement on the workforce transitions of their spouse or peers. And for the most part, they embraced retirement. The changing demographics of today's workforce make this group a diminishing subset of women, but their narratives illustrate the persistence of retirement as a subjective status and as a marker of personal identity that created an opportunity for these homemakers to finally square their roles with those of their peers. Their experiences highlight the heterogeneity of women's retirement identity and how the constraints of social norms around retirement can be rewoven to achieve greater contentment in later stages of the life course.

Chapter 7: Conclusion

Retirement is the ugliest word in the language.

—*Ernest Hemingway*

Social norms around conventional retirement can constrain a person's identity and sense of purpose, contributing to feelings of discontent. Some researchers have called for an end to the use of the term *retirement*, but my findings support the notion that retirement is a widely used and broadly understood term—it just means different things to different people. Retirement can be embodied by people doing something completely different from their preretirement work, whether or not it is the result of an early retirement, as well as by those who are "working in place" or pursuing "fulfillment employment" in their retirement. Defining retirement as an age-specified exit from employment is anachronistic. This book contributes to a more nuanced understanding of later career transitions and outlines how preretirement work skills can be applied to address some of the sources of discontent in retirement. It also illustrates that the true challenge for aging societies is to reconcile the blunt ways that age stereotypes are used to influence assumptions about productivity, retirement, and postretirement employment decisions.

2

Renegade Retirement and the Greedy Institution: THE DOCTORS

From the moment they enter medical school, doctors are groomed through institutional efforts to view their professional role as paramount. In many ways, they are conditioned to embrace a career trajectory that emphasizes work above all other aspects of life. Because their work can have life-or-death consequences, doctors are expected to always make the right decisions about their patients' care. Then, at precisely the right moment, they are expected to know when to retire.

For the most part, doctors tend to operate as self-employed professionals. As such, they rarely have access to public pension plans and must plan for retirement independently. But their retirement decisions have unique social implications for health-care systems and patients. An early retirement or untimely death, even a retirement that occurs too late, can negatively affect patient care. Therefore, plans for succession become extremely important endeavors, even as the bulk of a doctor's time and mental energy is needed for day-to-day work.

Aging doctors also must consider significant safety concerns. Much of their work requires physical strength, dexterity, stamina, and high cognitive functioning. Although experience often compensates for age-related declines in each of these areas, mistakes can be costly. Doctors know better than most that it is hard to predict how long a person will live, and this uncertainty further complicates their financial planning for retirement. Thinking about retirement within the context of medicine is particularly challenging not only because it raises questions about financial stability and patient safety but also because it stirs up concerns about social responsibility and personal identity.

This chapter focuses on the work experiences and transitions to retirement of five doctors. Although each took a unique path, their stories collectively exemplify the challenges that emerge when a profession demands total commitment. The successful doctor must, to some extent, reject traditional norms about the boundaries between work and other aspects of their life, such as family. He or she must be confident and quick thinking, if not egotistic. They are responsible for saving lives, and also for knowing that working past a certain point in their lives may endanger patients. Each doctor I interviewed had different reasons for and ways of retiring, but they all had to confront the reality that their life before medicine was but a faint memory in retirement.

I start with Emil, a retired gastrointestinal surgeon, who explained that retiring felt like becoming a renegade. Emil felt like a deserter and struggled to find a new sense of commitment as he disconnected from the role that had consumed his adult life. Allan, who retired from emergency medicine, shared his challenges and the sense that he had continued to work for too long. Wendy had been a family doctor for most of her adult life; her story acknowledged the complexities of being a woman in medicine, balancing work and family, negotiating the struggles of extramarital affairs, and re-establishing her sense of self without the title "doctor" in front of her name. Walter was a rural family doctor who struggled to replace his position within his community when he desperately wanted to retire. I end with Robert, who was a pediatric cardiologist, as well as a highly accomplished academic, who struggled through multiple retirement parties and refused to succumb to the traditional definition of retirement.

RENEGADE RETIREMENT

Emil, Gastrointestinal Surgeon

Emil's retirement was like losing a part of himself. One of the first things he shared was his sense that "to retire is to become a renegade." He explained, "You give your life to become a doctor. Leaving is like abandoning ship, cheating on your wife, and losing your shell." For Emil, being a doctor was important; being a retired doctor felt trivial.

Social constructions of the good doctor depict a devoted and self-sacrificing person who can immediately jump into his or her work role. Whether they are interrupted during their workday or awakened from the fitful sleep of being on-call, surgeons are particularly adept at tuning in and focusing on the important tasks required of them. To turn this role off is akin to turning off a large portion of the self. And deciding to exit this role can feel like a mutiny. Leaving paid work means leaving a professional role that society counts on us to perform, like lifting a veil of comfort, removing a source of pride, or stepping out of a zone of familiarity.

Emil did not "live to work" like some of the other doctors I interviewed, but to say that he loved being a surgeon would be an understatement. His whole face lit up as he described how he had been "the best." Emil had always felt an internal pressure to excel. He thrived on his professional accomplishments and the sense of satisfaction he received from his work, and when he thought about retiring, all he knew was that he wanted to leave at the top of his game.

Emil's career began when he moved more than six thousand miles away from his parents and siblings to attend medical school. He recalled that his training was overwhelming at first, but he was grateful for the positive ways in which it molded him. Medicine taught him to be disciplined, adaptable, and empathic. His career also provided him with the feeling that he was playing an important role in the world.

In his 20s, Emil married his wife Juleen, who was a nurse at the hospital where he began his career. Emil repeatedly described medicine and Juleen as the loves of his life. Together, Emil and Juleen had two sons, both of whom brought him worry but also great pride. As he showed me a family photo, he explained that the worry stemmed from thoughts about his sons' careers and wondering when they would establish themselves.

Being the Best

Emil retired at 68, after more than four decades as a surgeon. In his 60s, Emil came to the realization that he could not continue as a surgeon indefinitely. He started to feel that he was slowing down and worried that he was no longer at the top of his game. He told me about a senior colleague he felt had stayed on too long: "There was one man I knew. He was a titan when I was a trainee. He had a retirement party when he was 81, and very few people attended. If he'd had this party when he was 70, there would have been 200 people in the room. But he was so disappointed, you could see how upset he was. He was looking around, wondering where all the people were. Well, nobody cares anymore. To end up like that was not appealing to me."

There is an inherent struggle for doctors, particularly surgeons, whose work is physically demanding, but this struggle could transcend professions. It begs the question—how do we balance the rewards that are associated with being the best against the fear of an imperfect legacy that might accompany retiring after our prime? When Emil performed well and the surgery was a success, he was rewarded with the gratitude and acclaim of his patients. This happened often. Emil shared lots of stories about patients who acknowledged the various ways he had saved or improved their lives. He was also rewarded with an income that was well above average and allowed him to live comfortably. Emil wanted to maintain the status of "being the best" indefinitely, and the only way to do that was to end his career before he was really ready.

Emil loved his work, but he admitted that it became more stressful in his later years. He was concerned about being able to keep his hands steady and mentioned that his vision had become somewhat inconsistent. His back bothered him, which made standing during procedures less comfortable. He did not want to be remembered for needing special accommodations at work or for mistakes made as a result of his age. Yet, retiring also felt like dropping out of the society Emil had grown into.

An Allegiance to Medicine

Emil had a sense of allegiance to medicine. Over the years, he had formed personal connections and made numerous friends who were all one or two degrees of separation from his role as a surgeon. Emil described a core group of fellow surgeons who watched each other's children grow up, attended each other's children's weddings, and sometimes even attended each other's second and third weddings.

He laughed as he recalled moments early in his career that were formative in creating a sense of allegiance with his contemporaries:

When I was on-call on the weekend, it wasn't one day and then you get to sleep the next day. I was on from Saturday morning at

8:00 until Monday [night]—no break. You were there all weekend and Sunday night. . . . When you finish your work, that was
when you got to go home. It was enough to make me sick on a
few weekends. Especially the one that I won't forget where seven
or eight people died of cardiac arrest and whatnot—very stressful. I wouldn't wish that on anybody today, but we were devoted,
we couldn't just take off the minute our shift ended.

Medicine's emphasis on commitment to work and loyalty to colleagues had very stressful phases, but it also created a sense of community that Emil treasured. His personal life and work had always
been interconnected, making it difficult for Emil to retire. In thinking about retirement, Emil explained,

Social interactions are very, very important. The feeling of
importance, of belonging, of contributing to society, continuing to contribute what you can to society. That's what drives
many of us, and many of us were idealistic when we were
very young and we still are. That idealism still remains with
us after many years, despite the ravages of practicing medicine . . . there are many ups and downs during those years,
but we still have a good feeling for making a contribution.
When you retire, it's very difficult to go from 100 percent to
0 percent, from one day to the next. You lose a lot. I lost a lot.
Not just the money. But I lost the friendships and that sense of
being important.

It was clear that Emil had a strong sense of allegiance to his peers
in medicine. At the same time, he expressed a sense of dismay for
his younger colleagues. He saw the younger generation as more
privileged and self-absorbed than his own and worried about the
state of medicine after his generation retired. He said,

The younger generation are 'more normal' if you will. Some people call it that. They're not as driven. They're not as dedicated. Maybe that's a little harsh, but I don't think they are as dedicated. My first priority, no matter what I was doing, was always to the patient. I always forced my secretary to get back to my patients the same day they called. If you try and call a doctor today—I don't know if you've tried recently, but try to call a doctor, you'll get an answering machine, nine times out of ten. Many of them, you can't even leave a message. They'll just tell you to go the emergency room if you're sick.

As he described the generation of doctors that was supposed to succeed him, he admitted that some of the changes put in place had made medicine safer. He saw medicine as a better working environment than when he first entered the profession and admitted that surgery was much more difficult to enter now than when he had entered. Nonetheless, he had not retired to make room for the next generation.

The Retirement Time Stamp

Emil retired at 68 because that is when his father, who had also been a surgeon, retired. His father's retirement had created a time stamp in Emil's head. The magic age to retire was 68. Because his father's health quickly declined after he retired, it also forged a link between retirement and death. Emil sensed that he had more time than his father did (his father only lived a year into his retirement) and wanted to enjoy that time. He and Juleen timed their retirement together so that she would stop the part-time interior design work she had been doing for several decades. Emil imagined spending time in retirement relaxing, catching up on golf, reading fiction, and biking. He took pride in the idea that he would be remembered by his colleagues as someone who went out on top and not as someone who stayed on past his prime.

When he retired, Emil tried his best to remain active and in contact with his social circle. But he discovered a big difference between being an active doctor and being an active *retired* doctor. Emil learned that maintaining his social connections with friends who had not yet retired was difficult. Once he closed his practice, Emil felt closed off from medicine.

When I asked Emil about his retirement party, his face fell. He had two retirement parties, and as much as he loved parties and the attention he received, he did not reflect fondly on them. He had been disappointed by friends who were too busy to attend and saddened by the reality of what was transpiring. His retirement parties were the signal that he was past his prime. And there was no returning from that point.

Almost immediately after his second retirement party, Emil said he felt a sense of longing for his work. He missed the "rush" of the operating room and the sense of importance he had felt when he was asked to consult on a patient. The decisions in his retirement felt inconsequential. He described feelings of "withdrawal" from his role as a surgeon.

Medicine Is Addictive

At one point, Emil described his work as "addictive." It had brought him a "high" that he couldn't find elsewhere. In the operating room, he had been in total control, focused to the point that surgery was almost meditative. He cherished that feeling.

If, however, Emil was an addict to surgery and his initial retirement a withdrawal, it is fair to say that at 72, when we talked, he was in recovery. When he made dinner reservations, he still used "doctor" in front of his name and still loved thinking about his days as "the surgeon." He missed his title and his colleagues. Emil described several years of feeling that he had tricked himself into retiring. He came to acknowledge that the idea of having an untarnished legacy was both a myth and an unsatisfying goal.

True to his new role as a "renegade," Emil struggled to find a new faith. It took a full four years, but, in large part because of Juleen's efforts, he was starting to establish a new social circle. He had simply grown tired of missing work and was beginning to creatively carve out new ways to find purpose in his retirement. Emil was grateful that he had been granted more years to live than his father. Yet, in several ways, he struggled with this time. He never grew unaccustomed to having time on his hands and felt awkward about following a schedule that so closely resembled Juleen's. Although he was certain he would eventually adjust to a life outside of medicine, he was also sure that his retirement had signified an abandonment of his primary purpose in life.

RETIREMENT CAN BE HARD ON THE HEART

Allan, Emergency Room Doctor

Like Emil, Allan struggled to fill the gap in his life that remained after he retired from medicine. But Allan's story differs somewhat dramatically from Emil's, particularly because Allan's retirement was very much an unplanned and unwelcome transition. Although Emil feared the idea of retiring after his prime, Allan never thought about his potential legacy. Instead, he worried about the void that would be created by not working. Allan also had financial obligations that obfuscated his ability to retire. He had seen his share of trauma and heartbreak—he had made lifesaving decisions for his patients and had informed families when a spouse, parent, or child had died. The statement carried a certain weight, then, when Allan said that retiring was the hardest thing he had ever done.

Allan had been an emergency room (ER) doctor for more than forty years when he retired. He married twice and had five children, but work had always come first. He told me right off the bat that he had always wondered, "What's your value as a person when you're finished—if you're finished being a doctor, what's your value? And what are the things that make you happy, make you feel fulfilled? What will fill the void of work?"

Allan resented being retired. He felt robbed when he had to surrender his medical license because of claims that he was no longer competent. He was "pressured to retire" when a set of families filed lawsuits against the hospital where he worked. Needless to say, Allan never had a retirement party.

Much like Emil, Allan enjoyed being in charge and felt a sense of personal satisfaction from being a doctor. When his work was taken away from him, he initially missed it "like a baby that is ripped out of a mother's arms." Allan had been grateful on an earlier occasion when he very nearly avoided mandatory retirement, but he had never expected that he would be *forced* to stop working. He gave his life to the job. Administrative decisions had been made that he felt negatively affected his work. At one point, he described the work ethic that permeated the hospital:

> It's almost like shift work that you're doing, and there's always the difficulties of taking over from people you don't know well. I think that's one disadvantage, and I see that . . . and people don't care so much about their patients because of that, because it's no longer their responsibility. It's like, when you have a shift

from eight to eight, you care about the people from eight to eight. You walk out. All the people who are left there, at 8 p.m. when you leave, you couldn't care how they do after that. It's somebody else's job, right?

The "Doctor Hat" Is Always On

When I asked Allan if he had typically brought his work home, whether it was paperwork or simply thinking about cases after he left the hospital, it was clear that he did. He reminded me that his shifts were long and demanding, and the work had to get done somehow. His work often required quick decision making, and at a certain point, it became more effective for Allan to simply stay in his persona as a doctor all the time instead of switching to another role—like father or husband—once he came home. I asked about his family life, and whether he had ever missed one of his children's birthday parties because of his busy job. He said,

> Birthdays were always happening. I don't put some kind of special value on a year. I save people so that they can live richer or longer lives. So, yes, I know I missed birthday parties. I still do. And I don't send cards either. But I've always concerned myself with the bigger picture. Some of my colleagues are all about buying things. Thinking that somehow you get more points in life if your gift is the most extravagant. For me, it's always been about helping people have more time.

Allan explained that he never took off his "doctor hat" and felt that he was always expected to be the leader. At home or at work, he was the one who had to make the tough decisions and instruct others even when he did not have full information. He described situations when there just wasn't enough time to gather all the details at work and times at home when he didn't want all the details; nonetheless, he had to make the "big" decisions. Allan had to stay apprised of numerous different types of conditions and treatment options, all of which meant he was always working to stay on top of it all. This made him the de facto leader when a patient had a complex medical situation and there was little information to work from. He learned to adapt to this position, but had a hard time, emotionally, unlearning the role.

His first marriage ended when his two oldest children were in high school. His second wife, Lanni, was a nurse who worked at the same hospital. Together, Allan and Lanni had three children. Allan wanted to be able to provide Lanni with the lifestyle she desired. Over the years, he had bankrolled private school tuition, music lessons, ski trips, orthodontist visits, college tuition, weddings, and house down payments for his two oldest children. He wanted to be able to do these things for his younger children as well. In retrospect, Allan claimed that his financial obligations had prevented him from planning for retirement financially, and his drive to stay focused at work had kept him from planning for retirement mentally.

Allan did not have access to a group pension and had left no financial safety net for himself. Put simply, he had never foreseen his retirement. In addition, he had never been a good sleeper; sleep deprivation and anxiety had been a regular part of his job.[1] Retirement brought on a new type of sleep anxiety. In a time that many expect to be restful and leisurely, Allan worried about his children, his wife, and his ex-wife; he worried about what had happened to his career and about what would become of him.

Forced Retirement and Regrets

Some of Allan's initial dismay in retirement was compounded by his disappointment about the legal actions against him. He had not taken time to make a backup plan and was not sure what other career options, if any, were available to him. At times, I wondered whether he had been responsible for patient deaths, and if so, how many? We did not talk about any specific incidents that pertained to the legal case leading to his retirement, but it was clear that Allan had posed a threat to patient safety in his later years of practicing medicine.

Although experience can compensate for much of the traditional wear and tear that comes with age, making the experienced doctor more efficient at decision making and practice, advanced age can also turn a world-renowned expert into an error-prone individual. In emergency medicine, there is little room for error. Allan described himself as more comfortable with and better at certain aspects of his job than others while he still had his medical license in his later years. And he was adamant that he should have been allowed to retire once he had his financial life in better order.

Needless to say, Allan had not left medicine when he wanted to, and he regretted his own failure to create alternative career options. In the end, Allan felt remorse in his retirement about not having spent more time thinking about things outside of medicine and especially that he had not spent more time with his children. He explained,

I always had to work, always brought work home. How did I balance it? Not as well as I would've liked to, I admit it. When my kids were young, I was always really exhausted. I was often quite late getting home because there were always so many new admissions at the hospital in my later years that we had to take care of. There were always so many sick patients that I just always got home quite late. I didn't make my wife very happy. You know, in retrospect, maybe I should have traded shifts more often with someone.

Less Than Zero

Allan was resolved that he had always given more than 100 percent to his work. Being forced to go from operating at overcapacity to stopping work entirely when he retired made Allan feel as if he was worth less than zero. He described feeling devastated that he was not only unable to maintain his practice but also that the nature of his retirement severed so many of his social connections. He felt disrupted and disoriented. Allan often resented the fact that the physical decline, which accompanied his aging, was not as serious as many of his peers who were permitted to continue working. He saw himself as still capable and able to contribute to medicine in meaningful ways, but it was clear that others held a different view.

His focus on work had made him a successful doctor. His ability to tune out other aspects of his life had enabled him to achieve high regard in his area of medical expertise, but this same ability made it difficult for him once work was removed from his life. Allan had saved many lives over the course of his career, and, in many ways, his work accomplishments obfuscated his interest in and ability to plan for retirement and to fully invest in a life outside of medicine. He never saved for retirement or spent time thinking about what he would do without work, because he was always working. His abrupt retirement spurred a deep sense of personal loss.

Allan told me that he wanted to spend more time with his family, but he had taken on part-time pharmaceutical-related consulting work, which ended up consuming more time than he had hoped. This postretirement position, however, was helping him regain his sense of purpose while addressing his financial situation. At the end of the day, Allan was grateful to be working again. Throughout his career, Allan had learned the importance of being resilient both physically and emotionally. His career had taught him that sometimes surviving is about forging ahead, and sometimes it is about adapting. In his retirement, he saw with great clarity how he should have made adjustments earlier to create a more sustainable career. He also saw clearly that his work brought him a sense of affirmation that was difficult for him to live without.

Within medicine, a work culture favors the individual who is willing to work at 110 percent capacity. Medicine also fosters independent doctors, who are expected to be fully dedicated to their patients at all hours and also expected to make time to know precisely when to stop working. But with age and financial obligations, it can be difficult to know when to retire and how best to do it.

DOING IT ALL

Wendy, Family Doctor

Wendy experienced retirement differently from Allan, in that she made the decision to retire. Her retirement was also unlike Emil's in that she did not time her retirement with her spouse's. When she retired, however, she also felt a sense of having recklessly abandoned medicine.

From my first interview with Wendy, it was clear that she had always loved medicine. But it had demanded everything of her— until there was nothing left for it to take. Wendy had a successful career as a family doctor; she raised four children and had an insatiable sense of curiosity. She was bubbly, outgoing, and warm. Wendy had a strong inherent desire to feel connected to other people and to understand how things worked. It was surprising to hear this upbeat, good-natured woman describe her initial transition to retirement as "devastating."

Wendy's formal entry into medicine started just before she married her husband, John, when they were both medical students in their early 20s. Wendy recalled loving the challenge of medical school. She knew that she was born to be a doctor. From the time she entered medical school, the rigorous schedule suited her well. Medicine was all consuming and demanded her full attention. She loved how important she felt studying medicine and devoted herself to the study of it. Wendy also appreciated that medicine felt like being in a small community.

Medicine allowed Wendy to enjoy affluence and aspects of a normal family life, while also allowing her to exist outside the realm of a "normal life" for a woman in her time. In addition to having four children and a double income, Wendy and John's luxurious home included pets, an in-home theater, and multiple forms of exercise equipment. They also kept more than one vacation home over the years. Wendy recognized that being a professional afforded her more than a generous salary; it allowed her to devote herself to her work in a way that gave her a distinct identity separate from being a wife or mother. She was aware that this was not an option for most of the other women in her neighborhood. She relished her uniqueness, and although it was demanding, she treasured her time at work.

Throughout her 20s and 30s, Wendy worked tirelessly. Her priorities were to help her patients and to make sure her children got the best start in life. For the most part, Wendy recalled few career interruptions. She gave birth to her children in quick succession, managing to mostly hide her pregnancies, when necessary. Like the somewhat-rare professional mothers in her day, Wendy had little institutional support for her role as a working mother.[2] She told me that she often read about younger women who complained about "wanting it all" and feeling bad that they "can't have it all at the same time"—meaning that they lament having to balance raising children while also trying to move up in their careers. As Wendy reflected on how it was different for her because she never *wanted* it all, she explained that her solution was simply to *do* it all. When she needed help, she hired help. It turned out that she needed the most help when they could least afford it, but, unlike the women who "want to have it all" that she reads about today, in her early days as a working mother, Wendy didn't think twice about how "having help" reflected on her character.

Wendy's trajectory into being a mother and a doctor was unfortunately plagued with major grief and misfortune early on. Roughly a year after she graduated from medical school, she had a miscarriage, experienced her mother's death, and was hit by a car (in that order). She claims that the close sequencing of these devastating experiences helped clarify her commitment to medicine. Wendy learned that, to survive, she had to be physically and mentally strong. Her children kept her grounded and acquiring new knowledge kept her going.

Her 40s were consumed with work. In her spare time, she focused on ensuring that her kids had the best nannies and tutors. At one point, Wendy described her children as her hobbies. She never took time to take an art class; instead, when time permitted she would drive her kids to their lessons and sit in the back to catch up on work. Beyond reading a few novels a year, she had not allowed herself time for interests outside of work. Even when she exercised, she saw it as part of her job. Seeing patients with issues that could have easily been prevented with better diet and exercise motivated her to regularly exercise.

For decades, Wendy lived, breathed, slept, and woke up with her primary identity as a doctor. Part of what made Wendy successful was her unwavering devotion to medicine. Another key to her success was outsourcing domestic tasks. She had a team of nannies who took her children to school, after-school lessons, medical appointments, and birthday parties so that she could maintain her commitment to work. She also had a maid and a gardener who took care of her home and garden long after her children moved out of the house.

Never Missing a Beat

Having this additional help at home meant that Wendy never missed her children's birthday parties, although John sometimes did. In general, Wendy rarely missed a beat when it came to important family events or with regard to her patients. She also prided herself on being prompt, never missing a meeting, always doing her duties when it came to being on-call, and being available to her patients. During our third interview, Wendy shared a memory box that included a combination of carefully folded notes from patients and select photo albums depicting what she described as the main events in each of her children's lives. Wendy was proud of each of her four children and lit up with enthusiasm as she described their personalities and funny situations that motherhood brought to her life.

The one key area in which Wendy missed a beat had to do with her husband's extramarital affairs with his nurses and "other women, too—for years and years." It was not until Wendy was first forced to face the fact that John was having affairs that she started to think about retirement:

A woman I'd known for years and years finally confronted me about John . . . Suddenly, I realized, I'd had no plan for my life. All my life, I had been planning this and that for my kids, for my practice, for him! I hadn't paid any attention to the financial advisors or what my life would be like. So, I thought about stopping everything right then. My first reaction was: I was going to get a divorce, retire, and move away, and start up an art school. How funny is that? I didn't know anything about art really . . . And I didn't change a damn thing, in a way . . .

Maybe Wendy didn't change her life in the sense of moving, divorcing, or closing down her practice, but she started to see the world in a different way. She realized that she was terrified of shutting down her practice in her early 50s. At that point, she had no retirement plan and her children were not yet established in their own careers. Her two younger children were still living at home, and the older two were interested in pursuing medicine themselves. Wendy felt that she could do a lot more to help set her children on good career paths and yet her own next steps felt foggy at best.

When she contemplated retirement at that point, she was also concerned for her patients. How would they deal with a different doctor? What was the right point to switch each person over, and who would be the best doctor for each patient to see? The idea of giving up her practice filled her with so much dread that, instead of retiring, she doubled her commitment to medicine. Wendy described her 50s and early 60s as her busiest, most productive, and most fulfilling working years. She remained where she was—at home and in her marriage—and unfalteringly admitted that, during this time, her practice was what motivated her to get up every morning and what kept her going until the end of the day.

Crossing Boundaries

In her late 50s, Wendy indulged in her own affair with Ed, another doctor, who was also married and had been pursuing her for years.

When I interviewed Wendy, in her late 60s, she was not timid about admitting that her relationship with Ed gave her the confidence to contemplate her later years in a positive way. She admitted that she had always thought of any person over 50 as "old." Those feelings were reinforced by images she had grown up with, in movies and by things her mother had said when she was a girl that linked beauty with youth. Even in medicine, younger and newer were usually better. Wendy feared looking old and feared that she would receive fewer referrals as she aged.

Wendy described her affair as both a defiance and an adventure—revenge for her husband's dalliances and something that helped build her own confidence to grow in her next stage of life. She also suggested that affairs were par for the course within the medical community. She explained, "Sometimes inappropriate bonding takes place within medicine . . . People spend so much time together, dealing with stressful, personal, and traumatic things . . . and they get these opportunities to cross lines. Doctors do that with nurses all the time."

When she turned 65, Wendy realized that she had put retirement on the back burner for fifteen years. When it came to retirement among the doctors she knew, 65 seemed to be the "magic" number. It was as if she felt that crossing the boundary between 65 to 66 years old without retiring would be wrong. John, whom she remained married to, expressed no interest in ever retiring. But Wendy imagined that she would like retirement and having the time to develop other interests and enjoy life. She described commercials and advertisements that made retirement look fun and admitted to feeling tired at work more often when she entered her 60s.

About three months after Wendy announced her retirement, she had a retirement party and quickly closed down her practice. Some of the nurses in her clinic organized the retirement party. John and three of their children attended, as did a handful of other doctors she had shared patients with over the years. She described the party as a last glimmer of sweetness before the bitter reality set in.

Once Wendy transferred all her patients over to other doctors and completed her last paperwork, she felt devastated:

> After I failed to renew my license, the next day, I woke up, and suddenly it hit me like the car [that had hit her in her 20s]. I was sore and tired and so confused. I thought I'd wake up the next day and feel this surge of energy. Instead, I woke up and I felt the pain of losing my mother. Forty years later, I was feeling all the sadness I had when I lost that baby. And suddenly I felt the shame of having had an affair. I thought I'd be enjoying life. But I think I had been so preoccupied with setting things up so they'd run smoothly . . . I had been so busy with all the paperwork and everything else, that I never considered the reality of it. I had a fantasy of retirement.

Wendy was tired and lonely. She realized her work had totally consumed her. She had become accustomed to jumping from one thing to the next, without taking time to breathe in between. In short, Wendy was not used to being on her own or following an unstructured schedule. She always had her patients and her children; in her later working years, she had two men to think about. When she retired, her patients were gone, her children independent, John remained working, and Ed's health declined suddenly.

Permanent Weekend

Wendy had run a successful medical practice, but she had never maintained a flexible or independent schedule. She never had the option of taking maternity leaves and, until she retired, her only vacations had been short trips with full itineraries. Wendy lacked hobbies of her own and despite being an outgoing person, she had failed to develop a social group outside of work. As she explained,

When I first retired, I somehow thought I would relax and also go, go, go. Isn't that funny? I just imagined getting rest somehow and also that there'd be all these things I'd suddenly be able to do, things that I had just sort of put off. I'd been so busy all those years that I didn't even have time to think about what it was I was going to do when I retired. I just had this feeling that if I had more time, I would do other things . . . But when I finally did it, it just hit me like a brick wall. I didn't sleep well, and I didn't do so well. I looked around, and it seemed like the things retired people actually did were just not the kinds of things that ever interested me. I went from this very rigid schedule to where suddenly there was no difference between a Sunday and a Wednesday. It got to the point where it really depressed me.

Wendy described the discontentment she experienced in her initial transition to retirement as one of the lowest points in her life. She had focused on her career to the point of excluding most other interests, and she felt that she wasn't really good at anything outside of medicine. Wendy regretted not having spent more time with her children and not having developed closer friendships. Suddenly every day was like a weekend, yet she had no one to have fun with. She was limited in her descriptions of John, except to say that he consistently remained focused on his work.

Retirement was a disappointing counterpart to medicine. Medicine had kept her on her toes and maximized every aspect of her body and mind. As a family doctor, Wendy literally spent years on her feet. She made quick decisions that required a wide range of knowledge—treatment options, referrals to specialists, and complications—about a wide range of medical conditions. She dealt with the constant challenges of maintaining a practice, dealing with staff turnover, being a good colleague, and putting her patients first.[3]

Remembering What Had Always Kept Her Going

Wendy had always been incredibly resourceful. In her first year of retirement, she spent a great deal of time visiting her children and traveling on her own. Then, after trying to find excuses to meet people for lunch and testing out different ways of living out her flexible schedule, she eventually remembered what had always kept her going: learning. She realized that she needed to keep busier and to create a more regular schedule for herself. She started by taking a pottery class. Then she enrolled in an art history course. Eventually, she took up other history courses and, soon, a full course load.

Although Wendy did not end up starting an art school in her retirement, as she had once imagined, she did develop a deep understanding of medieval art and gained a range of experiences in applied art. Three years into her retirement, Wendy admitted to missing medicine as if it were a person torn from her life. She confided, "I started young. So, I don't really remember life before medicine. Life after medicine is hard. I don't think I'll ever replace it. I was a good doctor. I will never be good at anything like that again. There isn't much credit given to me for being a good former doctor. When your license expires, you expire, too, a bit . . . But I still have the will to keep learning!"

Wendy had never lived her life by "normal" rules. She entered medicine at a time when few women did, and she hired others to care for her children and her home. She entered into an extramarital affair and had a marriage that appeared to be consumed by work.

Wendy failed to engage in many "normal" activities, such as developing close friendships with other women or taking up hobbies. When she retired at 65, it was something she thought she wanted to do. But her transition to retirement was painful until she was able to reconnect with her core love of learning and to find a way to apply her intellect to a field outside of medicine.

REPLACING YOURSELF IS NOT EASY

Walter, Rural Family Doctor

Unlike Wendy, Walter had an added burden to face in his retirement, which was the challenge of finding someone to take over his entire practice. The experiences of Wendy and Walter both offer insight into better ways to prepare for retirement, but in many ways, Walter's retirement transition contrasts with the experiences of the doctors described thus far. Walter practiced in a small rural community. He had a close connection with his wife and retired much later than he would have preferred.

Walter and his wife Joanne never had children. Walter was the only doctor in a rural region with a small population of only 100 residents when he first began his practice. By the time he wanted to retire, he had more than 100 patients and could not find another doctor to replace him. Walter first tried to retire when Joanne became sick: "We diagnosed her cancer too late—ovarian—and she went from being sick to needing full-time care quickly. I tried to make it work with the nurses I knew. There were nurses that I trusted, but, at a certain point, I just wanted to be the one to care for her. I ended up closing up my practice for a time, but it was very temporary because I couldn't find anyone to take over . . . After Joanne died, I needed to go back to my patients."

Work helped Walter grieve, or at least it distracted him. Then, about five years after Joanne's death, Walter's mother's health started to decline. She needed his help each day. So, in his late 60s, Walter divided his time between caring for his mother and managing his practice. Joanne's illness and death had been so sudden that he was grateful for his mother's gradual decline, though he felt uneasy about describing his feelings at the time as grateful.

Once Walter's mother died, he was determined to retire. He didn't mind weekend interruptions, but he was having trouble dealing with night calls. He had always allowed patients to call him at home, but he could no longer go back to sleep when they called in the night. Although he never needed much sleep, he was starting to have a harder time functioning at work when his sleep had been interrupted. He got to a point where he was worried about making mistakes and harming his patients. He expressed his concern as follows,

I didn't want to be looking after patients and making mistakes. And it's such a changing environment, with all the electronic records from the hospitals. We've gone from a system where we had a very strong nurse-doctor partnership to a system where we don't have that anymore. What I had, that was a lot more work. I kept track of my patients all the time, on holidays, on weekends, because who else could? It used to be that when I was on holiday, nine times out of ten, my nurse would be on holiday a different time, and there'd be some continuity with that patient. Now, the way our system's organized, there's none of that. So, a doctor can leave and have a really sick patient with metastatic disease, and some of them go on for years, or they're in a sort of very acute and palliative stage for six months or three months and nobody really knows them very well. So, I would worry that something would get missed. We all know that is when mistakes happen; it's often when somebody else is covering for you or when there's turnover. One worries always about making a mistake with patients, which I think is a good thing, and as you get older you worry more that maybe you're more prone to it for whatever reasons. I'm telling you, I really wanted to be out.

Wanting to Get Out

Walter also wanted to get "out" because he had interests he wanted to pursue before his own physical decline. One of the most important things Walter wanted to do in his retirement was to visit with a few friends from his medical school days. Walter was not interested in traveling or pursuing new activities like golf; he simply wanted to reconnect with a few people he knew were still around. He viewed his interests as simple and described himself as distinct in several ways from other doctors. He said,

> One difference from my colleagues is that, you know, I didn't have children. I think if you have all this time in medical school and then you have children and you start your practice and so on, then, you kind of wake up at 55 years old and the children have left the house and you may not have any of your own interests. So, you think, "What could I possibly do? How could I develop any other interests at this time?" They could, but it looks so difficult. I think the only thing they do is to keep practicing [medicine], which, you know, sort of gives them something to do, for which they get rewarded. And work may be where they place most of their sense of self-worth and, you know, that's important. For some people, it's a big issue and I just think that they have a more difficult transition than I did.

Because Walter and his wife never had children, Walter felt that they would have time to find other ways to find meaning in their lives when he retired. He had never feared retiring. In fact, toward the end of his life, Walter regretted not retiring *sooner*. Walter lamented the fact that he might have been able to make Joanne's last few months more comfortable if he had retired earlier. But he also recognized that, after she died, his work helped him get through a very difficult period.

Finding a Successor

In his early 70s, when Walter was absolutely determined to retire, he found that it was very hard to find someone to take over his practice. After multiple unsuccessful attempts to sell his practice, he desperately tried to all but give away his practice. Walter contacted his medical association and his alma mater. He called everyone he could think of to try to make arrangements to hand over his practice. Walter could have blamed these difficulties on the small town where he practiced—its lack of amenities, distance from an airport, or other factors. Instead, he decided that there was something "different" about the next generation of doctors. Like Emil, he warned me not to get sick, because new doctors didn't have his work ethic.

As he pointed to a neatly folded journal article written by someone he knew to be a younger doctor, he told me, "Probably, like everybody, I don't think the younger generation works as hard as I did. But then, I don't know, my view is skewed, like, I've been there, and it killed me when I started. I think people just wouldn't start a new practice now and do what we did years ago. These aren't gonna be people that'll take care of you when you're sick down the road, another twenty years. You're gonna have to get sick nine-to-five."

Eventually, in his early 80s, Walter found a husband and wife team interested in "country living" to take over his practice. He practically donated the business to them, but he was relieved that they had come into his life. Walter had developed lymphoma by the time I interviewed him, when he was in his mid-80s. He said,

It's not curable, so I don't know how long I'm gonna live. I'm aiming for another five years, tops. I see my mortality. Not fearful. I don't fear death at all. I fear the preliminaries. How bad is it gonna be to get me there? So, just to give you the whole picture, I will not be in a long-term care nursing home. I have already worked out my plans when I need to go. When the quality of my life is bad, I'm not going to be here. My nephews all know that, so my aim is to have a few more quality years, and when I don't have any more quality, I'm out of here. I'm one of those very strong proponents of assisted suicide. I'm trying to give you the whole picture. I'm finding peace now. My retirement regrets are that I couldn't get out sooner. I should have let go sooner.

When Walter finally retired, he had a "low-key" party, attended by his staff and a few patients. He was pleased that he had that party and relieved that the patients in his community would have someone to look after them. But he was sad that his wife had not been in attendance and regretted that it took so long to find his replacement. He also marveled at the fact that it would take two doctors to do what he had done alone.

WHO MADE THE RULE THAT SAYS I HAVE TO BE DONE?

Robert, Pediatric Cardiology

Robert was distinct from the other doctors because he was also an academic. His retirement transition in some ways foreshadows the experiences of the professors in chapter 5. But he differs from the academics because medicine was so close to his heart.

Robert always knew he would go into medicine. Several of his family members had been doctors, including his father, uncle, and two cousins. Robert thrived in medical school and, for over four decades, he regularly worked 80 hours a week as an academic doctor. At 79, he found it hard to disconnect from medicine:

> During training, there was no life. Literally. I mean, I didn't do anything else during my training. I had a wife at home. And when I came on-staff, I worked all the time. You know, seven in the morning 'til nine or ten at night. I came in on the weekends. My academic productivity, promotions, teaching, and clinical work depended on being there and being focused. I was never home. I was always working and so on. They still think, my kids and my wife still think, I'm a little nuts— writing grants. Right now, I'm writing part of a grant. They say, "Why are you doing this at 79?" I have one grant left. They said, "Why do you need another grant?" I say, "I don't have enough [grant] money to do what I want to do, so I really want one more grant so I can accomplish some of the things I want to still accomplish with my research," which is, I find, very exciting. I find the stuff I'm doing interesting.

For Robert, his life was his work and his work was his life. To remove medicine from Robert permanently would be like removing an IV from a patient in need of medicine. To ease the pain of an abrupt transition, and to allow him to focus on his primary interests, Robert shut down his clinical practice when he was 75. But in this retirement, he held on to his academic work.

By the time he finally "retired," Robert had received numerous awards over the course of his career, including one for having trained the most junior specialists in his subfield of pediatric cardiology. He had hundreds of publications and numerous research awards. At least ten different retirement parties had been held in Robert's honor. But to him, they felt like funerals: "They are talking about you as if you are done. Finished. There is this enormous assumption that you have nothing left in you. It really was like being dead to them, even though they all thought they were being so kind."

At one point, Robert showed me his trembling hands. He probably understood the aging process better than most people, down to complex cellular mechanisms. He self-identified as retired, but he struggled to understand why retiring meant that he had to stop working. Even early in our interview, when he was explaining a typical schedule for someone in academic medicine, he couldn't help questioning why his work would have to end. He said,

> There's no question that if you want to be a star academically, publishing a lot, forty-fifty hours a week just doesn't cut it. You gotta work sixty, seventy, eighty hours a week. That's just, that's just the way it works. And I think a lot of people in academic medicine are very, very driven to be productive, to get recognition, and you can't do that on a normal workweek. It's impossible. It's just too difficult to be competitive with grants, with publishing, you know. It's just that I am driven by curiosity, scientific rigor, you know? I have to figure things out. I suspect there's also the desire for recognition, but I'm not sure how much of it is that. I have a contribution to make. I'm just not done yet. Who makes the rules that say I have to be done?

Taking Charge

Robert's drive to continue to contribute to his field made the decision to retire quite difficult—that is, until he realized that by retiring he could spend even more time on his research. The realization that it was taking him longer to do his work made him recognize that he needed to focus his time and energy on what was most important to him. As he explained,

> Part of it is this feeling of the demands that the institution, the university, and your department chair, and everybody demands that you perform at a certain level. That performance requires a lot of commitment, of time and energy, and so on. As you get older and your stamina gets less, you have to put in even more time because it takes you longer, like it could take you ten minutes longer to do this than it did twenty years ago. You may not be quite as productive as you were, but you're still putting in the time to try to maintain a certain degree of performance to meet the standards. So, I finally realized that they weren't respecting my time, and I need to take charge.

Robert's primary interest was his medical research, so he took charge by giving up other aspects of his career, including his practice and teaching.

Driven, intelligent, and highly dedicated—Robert's disposition allowed him to excel in medicine. In turn, the institutional culture of academic medicine had fostered in him an incredibly successful doctor. The combination of demanding work and a personality suited to it was ideal for continual advancement. In his clinical practice and through his research, he saved many lives. But Robert saw that his work had created a barrier to contemplating retirement. As Robert put it,

> What I haven't been successful at yet is finding other things to do. For example, if I go on a holiday more and spend less time working, I will maybe exercise more or walk more, do things like that, read the paper more, but I haven't actually been successful at developing a hobby other than medicine, outside of

medicine. Reading—I've a million books I want to read, but I always go to a medical journal first or a research article or something like that before I'll take that book up. I buy the book, and I have a stack of fiction on my desk, but then I just gravitate to the journals. When I'm in my medical mode, so to speak, it's very difficult to pull yourself out of it.

To say that Robert was unhappy with his retirement would be misleading. In retirement, Robert was able to focus on aspects of his career that he found most rewarding. His supreme focus on work was evidenced by the items he shared as reflections of who he was as a person. Without question, his work was meaningful as he flipped through a portfolio his wife had compiled for him filled with awards he had received over the years, and journal articles he was most proud of.

For Robert, work and other aspects in his life always formed a singular identity. Yet, when I asked him about whether he felt that being in pediatrics helped with his own children, Robert quickly let me know that this was an absurd question. His wife had done the childrearing, and he had three healthy children. His specialized medical knowledge did not apply to their situation.

Although Robert found the term "retirement" displeasing in that it imposed limits and implied that he wasn't somehow capable anymore, he nonetheless self-identified as retired. He had never been one to care much about what other people thought and decided to define his own rules for retirement.

THE GREEDY INSTITUTION

Medicine is a demanding line of work. It is a greedy institution that allows little room for doctors to pursue other spheres of interest.[4] Doctors are carefully selected into medicine, enculturated, and then often worked to the point of burnout.[5] They are awakened in the middle of the night, often to make life-and-death decisions. They are looked to as the leader, the one who carries out the plan that affects other people's lives. They get blamed if they are wrong, but when things go right, the credit they receive gives them a "high" like no other. Because of this, many doctors feel a profound loss when they retire. Each of the doctors I interviewed had a strong work identity. Although they varied in the type of medicine they practiced, their relationships with their family, and their reasons for retiring, not a single one fondly remembered their retirement party, if they had one at all. For these retirees, medicine was a true love. Without it, their lives seemed incomplete.

To retire and return to a premedicine life can constitute a negation of personal identity and career achievements. In many ways, it should not be surprising that a doctor's retirement can be a letdown. Going from having a waiting room full of patients to waiting around with nothing but time can be a less than ideal prospect.

Notably, the doctors I interviewed enjoyed relatively good health. Although it might sound ironic, their health may have exacerbated feelings of discontentment because they ended their careers while stilling feeling able to contribute. Each of these doctors struggled with their retirement because once they became enculturated in the field of medicine, they found it to be a difficult institution to leave. Their work had become a core part of their identity; retirement left them unsure of who they were.

Each of their experiences raised questions about age and retirement timing. For example, Allan's experience begs the question of whether medical institutions should be obliged to replace doctors before they pose any potential harm to patients. How can we reliably know when or if a doctor's age constitutes a threat to patient safety? Emil's experience suggests that perhaps doctors should leave when they are no longer "the best," but how can we know when this change takes place? The very personal decision about when to retire also has societal implications, because when doctors retire or die, it disrupts their patients' continuity of care.

Walter struggled for years to find someone willing to take over his practice. To have retired any sooner would have left his community without a replacement, and at times he feared that his retirement would be an abandonment for his community. Emil described feeling like a renegade when he retired. Transitioning from practice does not mean becoming indifferent to medicine, but retiring can feel like a dereliction of duty. Emil's experience exemplifies the tensions that can arise among individuals with strong work identities when they sever their roles as workers. Leaving medicine was like abandoning ship. For Emil and Walter, retirement also stirred up tensions between different generations of doctors. Although this was not their reason for retirement, evidence suggests that some doctors use their concerns that the younger generation is less devoted and capable as excuses for not retiring, fearing that institutions may crumble without them to hold the place together.[6]

Wendy was also a renegade in that she had betrayed societal expectations by entering medicine at a time when few women did. Both she and her husband were committed to medicine and renegades in their unconventional marriage. When Wendy retired, she had to find another passion outside of medicine. By studying art history, she was able to find some contentment. Allan was a renegade for staying on too long and betraying his Hippocratic Oath, working past the point at which could ensure the safety of his patients.

But perhaps the most clear-cut renegade was Robert, who, in his retirement, refused to succumb to conventional definitions.[7] Robert opted to give up certain aspects of his medical career to be a more efficient researcher in his retirement. Although his experience exemplifies the ways in which the greedy institution demands full, lifelong commitment, it also illustrates the notion of working-in-place discussed in chapter 5 and demonstrates that some retirees opt to continue to contribute in a manner that is similar to what they experienced before retirement.[8] Robert experienced retirement in ways that contradicted social expectations and struggled to understand why other people saw his retirement as the end of his career when he saw it as a more efficient way to focus on his life's work in medical research. Ultimately, Robert eschewed conventional understandings of retirement by plotting out his next research project and outlining his next journal article or his next grant application to support further medical knowledge, during his retirement parties.

Ethical boundaries get pushed when we consider doctors' retirement. Doctors take an oath to do no harm.[9] They are responsible for taking care of people when they become sick or are ill and at their most vulnerable. But what should become of doctors who grow vulnerable in their later years? To address some of the work demands they encountered, several of the doctors I interviewed had established norms to modify their personal lives. But they often did this at the expense of meeting family obligations, making social connections, and developing hobbies or exploring facets of life that tend to bring enjoyment, particularly in retirement. For those who have been totally committed, retirement can initially constitute an abandonment of their life's work or their value as a person. Within medicine, retiring is often euphemistically referred to as "transitioning from practice." Perhaps the idea of transitioning, in the sense of gradually letting go of certain work commitments, offers doctors the most promise, because it allows time for mending the gaps created by the hole that not working can create. Many of the skills, determination, and creativity that served them well as doctors offered promise for these individuals' ability to adapt and find contentment in a life after medicine.

3

Refined Retirement and Fulfillment Employment: **THE CEOS**

Some people may find it strange to feel sympathy for wealthy executives who have the financial means to enjoy a refined retirement, but their experiences, too, show how a consistent, career-focused life can become an impediment to contentment in retirement. The chief executive officers (CEOs) I interviewed for this book had excelled at developing their careers; however, they were not as competent at developing a life distinct from their work identity. Each advanced in a career that rewarded a deep commitment, and their work tended to penetrate every aspect of their lives. Then at a certain point, usually somewhere around 60 years old, each was expected to relinquish their position of power and forgo the part of their identity that had been such an important source of fulfillment.

Media portrayals and advertisements foster images of wealthy retirees who spend their time playing golf, traveling, enjoying cruises, and spending money. They look vibrant, happy, and otherwise satisfied with their lives. In his book, *Cultural Aging: Life Course, Lifestyle, and Senior Worlds*, Stephen Katz discusses how mature adulthood has been reimaged through popular culture in ways that commodify values of youth.[1] Representations of the refined retiree take us far from early conceptualizations of retirement as an age-graded exit from full-time employment, originally created to address concerns about later-life poverty.[2]

This chapter focuses on the experiences of five retired health-care CEOs who shared a common sense of discontentment and ennui when they retired, illustrating that media depictions oversimplify this important life transition. I begin with Ted, who retired of his own accord when he was 55 years old. By all accounts, Ted should have enjoyed his refined retirement, but instead he struggled with his sense of self when he stopped working. Next, I present Steve, a gay man who rose steadily to the top of his career, but who then faced a sharp plummet when he was forced to retire. Steve's experience illustrates the pain of involuntary retirement and unmet retirement expectations. Then we meet Bob, who was plagued by his own longing to be back in charge—a feeling he likened to "longing for a mistress." Finally, I discuss the stories of two trailblazing women: Elizabeth, who had planned well for her retirement yet struggled to balance being a mother, a provider, and someone who identified strongly with work; and Clare, who was not sure whether she had been more challenged by retirement or her battle with cancer.

REFINED RETIREMENT

Ted, CEO of a Large Nonprofit Health Plan Organization

Ted prided himself on being a family man. He had always been ambitious at work, cared about his community, and had lots of hobbies. He led a privileged life. He was generous to charities and generous with his time with me. During our third interview, Ted shared his secret ingredients to having a good life: being good at his work, staying happily married, and remaining healthy.

Ted had always imagined a picture-perfect retirement for himself and his wife, Kate. He thought that retirement was something successful people did at 55—he clarified that perhaps this was just an impression he'd gotten from watching commercials and movies when he was growing up. Regardless of his reasoning, Ted put away extra money for retirement, diversified his financial portfolio, and adjusted into more conservative investments as he approached 55. He had worked hard all his life, saved, and owned several investment properties. When he retired on schedule, at 55, Ted began his refined retirement. By his own estimation, he should have been content in his retirement.

Instead, despite his good health, he lacked the secret ingredients to a good retirement. He missed his much-loved job and found it frustrating to spend full days on the same schedule as his wife. Ted missed the structure of work. He felt remiss for not receiving a paycheck and his good health made him feel particularly unproductive and unsatisfied.

Even the quietude of retirement was disconcerting for Ted. He traveled, played golf and tennis, swam, ran, skied, and read (he was a fan of murder mysteries and what he called "airplane reading"). But these weren't enough to keep him feeling fulfilled in his retirement. In part, Ted had an added layer of challenge associated with his transition to retirement, pertaining mainly to his field of work—health care. He felt that his work had always been associated with an important mission and a clear contribution to society. He explained, "You feel that you belong to a very big, important world, and being a CEO in that kind of space is equally gratifying. There's constant affirmation of the value of what I was doing. To walk away is quite difficult actually. I don't believe there's any other place where the mission is more pronounced than it is in health care generally."

Work Had Been Gratifying, Retirement Stirred Up Questions

For Ted, being retired stirred up questions about the significance and purpose of his life. In his initial transition to retirement, he became more active within his church community. Ted explained that retirement led him to suddenly find time to think about things that had been pushed to the back of his mind. He said, "You wonder things like: am I going to live 'til my grandchildren are old enough to really know me? I started going through all that kind of stuff in my head like, 'What is my purpose? And what have I contributed?' I questioned everything because I sort of felt like I lost sight of everything when I retired."

Ted's career featured a steady progression to higher paying jobs. To retire was to flatline after all the time he had spent rising through the ranks and proving himself. His experience as a CEO was demanding; he had grown accustomed to constantly being scrutinized. Being in charge gave him a chance to be his best self. He said,

> When you're a CEO you have to anticipate or should know that people are looking at every aspect of your life: your car, your clothes, what time you arrive, what time you go home, how often you go to the washroom, what you order in the cafeteria. Everything. Absolutely everything. There's no such thing as being anonymous or one of the crowd. I had to get used to being aware that I was being watched and that casualness had to be very deliberate and very well acted. It's important to be aware of how you're behaving at work and at the shopping mall so that it's not inconsistent. You have to learn to be yourself at both places, you have to be your fantastic self at all times so nobody will become confused.

When Ted retired at age 55, he had a big party with more than 200 guests. He couldn't remember much about it except to say that it was "a big to-do about nothing." Still, he remembered feeling that the timing was right. Ted said,

> I had reached my 100,000 hours by age 55. I spent many years leaving the house for work before my sons were awake. And I'd have some reception a couple nights a week that kept me out until late. And then there were always at least a few traveling weekends. Toward the end of my career, sometimes I'd have an earphone in each ear for different conference calls. . . . I had been super productive and I thought retiring at 55 was the ultimate signal that I had achieved success.

No Longer Grounded

Almost immediately after his retirement party, Ted vacationed with his wife in Europe for a month. This trip marked the longest time he had gone in his entire life without working. They had a full itinerary and met up with friends and one of their three sons. But when they returned home, Ted no longer felt grounded. Questions about what he was doing with his life and the prospect of no longer being needed were difficult for him to get a handle on.

Ted explained, "When you leave, it's not like nobody calls, but your phone is very quiet . . . it's as if you died and you are no longer needed, right? Your CEO successor doesn't call. Nothing. Zero. It's an adjustment because all of a sudden you're not needed. Even though you plan to leave, it still is a harsh adjustment."

There were lots of details Ted had never considered:

> There was a bunch of logistic stuff that I didn't appreciate during my career. Like how much I had depended on my office team. I thought that when I would be on my own, it would be easy to

transition appointments. But then, it wasn't easy and my wife wasn't about to do that for me. She had her thing and I found it very difficult to be with her all the time. I mean I love her and I love being with her, but I've never been around her so much. She has a funny way of getting through the day and some of the things she does are just tedious for me. I have a need to contribute in a different way to society. I feel the need to be productive. I think it's embarrassing to forget your appointments. I had a really hard time just with managing my time because I'd never had so much of it.

Ted also found retirement challenging because he took so much pride in being a provider and in distinguishing himself from his father. When Ted was four, his father left. His mother had singlehandedly raised him and his older sister. Although Ted would hear about his father from time to time, he never saw him again. What he knew was that his father always had a hard time holding down a job, had married another woman, and started a new family with her.

Productivity and Fulfillment

Ted was determined to be a more involved father, and he had strong ideas about how he and Kate would raise their boys. He also resolved to be a good provider for his family, with Kate as a stay-at-home mom. In his retirement, Ted was still able to provide financially for his family, but not working detracted from the distinguished image he had of himself.

Around two years after Ted retired, he had a feeling in the pit of his stomach that told him to return to work. He was healthy and wealthy but being able-bodied and not working was problematic to Ted. Living out the "golden years" of retirement did not sit well with him. He realized that, for him, being successful was intimately connected with being a member of the paid workforce. Working allowed him to maintain not only the lifestyle he and his family had become accustomed to but also a core part of who he was.

The concept of "successful aging" has been popularized in the academic literature most prominently by John Rowe and Robert Khan, who describe successful aging as the attainment of three key states: low disease-related disability, high cognitive and physical functioning, and active engagement with life.[3] For Ted, the achievement of these three states made him all the more dissatisfied with his retirement. The concept of "productive aging" has since emerged from theoretical work on "successful aging" to emphasize the importance of remaining engaged in constructive activity—in particular, on extending the working lives of older adults.[4] In keeping with this concept, to quell his desires to be productive again and reestablish his sense of success, Ted began consulting part time.

He eventually found himself moving into a partnership position and four years into his retirement, Ted went on to co-own a small consulting firm. He explained it was about finding fulfillment:

> At first being retired was like being captain and then kicked off the football team. You miss the guys. You miss making the calls. Getting into retirement is hard. It's hard just to stop and lose your network of people. Our whole social life was around people we knew basically from work. We had a pretty tight group . . . I had to go back in when I retired. And I found that working again helped me feel fulfilled. That and the church really helped. I got much more involved with the church when I retired and, through it, we are doing important work.

Ted's work had instilled in him a need to contribute, and he enjoyed being rewarded for working hard. These rewards were not limited to financial success; working also provided him with a sense of fulfillment that could not be replaced by other activities. Ted had spent most of his life focused on moving up into increasingly important positions throughout his career; in contrast, retirement had the potential to turn into a downward spiral. Although Ted struggled to find the secret ingredients to being successfully retired, reengaging in paid work and getting involved with his church helped him find a greater sense of contentment.

A DISTINGUISHED CAREER

Steve, CEO of a University Health Network

Like Ted, Steve imagined that he would realize later-life success by not working in his retirement. But, being catapulted into retirement by means other than Steve's own created feelings of discontentment. Ted's and Steve's career trajectories and retirement experiences have many contrasts. Most notably, Steve never considered himself to be a conventional person. He explained, "As a gay man, I was accustomed to having a side of myself that was hidden and separate from work. I never held myself to normal standards. I always dressed better! I was always smarter than the people I worked under. I worked harder, and I think I cared more about quality and making things better."

He saw his relationship with work as different from other people's because he didn't quite feel that he fit the mold of a CEO. He remembered a mentor telling him that if he wasn't a male with a wife, two kids, and a dog, he could never become a hospital CEO. But Steve worked his way up the ladder, rising through the ranks of hospital administration with no wife, no dog, and no kids. He won the trust and respect of his co-workers by distinguishing himself and by excelling in his commitment to his work.

When he became a CEO, he continued to distinguish himself not only by setting a good example but also by being disciplined and careful. He clarified,

> I had to learn how to be more judicious in how I used humor, how I used certain language, and what I appeared as. People want things out of a CEO. They have a whole body of expectations that need to be fulfilled. Some CEOs want to be 'one of the guys.' That's not what the guys want. I've seen colleagues out there boozing it up with their fellow employees—what a disaster! I've seen just a couple of examples of those disasters in my career, and you just do not want that. So, I think it's a bit lonely in my career; you're by yourself. I've always been given the opportunity to go make the big mistake, and I don't think I ever did, though others might disagree.

In part, Steve admitted to being motivated by the money. But most of his motivation came from being recognized as the one in charge. Once becoming a CEO felt like a realistic option, he had spent almost every waking hour working toward that goal. The CEO title came to Steve in his late 40s—he recalled the evening he received the news as the peak of his career: "I was naively optimistic about what being CEO would be like. I had a fantasy of it. The night we went out to celebrate was in many ways the last time I really felt optimistic in all senses of the word. I imagined feeling distinguished, and the experience was more like being singled out for everything."

Being CEO was incredibly demanding. Steve had to bear the blame for everything. His work left him little time with his life partner, Russel, who was also a busy and driven professional. Steve never stopped working. He had many social engagements that were part of his job, but each event became less fun and more work. In retrospect, it was clear to him that he had not lived a balanced life by any means after taking on the role of CEO. Yet, Steve distinguished himself in it. He showed me regional awards his hospital network had received and news clippings of public praise.

Steve knew he couldn't keep up the pace that his work demanded forever, and he had an exit strategy that involved retiring at 65. He figured that was an age when he would still be young enough to enjoy his successes. Maybe he and Russel would live the "good life," taking cruises around the world. He never worried about how he would fill his time. But a full ten years before age 65, Steve's hospital was embroiled in a major legal matter and he was forced into retirement.

Retirement Was a Euphemism

For Steve, the term "retirement" was used as a euphemism—a tidy way to publicly describe what was actually a termination. When he learned from the chair of the hospital network's board that he would no longer be CEO, Steve wasn't even sure how the newspaper would report it, but in all printed and public accounts, he had "made the decision to retire."

He remembered that time as "terrible." He explained,

It was horrible. It was like post-traumatic [stress]. I mean, I had dreams about the termination conversation for months. It was great to have some free time, to get off the treadmill. Yeah, and not work fifteen hours a day. That part was great, but from an emotional perspective, it was terrible. I had a really hard time trying to figure out what was going to happen next, because it was bad. I was not happy about what transpired at the hospital. I had to take the fall. I was also not happy with how I had to leave. But then I was like, "Ok, so this happened, it's terrible, it's horrible, unanticipated." But I realized, "You've been through crap before, and life goes on." So, I "retired."

Steve hasn't been able to eat beef carpaccio since the night he had dinner with the chair of the board, who informed Steve that he needed to step down. From news accounts, I was able to learn that some money had been mismanaged in the time leading up to Steve's retirement. But the press seemed to paint him in a positive light, with no direct links between his retirement and the financial mismanagement.

Steve described his retirement party as one of the worst parts of his transition. At the party, which was imposed on him suddenly, a board member pulled Steve aside and told him with tears that he felt awful about the way things had turned out. But Steve had no time to react—he simply had to go with the plan. He had to pretend that retiring was his choice and that everything was going according to plan.

I Don't Know How to Do Nothing All Day

Steve felt robbed of the opportunity to plan his retirement. And when he was suddenly not working, the idea of taking cruises seemed bizarre. Russel was nowhere near ready to retire, and Steve was despondent: "I was angry and dejected. I really wanted to be working, but I couldn't exactly apply for another job right away. The papers said I wanted to retire. I think we all know that we're supposed to retire eventually, but for some of us, it is sooner rather than later."

For a while, Steve brooded. His notions of retirement turned quickly from the commercial images to negative ideas about humanity, laziness, and boredom. He looked at retired people he knew, like his older brother's wife, and resented their lack of productivity. He explained,

> I love my sister-in-law dearly, but she does nothing but look after herself and have lunch and go to lunch. She invited me to a dinner party with some of her friends when I first retired. And I just kept thinking, "How do they do not do anything?" I kept thinking, "How can they do nothing all day?" I do not get it. I truly don't get it. I don't know how you do nothing. She doesn't volunteer; she doesn't contribute to anything. Like, what is that? Is it something about your upbringing? Is it something about the environment you were brought up in? What is it? I do not know. I do not understand it. My brother is a lawyer, he is still working and he is past retirement age, which is how my sister-in-law can do nothing. I always remember my mom, even though there were five of us, she did volunteer work and she did all that stuff for the church, so she was always busy. So maybe it is just the environment I was brought up in. I do not know, but doing nothing is terrible.

Steve received generous financial compensation, but he could not buy fulfillment. He spent a painful year not working, floating between lunches and restless vacations. A little over a year after his retirement, he found a position on an executive pharmaceutical sales team. When I interviewed him, almost a decade later, he was still in that position. He explained,

> [I am] working like a dog and loving it. Retirement was a kick in the pants. I spend a good amount of time with golf clubs

and tennis balls, but no way in hell am I going to not work. I was never a refrigerator nurse, by any means—you know the ones who were working because they needed a new refrigerator. They weren't working because they wanted to work. I didn't just want to work, I loved to work, I needed to work. I get emails from my buddies saying, "When are you coming back, can you golf?" And I like golfing but it just cannot be my life. And then one of my friends said if you practice more you would be a better golfer and I said to him, but you know I don't really care about my handicap. I'm working on projects now because I like the people, because the projects are stimulating and the compensation is good. If I do it right, do it the way I think it needs to be done, there will be value for the company. But this is not a stepping stone for anything. This is for my sense of well-being.

Work was integral to Steve's sense of self and that didn't change when he abruptly retired. Working made Steve feel productive and valuable. He dreaded the idea of being "cast out" ever again. The skills he acquired as a CEO served him well as he repositioned himself in the workforce, and he was adamant that he would never let himself be vulnerable enough to be pushed into retiring again.

Even so, Steve identified as a retiree. He said,

To be successful in retirement, I think you've got to have a lot of capacity for things that are not clear, things are murky, things are political in life and in retirement, you have to seek out the kind of work you find enjoyment in. People always watch you the closest when you're dealing with the most difficult problems. They want to see how you're going to handle it. If you handle that well, then you gain a lot of trust, credibility with the staff. I've always kind of enjoyed dealing with emergencies and difficulties.

It's always been a kind of adrenaline rush. But not working at all that is another story, it's a story that is the opposite of an adrenaline rush in a bad way.

In *The Hero's Farewell: What Happens When CEOs Retire*, Jeffrey Sonnenfeld describes how the departure style of a CEO holds important implications for their adjustment to retirement.[5] Research suggests that adjustment to involuntary retirement is particularly difficult.[6] And for Steve, after a life of moving into positions of greater control and autonomy, a forced retirement was particularly devastating. The experience dampened his fantasies about enjoying cruises with his partner, forever remolding his conventional ideas about retirement. Although he was still young and in good health when I interviewed him, Steve was adamant that he would never retire in a way that meant *not working*.

A WOUNDED VET

Bob, CEO of a Health-Care Consulting Firm

By his own estimation, Bob was destined to become a CEO. He had always been good at getting what he wanted, and he prided himself on being a good leader. When he retired, he lost a bit of his sense of self. Bob was in his mid-70s and five years into retirement from his position as CEO of an international health-care consulting firm when we began our interviews. One of the first things he told me was "I think I was made to be a CEO. I think of my career like being in the army. You'll never be a good soldier unless you've got a bit of war behind you. But being retired can feel like being a wounded vet."

Bob had always enjoyed being in charge, but he also expected that he would quickly acclimate to retirement. He had always adapted quickly to career transitions throughout his life and figured that it wouldn't take much time for him to get accustomed to reading his favorite newspapers, going for a walk, and then having a lunch date before spending some time with the grandkids. He suspected that being out of the loop would require some getting used to, but he also thought that he might *like* being less integrally involved with work and having more flexible days.

Hiring people, moving money around, moving people around, moving himself, and being on the go were constant features in Bob's career. He enjoyed making big decisions and helping a company grow, and even the distasteful task of firing people seemed like it was useful, in that Bob figured it would help him mentally prepare for retirement: "When you have to let people go, they don't send you Christmas cards anymore and people look at you differently, but I never let it bother me. I told myself, 'We all have to leave at one point or the other,' and I always imagined I was going to be one of those guys that did it with honor."

Knowing When to Move and When to Leave

As his two children were growing up, Bob relocated for a new job every few years. He described five moves in a ten-year span before his children went to college. Sometimes the whole family moved with him, and at other times, Bob worked in a different state from his family, often for years at a time.

Although he moved often, Bob had always made time for hobbies. During our second interview, Bob brought some photos of himself golfing at a famous course with colleagues. He also showed me pictures of his sons and his wife on his phone, but he paused the longest on the golf photo. This picture clearly triggered a fond memory. I was struck by the deep connection Bob had between his work and leisure. His golfing had always intertwined with work, and it was clear that his time spent on leisure activities throughout his life was also time spent working or thinking about work.

At age 65, Bob announced his retirement. He thought that was a respectable time to make his exit. Retiring was not about the pension or a generous financial package (although he got both), it was about an internal pressure he felt to leave while he was still in charge. For Bob, it was important for a leader to have a keen sense of when to leave. Remaining in a leadership position in health care for too long could cause problems for the organization; health care thrives on vitality, youth, and new ideas. Bob also felt some external pressures. He sensed that people expected him to retire at 65 because that was the traditional retirement age, and he did not want to be the kind of person who was remembered poorly for having stayed on too long.

Several lavish dinner parties marked Bob's retirement. More than 400 people attended the first one, and Bob was very much enjoying it up until one of his friends, Joel, shockingly went into cardiac arrest. Bob explained that his friend survived, but the incident was a big wake-up call to him and several others in his social circle. Joel's near-death experience also helped Bob realize that lives are fragile, and any one of them could knock off at any time. Bob would face health scares with his lungs and, later, his heart. These experiences helped Bob come to recognize that although he cared about how he would be remembered when he died, he had no control over who would be at his funeral or what people would say about him.

About a week after Bob's last retirement party, Bob and his wife Patricia went on an extensive trip through Asia. He explained,

> She saw the trip as a shopping spree. I saw it as a turning point. I
> enjoyed the freedom at first. Freedom, yeah, freedom. That's the

word I feel covers it. At first when I retired, I felt freedom. And yet, I felt lost because suddenly I realized what I had given up. I almost didn't know who I was at first. The biggest fear is that you go from being known to an unknown. Very, very quickly and if your identity is tied up in that "being known," then it all becomes inconsequential, *you* become inconsequential.

My Heart Still Flutters

Bob thought he was going to continue enjoying feeling free, but instead he missed the feeling of being important, being in control, and being connected to and through work. He described thinking about work in his retirement as akin to having an affair:

> You find yourself secretly thinking about that person. Maybe she'll call you or send some sort of message that she still thinks of you. When you retire, you're supposed to move on and be happy about the choices you made. And I'm thinking . . . a call to get my opinion really wouldn't bother me at all, I wouldn't want it all the time. It would be like a little reminder that they're still interested . . . Except that I know that I'm better off without it. My heart is literally better off without all that. But my heart still flutters thinking about when I was in charge.

In his retirement, Bob realized he could never go back to being a CEO. Although he was grateful for his time in that role, he found it difficult to replace that feeling. He continued to describe his work life as analogous to a romance, which was evident through his choice of words. He had been on top of the world for a good amount of time, but that "relationship was over and there was no going back." He began to feel that he had given up his role too early.

Maybe he could engage in a "rebound"—a new job to help him get over the one he'd "lost."

So, Bob rechanneled his energy into doing things that brought him a sense of fulfillment. In time, he went to see a consultant, less for the financial advice and more for advice on how to spend his time in retirement. With the consultant's help, Bob decided to get involved with helping run a charitable organization that assisted people with mental and physical impairments through exposure to animals. This work gave him a goal to focus on, meetings to attend around the world, and a way of helping others.

In our last interview, four years into his retirement, Bob summarized his experience as follows:

I was prepared for retirement because I spent my adult life moving around, recreating myself in some phases, and you go through different phases. I worked with some people off and on for over a decade and you miss that interaction, you get quite close. When I retired, for example, I missed having a secretary. I had to do things myself that I've never done, obviously. You get older and don't have the energy for certain things. I made the decision that I wasn't going to pursue any employment opportunities that I didn't create myself. I had to adjust to not being in on the "big action." I worked long hours my whole life, and I did a lot of stuff that I really enjoyed. So do I do anything different today? I realize—no, I just don't have a team of a hundred and fifty-eight thousand people around the world to back me up. I think my wife really knew that retirement for me wasn't that I would just stop working. It just took me a little while to figure that out too. I mean, I'm in a very fortunate position in that I don't have to work for money. But maybe I'm unfortunate too, in that I need to be working for my own sense of who I am.

The premise of role theory is that difficulties in the adjustment to retirement, or feelings of discontentment associated with retirement, derive from the loss of status and identity associated with the paid workforce.[7] Thus, retirement was unsatisfying for Bob because, like many other professionals, work was a critical piece of who he was. The stronger the connection between personal identity and work identity, the more likely it is that an individual will seek postretirement employment or bridge employment.[8] Increasingly, people are reentering the paid workforce, and they are doing so not because of financial need but because it provides them with a sense of connection to society.[9]

Bob processed normative expectations about when he would retire. Ultimately, however, retirement did not suit his desires, and he was driven to reenter the workforce. This return to work gave him a better sense of who he was. Although research has suggested that men are more likely than women to experience feelings of loss in retirement, the connections that exist among work, personal identity, and adjustment to retirement are changing for women, too.[10] For the first time, large numbers of women are approaching traditional retirement age after years of paid work experience. Women currently account for just over 4 percent of the CEOs in Fortune 500 or Fortune 1000 companies, but their experiences are paving the way for future generations.[11] I discuss two of these female CEO's retirement experiences in the next two stories.

WORK HAD BEEN A WAY TO A BETTER LIFE

Elizabeth, CEO of a Large Community Hospital

Elizabeth had always been independent, a planner. She thought about retirement in her 30s, began planning for it in her late 40s, and started practicing for it in her late 50s, which was roughly ten years before she actually retired from her position as CEO. To her, "practicing" initially meant making time in her schedule, three days during the workweek, to take a walk at lunchtime. Then she joined a reading group, started going to seminars about retirement, and attended retreats held by financial investment firms.[12]

Being such a good planner helped Elizabeth rise to corner office at a time when few women did. She had not come from a wealthy family, and from an early age, learned that money was valuable. Earning money helped her establish her independence, which suited her nature well as a young woman. She viewed herself as:

> a sort of more practical person. And I've always been indepen-
> dent. People from my social situation always knew you would
> look after yourself. It became quite clear to me very early that I
> wasn't going to be dependent on anybody. Whatever successes
> I had, I achieved on my own. I was the one who always looked
> after everything. I worried about my retirement because I loved
> the challenges and the variety in my work. I worried about
> retirement for a long while, so I tried to plan for it.

In highly economically developed countries, effective financial planning for retirement is the hallmark of successful aging. Commercials and billboards convey its importance, and many books have been written about how proper financial retirement plans make retirement easier and more enjoyable, particularly for women. Much less is said, however, about what women who loved their work actually are supposed to *do* in their retirement.

For Elizabeth, work created meaning and variety. Although she always lived in the same part of the country in which she had been raised, Elizabeth made many career transitions as she rose to positions with increasingly greater authority. She thrived on being busy and making use of her organizational skills. Many other people would have viewed her work as a constant source of stress and anxiety, but for Elizabeth, work had always been stimulating and enjoyable.

Work-Life Balance

At a young age, Elizabeth realized she was smart and that work offered her a way to escape the negative behaviors and patterns she had observed in her childhood. Elizabeth grew up in an alcoholic family. She never imagined that she would want to have children or get married. Yet, in her late 30s, Elizabeth married, and, at 42, she gave birth to her son. Elizabeth worked until the day before her caesarean section.

After her son's birth, Elizabeth found it difficult to balance work with all the extra demands on her time. She explained,

Once my son was born, he was always number one. But I never stopped caring about work and I never stopped working. In fact, I'd often be distracted in the middle of a conversation with someone, with my son, and he'd know I wasn't there in spirit because I was always thinking about work. I'd say, "Oh, sorry. What was that? Where . . . where were we?" That was the reality most of the time. When he was younger, I just couldn't turn work off.

Elizabeth told me her ex-husband was a "less-involved parent." She recalled a time at her son's birthday party before they divorced,

A friend of mine remembers seeing me and him and our kid at—a really funny story but it's true—she remembers seeing us at the Old Spaghetti Factory. You know the Old Spaghetti Factory? It's one of those really noisy places that have birthday parties, and while I was supervising the birthday party, my ex-husband had his earphones on and was reading the newspaper [laughs]. And you know it was really loud, and he hated places that were really loud, and I don't remember being aggravated with him for that. I thought that in his own way, he was participating. But when I separated from him, this friend of mine said to me, "I know that sometimes you had to put up with quite a bit from that man," and I said, "Oh geez, I don't even think I was mad at him about that, it was just par for the course."

Elizabeth divorced when her son was 4 years old, and she never remarried. When her son was younger, she hired help to assist with cleaning her house and bringing him to and from school. She said, "What I cared about was being at school events, doing outings with my son on our weekends together. I remember one time I said something about being the pizza mom for his class. I was going to take one turn to be the pizza mom, and my son said, 'You're doing *what*? You're the pizza mom?' "

Elizabeth cared deeply about being a good mother. She expended a great deal of energy trying to separate her work from her role as a mother. Sometimes Elizabeth would have to attend work events during weekends, and on occasion, some of the men in senior management would bring their wives and children. But Elizabeth never brought her son. She drew clear lines between her professional and personal life—except, perhaps, when she used her weekends to catch up on work or do personal maintenance like ensuring that her hair was dyed to avoid showing grays. This sign of aging wasn't acceptable, she believed, in her professional role. When she had to attend work events in the evenings and on weekends, Elizabeth usually arranged for her son to be with his father, but she also relied heavily on babysitters.

Since the feminist revolution of the 1960s and 1970s, working women have faced this enormous challenge. For professional women, like Elizabeth, retirement poses a threat to this carefully cultivated balance. Elizabeth felt that she had been able to maintain a continuous and upwardly mobile career path while still balancing her personal commitments; the idea of losing her connection to the workforce through retirement threatened her sense of balance and precipitated a period of grief.

Work Fulfills Financial and Emotional Needs

Throughout her life, Elizabeth also battled alcoholism and depression. She decided that it was time for her to retire when her full retirement pension took effect at age 65. At that point, Elizabeth entered into a major struggle with alcohol. She described her transition to retirement as a deep dive into unknown waters. She had expected warm waters, but instead she found them to be frigid and uncomfortable. Resilient as she was, Elizabeth fell adrift.

But despite this, and as would be expected of a good planner, Elizabeth had planned a set of her own retirement parties. She hosted three retirement parties at restaurants around the city, making sure to invite people whose connections might be useful to her in retirement. Each of the parties served a function, just as Elizabeth intended to serve a purpose in retirement.

At the time of our last interview, Elizabeth described herself as being in a stage of recovery. She was in her early 70s and doing consulting work. She showed me her eye-catching webpage and talked about her plans to take her consulting work to a broader market. She said that, other than her son and cousin, she had few strong personal connections that she cared deeply about. She took pride in the fact that she was still earning an income, and her focus on personal finances had by no means faded in retirement.

Work afforded her with a connection to society and a lifestyle that she did not want to give up. She described a recent trip as follows:

> Somebody paid my way and I got to go to Madrid last month. I stayed at the Ritz. The Ritz, where Alec Baldwin was. I met him in the revolving door. But, you know, I'm not ever going to afford that if I'm not working. That's a feature of my current life that I won't always have. I fly over 100,000 miles a year, or I have until very recently. I get to be super elite so I can get all the points on the days I want, and that's gonna disappear. You know, a lot of those things change when you retire, because you can't really afford to pay for that. But while I keep this up, I can afford my expenses. I live in a house. I like it. I'd like to stay there. One of my cousins is living with me right now and, actually, my son has been home recently for a while. I like to be able to stay in my house. So, I'm crunching all the numbers to see whether I can really afford to stay. You know, those are all the things you have to think about giving up. And so, it's always a little tempting to think, 'Oh, if I work a year more, couple of years more, I'll be more secure.' Everybody, women especially, worry that they're gonna outlive their money. I think the financial piece of it is a big piece of dealing with retirement, even if you have money. I'm still trying to see that I have all my financial ducks in a row, but I still can't figure out what I will do with myself when I don't have to check my e-mail every minute.

Elizabeth was likely the most "prepared" retiree I interviewed, but even for her, retirement was a rocky transition. "Some things, like how to wrap up your whole life, just can't be planned," she told me. She had always worried about independence, as expressed in fears surrounding financial security and isolation. Elizabeth had focused on carefully separating her roles as a professional and as a mother, but along the way, she had allocated little time for friendships, relationships, or interests. She did not enjoy her reading groups as much as she thought she would when she had begun practicing for retirement; instead, she realized that *work* fulfilled her financial and emotional needs.

By continuing to work as a consultant, she was able to remain on the "net positive" side of life. She brought in an income as opposed to simply drawing on savings, and she gained a sense of contentment through the intellectual stimulation and social connections that work brought her.

In this way, Elizabeth's retirement looked a lot like the experiences of the male CEOs I interviewed. Retirement wasn't a time for indulgence and leisure, nor was it a chance to explore new endeavors. Instead, retirement was a reminder that work had dominated her sense of self. Elizabeth was once again a trailblazer who didn't fit into what she viewed as the traditional role of women.

MOVING UP AS A WOMAN IN A MAN'S CAREER

Clare, CEO of a Private Hospital

Clare was not a careful planner and was never as concerned as Elizabeth about money. Clare was always the best and the tallest student in her class. She never had children and never joined a book club. She was good at sports, liked being in charge, and *loved* working.

Clare married her high school boyfriend, Larry, in her 20s. But over time, she realized that she was far more ambitious than her husband and then their marriage was doomed. After their divorce in her late 20s, Clare went on to graduate school and began to advance through various positions at work. She explained, "I always knew that I wanted to be a manager and then, when I became a manager, I thought, 'well I want to be a bigger manager.' Once I sort of 'nailed it,' I thought okay I have got to move on. It's sort of like flipping houses. It's like, okay, I have fixed it all up and it's time to move on. And then when I got to be a bigger manager, um, then you know another opportunity came along and I applied for it and I just kept at it."

Clare moved up the ranks, from filing clerk to CEO of a private hospital (and many health-care positions in between). According to Clare, being a woman in a male-dominated career was difficult at times:

> I guess as a woman, it can be tricky. Every other woman thinks you're after her husband even if you're not. Living in a couple's world and all of a sudden not being part of a couple was very difficult. Monday to Thursday your friends were there for you, but Friday, Saturday, and Sunday, they weren't. So, you either have to create a whole new network of friends and that's more difficult because of your work and the lifestyle you're leading or you just throw yourself into the work. I loved my work. I loved my job but my social life has been pretty scarce.

Being an older, single working woman was particularly tricky for Clare. She was always cognizant of the fact that being a woman meant that she received greater scrutiny. Women in her field had less room for error. But Clare's dedication to her work and "some luck" helped her thrive and rise to the position of CEO. She remembered, "I had the motivation and drive to fully focus on my work. I was ready to be at the top of the ladder. But it's always harder as a woman. I needed more luck than a man might have needed and I really had to put in my dues."

Like Elizabeth, Clare felt that her career benefited from continuing to look young and healthy. When she developed breast cancer, Clare saw her treasured career dissolve. She tried to keep working after her diagnosis—she never wanted to retire—but her oncologist told her that she would be crazy to continue working. As soon as members of the board that oversaw her hospital got wind of her illness, Clare felt she had no other choice than to retire.

I Don't Know Which Was Worse, The Cancer or Retiring

Within a day of announcing her diagnosis to the full board, hospital staff contacted her about the assembly of her retirement package. And within a few weeks of the announcement, she was given a retirement party. Clare described her party as a blur; it felt rushed, she felt sick.

She felt as if she were being pushed out the door:

> When I retired, I had unfinished business. I was not ready to stop, but I am a bit of a sap. I like to look after making things better for people. Never mind, who was looking after me in all that? I think retirement was, for me, like leaving unfinished business, retiring not at my own choice but because of an external event and external pressures. Had I had planned it, I mean if I always planned to retire and, you know, go live in Hawaii, or something, if I had a plan in place I think, it might have been easier, but I found retiring unbelievably difficult. So, you are dealing with cancer, and that is hard, but retiring was intolerable.

Retirement, like cancer, wasn't something Clare wanted or was prepared for. Her transition to retirement was cold and lonely. It was a time that marked the end of what had brought meaning to her life for many decades. She described her retirement much like her cancer diagnosis: malignant. She said,

> It was an awful time for me, because you have to lie on the machine and you are in this great big cold room by yourself and you're stuck in the machine. As a patient, I was treated really well, but the whole emotional piece around it, nobody pays any attention to that, and that's the thing—you end up dealing with going through that by yourself so you are dealing with the cancer and being alone, but I was also dealing with the loss of my career. I don't know which was worse, the cancer or retiring, you know? But they coincided, which makes it worse.

Not only did the timing of her diagnosis and retirement overlap, but her memories of adapting to retirement were intertwined with the experience of going to her chemotherapy treatments and her subsequent recovery. She attended her treatments alone, and those experiences caused her to question the ways health-care systems often left patients to fend for themselves. She also questioned the priorities she had set throughout her life: her heavy focus on her career, leaving little time for a life outside of work. She was aware that some of the men who achieved similar positions of prominence had families, and even second families (after the first ones ended in divorce), but Clare could not see how it would have been possible for her to have both in her own life. She resented the idea that a person who had devoted herself to improving the health of others would be brought down professionally by her own declining health. As Clare emerged from the other side of her battle with cancer, she came to resent even more the idea that she had been forced to retire.

The Challenge of Getting Over Working

Several years into her retirement, Clare tried to adjust to life without work. Her experience with cancer did not generate a new sense of purpose in her life. Instead, she recovered, held firm, and resolved to work again. She was quite frank in explaining that she had a hard time filling her time when she recovered. She asked, "What do you do all day? I tried golf and I golf pretty well three days a week. But more than that was pretty boring. The women that were there golfing were all the wives. They were women who never worked and all they could talk about was who was sleeping with whom or whatever and who was buying which product. I mean it was boring shit to be frank."

I interviewed Clare for the last time during her lunch break at the office where she worked as an executive vice president. Clare was approximately 80 years old at time, but uncomfortable sharing her exact age with me. At one point when she talking about her age in general terms, she checked to ensure that the door was closed because she didn't want anyone from her office knowing how old she was. Despite her self-consciousness about her age, Clare thought that age and her life experiences enhanced her sense of humor in ways that favorably distinguished her from younger executives. Clare laughed as she shared stories of times when she handled antics better than some of her more junior colleagues, like the time when a mischievous patient pranked the hospital by ordering dozens of pizzas or the time that a patient advertised hospital furniture and equipment as for sale and gave the hospital address as the pickup location.

Clare was good at addressing patient needs and had honed her skills with age, particularly her fundraising skills. Clare explained that her key to success was making herself essential. In her current role, she had saved the hospital multiple times. Given these successes, she decreased the likelihood that she could be pushed out again anytime soon.

She summarized her position as follows: "At this point, I don't have many needs. Shit, I could just stop working anytime and I'm quite sure I wouldn't outlive my money. I don't have kids, although I have several organizations I will leave money to. But, you know I worked all my life. My work was always a big part of who I was. I don't know how you get over working, I started work when I was fourteen you know?"

FULFILLMENT EMPLOYMENT

Although each of the CEOs I interviewed retired in a distinct way that spoke to their personal struggles, the CEOs whose stories are shared in this chapter also reveal many of the contemporary challenges that arise from unrealistic, out-of-date, and ageist expectations about retirement. All eventually sought out new work in retirement, but not for financial reasons and often in spite of health aliments. Their work had been an important source of personal fulfillment, therefore each had to find a way to tailor their retirement in a way that helped them regain their sense of worth.

In contrast to popular portrayals of the refined retiree, these CEOs longed to be productive. And being productive clearly translated into engaging in paid work. Their stories would have been much simpler and fit more easily with media representations of wealthy retirees if a retirement filled with leisure activities, hobbies, grandchildren, or volunteer work had satisfied them.[13] Instead, they experienced a sense of discontentment when they relinquished their work responsibilities. They shared a sense that something meaningful disappeared from their lives when they retired and stopped working, which was regained only by reengaging in the workforce.

The concept of *productive aging* has long involved contentious debates among scholars who have argued about its emphasis on health, physical activity, and economic contributions, raising concerns about excluding less able-bodied people or those who might contribute in ways that lack clear economic contributions to society or that are harder to measure. Likewise, the concept of *successful aging* promotes the idea that to be considered "successful" with age, one must remain healthy and engaged, avoiding isolation and decline.[14] Refined images of a retirement spent golfing and traveling on luxury vacations exclude people who do not have the good health or financial means to retire in ways that illustrate some of the exclusivity that can be associated with notions of productive and successful aging.

Though volunteer work has been promoted as a salubrious and important way to remain productive in retirement,[15] each CEO I interviewed yearned to do more than volunteer work in their retirement. They had earned high wages throughout their lives and being paid for their work was something that they were accustomed to. They saw paid work as a reason for other people to take them seriously and as a sign of a person's worth and ability. Family and leisure activities could not replace the type of fulfillment they experienced through paid work. Even though their finances were abundant, they viewed their paid work as a way to continue contributing to and giving back to society.

The "third age" is another relevant theoretical framework to consider here, in that it recognizes retirement as a time to reflect and to feel a sense of fulfillment after the phase of life during which work and family obligations are dominant.[16] In contrast, the experiences of these CEOs illustrate challenges associated with trying to disconnect from a life that was once career-centric. While these individuals had been quite good at building their careers, they had been less effective when it came to building a life outside of those careers.

Perhaps the experience of having been at the top of the ladder, as CEO, made the fall down to retirement even more difficult. The fact that each remained relatively healthy in retirement was a critical factor in their longing to remain productive by continuing to work. For these CEOs, the idea of enjoying life without work before physical decline and dependency set in wasn't enough. Ted was confident that he had the secret ingredients to a good preretirement life, but he was less sure about how to achieve a satisfying retirement until he returned to work. Steve struggled with the sense that something meaningful disappeared from his life when he stopped working. Bob likened his secret wish to return to work to that of longing for a mistress. Although he enjoyed his newfound freedom traveling through Asia with his wife, Bob was uncomfortable because, all the while, he craved the feeling of being desired by work. Elizabeth planned carefully for her retirement, but she never anticipated and prepared to cope with her feelings of being disconnected from society. Even as Clare regained her strength after retiring because of her cancer diagnosis, she questioned how to "get over working."

In retirement, each of these CEOs longed for the familiar. Becoming a CEO requires dedication, ambition, and a willingness to be exposed. By definition, a CEO is the highest-ranking executive with the responsibility to oversee, or delegate the oversight of, numerous employees. Their salaries and work obligations loom large, and their organizations reward leadership efforts that demonstrate productivity.[17]

As health-care CEOs, each had work responsibilities that affected the financial health, morale, and overall functioning of a hospital or health-care organization. They faced challenges specific to maintaining the highest standards of safety to minimize patient harm and often had to shoulder the burden of responsibility when medical errors took place, labor unions went on strike, infections were spread, and other health-related incidents took place. To excel at work, they had to know how to work well with people, work well under pressure, and lead people at every rank. They each had at least thirty years of professional experience and worked for at least five years in their role as CEO.

Elizabeth and Clare began their careers at a time when fewer women participated in the paid workforce. In part, because of this rarity, little research has been conducted on the experiences of female CEOs, and much of this research has focused on gender-based obstacles to career advancement.[18] Their work and retirement experiences illustrate some distinct concerns for women as well as remarkable similarities in terms of their dedication to work with the men I interviewed.

These five CEOs had not led what we might consider standard lives; their ambition, career achievements, and income were all above average. They devoted large amounts of time and emotional energy to their work. In turn, each derived a strong sense of identity from and received high compensation for their work. Even among their familial relations, it was clear that extraordinary amounts of time had been spent focusing instead on careers. Yet they held surprisingly conventional definitions of retirement before they entered into it. When it was time for them to retire, they either saw the writing on the wall or were forced out of their positions because others determined it was time they moved on. They retired from their careers while still possessing tremendous capabilities and interest in contributing to society and continuing to work.

In her book, *Encore Adulthood*, Phyllis Moen draws on research from a broad set of people from across the United States in their "encore years" to demonstrate the positive impact of engaging in meaningful work on well-being and health.[19] The CEOs from this chapter highlight the importance of "encore jobs" and the wasted talent that can accompany traditional notions of retirement. Their experiences further demonstrate how, for some people, success in retirement can be defined by continuing to find fulfillment through work. Their experiences also reinforce the fact that retirement cannot be a single thing; one path will not satisfy all or even most people, whether or not they've passed the "magical age" that they associate with retirement. Finally, their experiences highlight a need to disassociate retirement from chronological age and to instead focus on capability and personal interests when making retirement decisions.

4

Early Retirement and Resilience:
THE ELITE ATHLETES

To become an elite athlete requires total commitment, some
degree of luck, and cooperation from the body as well as the
mind. In sports, everything can change in the blink of an eye.
Elite athletes can go from being on top of the world to being out of
the game forever within seconds. Even if an athletic career does not
end suddenly, it is by its nature a short-lived endeavor. The average
professional athlete's career is over by age 33. Across most Olympic
sports, the elite retire even sooner.[1]

Elite sports require incredible physical and mental energy. The
ability to focus on a singular goal is paramount. This need for focus
is why elite athletes often rely on trainers and coaching teams to
care for ordinary tasks like preparing meals, coordinating travel,
and mapping out daily schedules, which renders the athlete even
less prepared for a life after sports.

The athletes I interviewed for this chapter traveled the world
and represented their countries at an Olympic Games. When they
retired, they felt like foreigners in their own bodies and minds.
They found it disconcerting, if not downright depressing, to transition from highly structured goals and training regimens into the
"ordinary" world in which their accomplishments were no longer

foregrounded and their talent, physical resilience, and sometimes ruthless competitive drive were generally unnecessary. Of course, although they identified as "retired", these athletes were in what most people would consider the prime of life as they parted ways with a deeply held work identity. Their retirement was not met with the age-graded expectations and rituals that accompany other retirements.

This chapter illustrates how the all-consuming processes of rising to great heights in sports can create very low points in retirement. To get near the Olympic podium, elite athletes must push themselves to the limit. Each of the four athletes whose stories are shared in this chapter represented a different country and sport, and were at different stages in the life course. By the time I interviewed them, some had multiple work experiences, and even multiple retirements. They began their athletic career very early in life and sacrificed a great deal to be the best in the world. While transitioning into retirement, recalibrating their sense of self meant tapping into some of the same traits that enabled them to persevere in their sport: resilience, mental fitness, and a competitive drive.

I start with Allison, a young woman whose years of work as a gymnast left her body wracked with pain more typical of a person at least twice her age. Next, I introduce Luiz, a judo player turned coach who retired at his physical peak, but at a moment when his fears of being replaced were also greatest. Then I focus on Ryan, who achieved an Olympic medal for his rowing team's performance, but who struggled to achieve satisfaction in its wake. This chapter concludes with Omar, an exceptional competitor who had multiple retirements and spent decades searching for ways to replace the adrenaline rush he experienced in his role as an elite runner.

EARLY RETIREMENT

Allison, Gymnast

When Allison represented Great Britain at an Olympic Games in rhythmic gymnastics, it was the highlight of her life and the pinnacle of her career. She had a beautiful face and a tall, thin physique. At 21, she became a retiree, and the world as she knew it fell apart.

Reestablishing her sense of purpose and engaging with the real world was disorienting, both physically and emotionally. She explained,

> To represent your country at the Olympics is the ultimate goal. The fact that I got to the highest level in my sport, there is nothing higher than that in gymnastics. I think I have always been very appreciative of my training, you know, and that my life has been very unique. I'm glad that I had opportunities to learn so much so far in my life. And I prepared myself for retirement. I think if I hadn't retired when I did, I would have just held on to it, you know? Like maybe that closure wouldn't have been there. I made it to the very top, so I wasn't compelled to go back in and to compete again for a few years. But retiring was still really disorienting and scary.

When she was just 5 years old, Allison was identified by a set of national coaches as showing potential in artistic gymnastics. Her parents agreed that she would start an intense training program. From that point on, her childhood was focused on training and competitions. Allison participated in her first major competition when she was 8. To prepare, Allison trained with some of the best coaches and facilities. That meant moving more than a thousand miles from her parents and siblings. She reminisced,

> When I was 8 years old, I went to Russia for the first time to train. So, I trained there for three weeks at a time. All of these decisions were made by my parents. When I was 10, I moved again, for three years to work with one of the best coaches because that is where she lived. So, that was a huge kind of change. I wouldn't see my family much. I went to school there and everything. As far as I remember, when I was still living with family, my parents came to my room one day and said, "Okay this coach has invited you to work with her. You will be staying with another family and you will be coming home on the holidays." And that was it. So, I was sent off.

The first move was shocking for Allison. She was homesick and unused to the intense physical training regimen that would soon dominate her life. She had three siblings at home; she missed them and the comforts of home. Still, the move brought advancement: Allison rose from fifty-fourth to fourth place on the national level over the span of her first year away from her family. She would remain at the top of the national rankings for the rest of her career.

Most of Allison's adolescent years were spent training in Eastern Europe. When she was 17 years old, she was selected as one of the top six individual artistic gymnasts to form a rhythmic gymnastics team to work on a four-year project for the Olympic Games. Up to that point, Allison had participated only in individual competitions. She had to adapt to the new dynamics that came with having more coaching staff and being on a team. Allison found that she enjoyed the extra support and companionship of the national team, but both of those benefits made her eventual retirement even more challenging.

Pushing to the Limits

Gymnastics filled almost all of Allison's waking hours. It challenged her and gave her a sense of purpose. In every training session, Allison was pushed to her limits. If she didn't feel physically and mentally exhausted, she didn't think it was a normal day. She had no time for hobbies or friends outside of gymnastics, and she never had an after-school or summer job. Allison was clear that training for the Olympics was "work."

On a good day, when the team got the routine correct, they spent eight hours training. When mistakes were made, their workdays were longer. Portions of the afternoon and evenings were allocated to schoolwork, but Allison was often exhausted, hungry, and distracted. Sundays were her day off, but even so, it had an important purpose: Sunday was for rest and rejuvenation, conserving energy and healing (however briefly) for the upcoming week.

Allison and her teammates learned to function as a unit. Their shared childhood was a far cry from typical in that they focused exclusively on their Olympic dreams. Allison recalled:

> When we would have one day to recuperate from work, we would all just lie on the beach like mummies. We remained absolutely still. We wouldn't move, [hoping] to regain some strength. The whole thing was very regimented, even our rest day. That day was not to have fun or whatever. Of course, we did things and were silly, we *were* teenagers, you know!

Being a Big Deal

In her adolescent years, Allison rarely saw her family. During this time, Allison was cognizant that her body could not withstand the constant pressures it had been under for most of her childhood. Her initial plan had been to go to college after the Olympics, and Allison had been accepted to a few schools. But, about two months before the Olympic Games, she was overwhelmed by speaking engagements and the media. As the Games approached, Allison and her teammates were in high demand to do interviews with news media and talk shows.

For a short period of time, they were "big deals" and that experience largely contributed to her decision to defer college. She said, "You know, me and my teammates, all of the sudden we were like big deals in a way. That's what it felt like. In a way, it was very overwhelming, except in a good way. And I just couldn't, at that point, see myself somehow being on top of the world and coming down and starting my five courses per semester a week later, literally, because I would be coming home and I would have less than a week and then start school."

At the Olympics, Allison and her teammates thrived in the spotlight and performed exceptionally well. She loved the attention that came with her fame, and her family shared in the excitement. But at 21 years old, Allison had reached what she described as the age limit for elite completion and decided to retire. Immediately after the Games, Allison traveled with her family for a few months and gave media interviews. She never had a retirement party, but she described this period after the Olympics as a constant party. When she returned home with her family, a new reality set in. She had to face a world that she had never been a part of. Allison felt like a foreigner in her home country and an outsider in her own family.

Losing Your Sense of Purpose

In leaving her team, Allison had to adapt not only to the loss of companionship but also to retirement's autonomy and independence. She was both scared and, well, a little bored. She said, "It's really scary because you lose your sense of purpose. What's interesting about retiring is that all of the sudden my name is still the same, but I am not a gymnast anymore. I remember it being really weird the first few months. When you meet people and they ask you, 'What are you doing?' And you're like, 'Nothing, I am not doing anything right now.' Even when I was 7 years old I was constantly working, you know?"

In addition, Allison became depressed, and her body went into shock when her rigorous training schedule ended. She had very little appetite and lost fifteen pounds that she really could not afford to lose. She explained,

When I retired, 90 percent of the pain was mental but there was definitely a physical component too. Everybody reacts differently. What happened with me was that I ended up losing so much weight because I guess first of all I wasn't very hungry because I was not having to train at least eight hours, six days a week. I was trying to force myself to eat and also I lost a lot of muscle mass, so I just became really thin then. It wasn't like, "Oh good, I lost weight and I am thin." It was really uncomfortable, so that's how my body reacted you know.

At 21, Allison's retirement was physically and mentally devastating. She developed chronic joint pain and learned that she needed surgery on both of her knees and her shoulder. Although she had achieved some fame, her Olympic career had taken a toll on her health and her independence.

Adapting to a New Routine

Allison's transition to retirement required that she create a completely new routine. For many years prior, her daily schedule was as structured and regimented as her team's complex Olympic routine. Her meals were planned, cooked, and served for her (with each portion carefully allocated). Her coaches arranged every aspect of the team's travel and monitored the girls' every move. Retirement was disorienting. She said,

> It's weird being part of the real world when you were never part of the real world, ever. I didn't even know what the real world was. There are so many factors that go into being the best at something and working toward being the best and taking a really long time to get there. Then, starting from scratch at something else, so that's one thing, but also not knowing what that something else is, is another thing. No instructor and no coaches telling you what to do, no one organizing your schedule for you. Like all this stuff is so overwhelming to figure out.

And because she had not profited financially from her Olympic experience, Allison was broke. So, while she was depressed, in physical pain, and finding her footing outside sport, she really needed a job. Not really knowing what other options she had available to her, Allison decided to try waitressing. She got a job at a bar, where she had to sport a tight uniform, but hadn't yet earned sick leave by the time she learned that she had to have surgery on her shoulder and both knees, which would mean a lengthy recovery. As a result, she lost her job (but given some issues that arose with inappropriate male customers, maybe it wasn't such a loss).

Recovering from the surgeries was difficult for Allison, who for much of her life had been accustomed to being physically strong and resilient. Her mother helped, but their relationship was strained after living apart for so many years, and her mother could not afford to stop working for the duration of her recovery. The pain was excruciating, amplified by isolation and confusion. She grew even more depressed and battled with painkillers.

Allison never imaged that she would suffer so intensely with the termination of her athletic career. Even at the time of our interviews, when she was only 25, she felt decades older, both physically and emotionally.

Although her family was finally nearby, they were not able to provide the financial or emotional support Allison needed. Her parents drained whatever savings they had to supplement the support the government provided for her training and to travel to her competitions whenever possible. And while she grew up isolated from her siblings, they saw her as the center of attention and harbored some resentment toward her accomplishments.

When Allison was down to only a few dollars in her bank account, she applied for and started receiving public assistance. Maintaining her resilience, she started to look for new work as soon as her body recovered from her surgeries. Even while she was still using opioids to address her physical and emotional pain, Allison realized that finding work would be the best way to adapt to being retired.

People were fascinated by and appreciative of her career as an Olympian, but she earned little respect for her retirement status. Allison said,

> If you did any other type of work for 16 years and then you said you retired, people would be like, "Yeah, you did retire." But it's almost like not taken seriously when you are 21 years old and you say that you're retired. I'm like, "You know what, I really did retire. I've been working full time since I was five in this field, you know?" So yeah, I think that's something unique to athletes because we retire when we are young and a lot of people find it difficult to relate to me. If I'm talking to an older person

in business or something and I tell them I've retired, they are almost like "no, that is not possible."

Recalibrating

Allison was used to doing things that most people would find physically impossible. She had learned to become fiercely independent and adapted to growing up with teammates and coaches in lieu of her parents and siblings. Her work as an athlete taught her to be disciplined and focused. But any expectations she had of using the skills that made her the best gymnast in the nation seemed unlikely in retirement, until an opportunity finally arose. Allison found a coaching job that brought her, for a short time, back into the world of gymnastics and gave her a sense of purpose.

Unfortunately, some of the young gymnasts' parents argued that she was too young and unfit to be a coach. In retrospect, she speculated that some of the parents were aware that she was struggling with opioids. Although Allison gave up coaching soon after accepting the position, the job was a major factor that helped her take control over her addiction. Coaching had given her the sense of purpose that she longed for. Allison then went on to work as a spokesperson at international elite athletic competitions.

By the time of my interviews with her, she was enrolled in college and studying to be a paramedic. Allison told me that she would always identify as an athlete. She proudly showed me her tattoo of Olympic rings and shared photos of her with teammates from meets held around the world. The athletic career that had once consumed all her energy was now a distant memory.

She saw retirement as an important wake-up call. Retirement forced her to rechannel the skills she had developed earlier in her life. She said,

The amount that you have to learn and the drive that you must have and the discipline and hard work ethic you learn as an athlete is amazing. Just the type of worker and professional that you become, you should be at a big head start in a way. Coming out of my career, I knew how to be a professional immediately. I knew how to work hard immediately. My body is weaker, but I am very strong and I know with certainty that I can go through a lot.

Although Allison was one of the youngest self-identified retirees I've ever interviewed, she had clearly done a lot of living. For most of her life, her primary identity was being a gymnast. The work was demanding. Although she was accustomed to wearing a tight uniform as a rhythmic gymnast, it is no surprise that she was uncomfortable in one when she was leered at while working as a waitress. She had moved suddenly from being around a supportive team of girls and receiving attention for her skill and beauty in sport into a state of physical decline, depression, and an awkward reintegration into her family and the "real world." Pain management would be a struggle for the rest of her life, but Allison was determined to revive her sense of self.

STOPPING AT THE TOP

Luiz, Judo Player

Luiz began his athletic career around the same age as Allison did, but in his sport, athletes faced a different life span, and thus his trajectory into retirement differed in many ways.

I first met Luiz when he was 36 years old. While he was showing me around the athletic facility where he worked as a judo coach, it occurred to me that I would have believed him if he told me he was still competing. He looked to be in superb shape physically. He showed me around the reception desk and each training room in the facility greeting each person we passed by their first name and kindly holding the door for everyone we encountered. There were no signs of the debilitating pain that accompanied his retirement.

Although Luiz's retirement had been his own choice, it was hard, motivated by an awareness of his physical decline and a desire to leave while he was at the top of his game. He said,

I thought retiring was going to be easy, but it was a shock for me. It really wasn't easy. It is very hard when you realize everything you have is because of your sport. I had to question whether I was sure I could afford another life away from sport again. I was afraid to start from scratch. My wife she said, "Whatever you do I will support you." She had a job. But the big question was me. In the end, you have to love what you're doing, and if you don't have that thing that drives you to work hard, then why you will do it? How will you do it? I always thought to stop when I was at the top of my career. But that is not so easy.

A Game of Survival

Luiz started practicing judo when he was 5 years old. He had developed an infection in his leg and could not walk properly, so the doctors recommended that his parents put him in a sport. They were not confident his leg would heal, but thought physical activity might help. Because his parents worked all day, Luiz ended up spending his days with his older brother who, like many of the street kids in his small town in Brazil, practiced judo. He was one of six children in a working-class family living in what he referred to as a "nonprivileged" neighborhood. For kids from his part of town, sports were the only way out of poverty.

Luiz quickly proved to be a strong player. He could pinpoint three traits that helped him get selected to move up the ranks in judo: his natural athletic abilities, his skill at judo, and a personality that allowed him to perform on demand. At age 14, Luiz was chosen by the federation to participate in an elite training program as part of the national judo team. He moved a thousand miles from his parents' home. All his expenses would be covered, with the exception of travel back home.

Being on the national team was a game of survival. Luiz had to constantly prove himself worthy of keeping his spot, so he spent most of his waking hours training. Each day, he played a mental game that meant balancing the positive thoughts so that nothing could interfere with his performance. He explained, "When I was an athlete, I did not even read the news. I did not want to hear about the airplane that crashed or kids that got killed because that would upset me, and it would take me away from my focus." He could be cut at any moment, which meant he had to constantly focus on his sport.

Focus

As he got older and more skilled and his body matured, Luiz was selected to represent his country at competitions held around the world. At 17 years old, he received his first professional contract and was placed on the Olympic team. At 20, he married the love of his life, Gabriella, and at 24, he reached the peak of his career.

He revealed a number of different motivations and pressures behind his drive to win:

When you are young, all you want is to succeed. It was a lot of selfishness as well because everyone was trying to succeed on their own. You have pressures from the family and everyone who expects you to "make it." When people are investing in you, paying for your traveling and covering all your needs, there is great pressure to perform well. In my sport, weight is very important. So, having the right diet and weighting in at the proper level were important parts of the program. We didn't have what they had in Europe and North America, but once I made the national team, I had access to really high-performance facilities and the best coach and support from the sports medicine side. It was amazing to have that and to have people believe in you, but you have to be so focused to handle the tremendous pressure.

Luiz represented his country internationally from age 24 to 28, roughly the peak years for men in judo. In that time span, he was a national champion, and he participated in several World Championships, the highest level of international judo competition, as well as the Olympic Games. Gabriella stood by him during his successes as well as his frustrations—like failing to medal at the Olympics. At that point, Luiz looked to his wife and realized that he no longer wanted to remain focused on himself. He was tired of keeping up with such an intense regime of training, dieting, competing, and being away from her.

Questioning It All

Luiz also began noticing that his body was not bouncing back like it once had. He needed more recovery time after competing. At 25, he had a training accident that required surgery on his foot. His doctor also explained that his lower back and hips were not going to hold out for more than three years if he continued to perform at such an intense level of physical activity.

Luiz's early descriptions of his decision to retire start with what sounded like a death sentence and evolve into an event which he had full agency and control over. He explained,

I was shocked when I heard that I only had a few more years. I asked the doctor, "How can you see that?" and he showed us the image. That was a kind of a shock for me. Because you feel pain every day but the amount of pain changes along the way, you know? When you are younger you feel some pain but then soon you are feeling fine. My doctor ended up making the recommendation that I was well enough to continue practicing judo and our contracts are extended based on the doctors' report to our managers. For me, retiring was more about the mental side. Suddenly, I didn't have the same motivation that I had when I was younger. I didn't have the same motivation to jump on a plane every month and go somewhere to be away from home and not spend time with my wife. One day I woke up and I asked myself, "Do you want to be doing this? Am I doing what I want to do? Do you still love what you're doing? Or are you still doing it for the financial piece? Or is it because you don't have any other thing to do?" And I started to question it all and I realized I wasn't on the right track anymore.

Luiz described his choice to retire at 28 as something he decided on his own terms, but it was clear that his prognosis was a factor preventing him from playing much longer. When he declared his retirement, everyone, except Gabriella, questioned his decision. But Luiz had never liked the idea of being replaced on someone else's terms. He had seen other guys forced out, and he observed how angry and dejected they felt. He knew of fellow athletes who took to drinking, drugs, and overeating to deal with the pain of rejection from their athletic careers. Luiz wanted to leave while he was in control and at the top of his game. Like some of the doctors featured earlier in this book, Luiz feared the idea that someday people might look at him as having stayed on too long.

Despite making an intentional decision to retire and having the support of his wife, the transition was onerous, and he questioned everything about it. He explained his transition to retirement as follows:

> I can't just erase 25 years of my life. When I retired, my body felt it a lot. I thought I was ready but my body wasn't ready physically. I thought I would like to eat the same amount of food that I would be eating when I was training. But you just can't eat the same because you are not burning that much energy or calories as when you are an athlete. When I retired, I became vegetarian because my wife is and she does all the cooking. I slept more than half the day for at least a year. I questioned everything and didn't want to do anything connected with judo for a while even though I became a coach. Above all, the most difficult thing for me has been dealing with the lack of pressure and adrenaline that you don't find anywhere else. For example, now I go to very important meetings. I go to business meetings. I am in high-pressure situations, and I don't feel even 10 percent of the intensity as I did as an athlete.

Detraining

Luiz's decision to end his career was a clear demarcation point in his life—it straddled the line between clear purpose and a prolonged period of the unknown. For a year, Luiz went through a process of monitored "detraining" in which his blood pressure was checked regularly, and he was advised about health habits. His wife helped him by cooking healthy food for him and monitoring his portion sizes. He vowed to never step on the scale again and was able to maintain a healthy weight. Nonetheless, he was saddened by giving up something he loved and though he still looked like an athlete, Luiz dealt daily with chronic pain in his hips, knees, and hands.

In addition to his physical pain, Luiz was lonely and struggled with his sense of purpose. He expected more of himself than what he was currently doing. He was eager to figure out how to maximize his potential. During our second interview, Luiz showed me a glossy card illustrating the charity foundation he had created for impoverished youth in his hometown. This was his prized accomplishment to date. He was reflective: "I think that, as human beings, I think we are supposed to be productive. I don't see it as productive to sit down in front of the TV or to read newspapers and books during the day. I have a need to be working toward something. There are definitely times when it is hard for me to get up. Physically, I ache a lot of the time. I also know I can be doing more."

Shifting Focus

As an adult, Luiz was constantly on the move. He was also quite social despite multiple mentions of his struggles with feeling lonely. When he retired, there were parties thrown for him in three countries. In the year following his retirement, he moved with his wife to Europe to work as a consultant on various sports projects, until he moved to North America for the first time to be a coach for high performance athletes. Working as a coach consumed him. He traveled around the world regularly. And even though Luiz had a schedule that was always plotted out at least 12 months in advance, he was consumed by a constant sense of restlessness.

Luiz reflected on the differences between being a coach and elite athlete. He explained that as an athlete, everything is taken care of by the coaches. But during competitions, everything falls to the athlete. In the end, the athlete alone must perform. Luiz explained that an athlete always needs support, and there is a great deal of luck in sports, but that it is the athlete who ultimately must be able to focus to push the luck in his favor.

Luiz struggled with what to focus on when he retired. But what he attributed most to his ability to cope with the loss of his athletic identity and his physical pain was having the ability to shift his focus away from himself and onto his family. He explained,

> Even family treats you different when you retire. When they know that you are not that champion anymore, you know, it's different. It's not about you anymore, what you gotta understand is that as an athlete everything goes around the athlete. It's all about your needs and what you're doing. So, when I retired from being an athlete, I had to realize that it wasn't about me anymore, it was about my parents and my wife. And for once, I realized I would like to attend their needs first, not mine.

After retiring from judo through to my interactions with him, Luiz lived in four different countries. He and Gabriella had no children and he claimed they had no plans of having any. At our last interview, Luiz invited me to watch him coach. At one point, he stepped off the mat to tell me again that he and Gabriella were moving to another country. He spoke to me about how being a coach was lonely and required almost as much travel and willingness to relocate as being a high performance athlete. He was now the one in charge of the scheduling, and although he was not performing, he had to be incredibly disciplined in his role. He had to ignore his own pains to inspire his athletes and be the best in his work. Much has been written about the special challenges that aging presents for athletes whose careers depend on physical performance.[2] For Luiz, however, retirement was a way to take control and take himself out of the running before he could be replaced. He was on the move again, in an effort to broaden his impact on the world through his coaching, while he still felt the drive to continue to rechannel his energies and the momentum available to him.

THE INCLINATION

Ryan, Rower

Like Luiz, Ryan had natural talent and the ability to focus almost exclusively on his athletic goal. Whereas judo has many championships—some of which are held in higher esteem than the Olympics—for Ryan's sport, rowing, the Olympic Games marks the highest level of competition. To reach his goal, Ryan had to put his athletic needs first. His ruthless, single-minded journey to the top made the transition back to the real world all the more painful.

As a child, Ryan had a natural talent for athletics. Tall for his age, full of energy, and extremely competitive, he played four sports regularly and competitively throughout his childhood. His competitive drive could make it difficult for family to be around him, but it served him well—just as it would in his retirement. He told me, "I was just always a competitive kid. I think, you know, there is nurture and nature and I definitely have the nature part of it, whatever it is that makes a person hypercompetitive. You know my parents will say that, ever since I was a little kid, I was running away from home, and I was kind of a hard kid to raise in that sense . . . When

I retired, I dug deep and realized, 'Other people do this, I can get through this, too,' because I am competitive."

In college, Ryan played football because he enjoyed it, and it earned him a scholarship. He might have gone pro, but he had to stop playing because of a shoulder injury. Luckily, he didn't lose his scholarship. Ryan was a good student who majored in economics, continued to play recreational sports, and had lots of friends. Toward the end of his last year of college, Ryan and his girlfriend from high school, Laurie, had a child together. This set them on a trajectory to move in together and, immediately after he graduated from college, he took a job working at a bank.

He remembers that year as a whirlwind of diapers and coffee. Although Ryan never mentioned the slightest regret about being a father, he hadn't planned on being such a young father. And somehow, as he started his first full-time job and embraced fatherhood, Ryan got the idea to pursue rowing.

At 21, Ryan was tall with a 6"5' wing span. He'd never been a rower before, but a football coach once commented that his build was ideal for rowing, and he knew he had the mental aptitude and dedication for extreme training. Half-jokingly, he explained,

I am really stubborn and, you know, I always commit to things that are detrimental to my own mental health and well-being. I have that "winner" personality type plus technical ability. When I played football, we did a lot of weight training in the offseason, we did a lot of powerlifting, and I remember my strengthening and conditioning coach commenting on how my form was really good relative to my teammates who were also athletes. So, I thought maybe I have some inclination there. I also had the benefit of ignorance in hindsight, of not knowing what I would sacrifice and what it would take to train for the Olympics.

The Ruthlessness

One day, he got the idea that he would row for the Olympic team stuck in his head. From that point, Ryan started training on his own whenever he could find time while he was still working at the bank. He channeled all his energy and stress into rowing and, in a short time, Ryan was training with the Olympic team.

The regimen was grueling: six days a week, four sessions a day (except Wednesdays and Saturdays when they had only two sessions a day). Although the team had a dietitian, physicians, physical therapists, a sports therapist, a masseuse, a head coach, and a cadre of coaching staff, nothing helped minimize the physical pain that went into training: "It's like being comatose. Rowing is an aerobic-power sport, so your muscles will slow twitch over and over again. It is pure pain sometimes. There's just no way to avoid injury altogether . . . I mean, rowers will get injuries where your ribs will just crack from repetitive stress. Your hands blister, they are cut up and there's a lot of numbing. You just feel miserable lot of the time."

To meet his goal of going to the Olympics, Ryan had to be completely focused. That meant putting his training above all other goals and interests for four years. He needed Laurie's support to achieve his goals. But to get what he needed from her, he had to be ruthless. Ryan said,

> I can't speak for everyone, but I believe you have to be very, very selfish if you want to be an athlete at a high level and be such a good rower. I had to be very ruthless. I think it probably applies to almost all athletes. Maybe 10-meter shooters can have a balanced life. I had to have a ruthlessness about me. I can be very cold and, you know, cold-blooded and calculating and ruthless even with [my son]. I mean, I think it was good because I gave him a lot of structure, to be honest. But there were times where

it was like, you know, I need to rest and I'd put my earplugs in to sleep during my day off, and I told him that he will not come in or he would lose his book time for the next two days. And it was tricky because my girlfriend, my ex-girlfriend, [Laurie] wanted to move on with her life, and I needed to stay put to continue my training. We'd been together for so long so, you know, at some point you manipulate people too a bit. I said to myself, "Ok I think that maybe [Laurie] wants to get back together, and maybe she thinks there's a future for us." I had to manipulate things to find a way not to push her away completely because if she took [my son] away, I would have had to follow them. [My son] is my whole life. I had to find a way to keep [Laurie] with me so I could also have my son in my life while I was training.

Doing what he needed to do included pretending that he wanted a long-term romantic commitment with Laurie so that she would support him by working and by taking care of their son. Most of what Ryan remembers as "good times" during those years of training were the times he spent with his son. At certain points during and after each training session, as painful as they were, Ryan felt a sort of high that he floated on and used to convert many of his dark, negative thoughts into what he described as a positive energy.

You Alone Work Through the Pain

Ryan had been self-absorbed during his training years, but he also had the support of his teammates and Laurie at home. In retrospect, Ryan was completely selfish and yet acutely aware of his narcissism. Reflecting back, he views that ruthless time in his life as both necessary and worthwhile. After four grueling years of training, Ryan and his teammates won an Olympic medal. It was the best feeling he ever had: "I mean, right after, it's just waves of euphoria, and to see that you crossed the finish line, it's just an unending orgasm you experience, basically, and then it recedes to just waves and you just realize, 'Wow, I am an Olympian.' Then you try to digest what that means and what you achieved. And then it gets dark, because retirement is hard."

When he retired, Ryan celebrated by hosting a small party with his former teammates, many of whom would return to rowing to train for another Olympic Games. They had won a medal for their country together and that was something they could always celebrate. But after Ryan's athletic career ended, he never felt truly supported by his former teammates. He felt a big contrast between suffering together as team as they worked to achieve a goal and the sense of loneliness he experienced in the wake of achieving that goal. About a year after his Olympic performance, Laurie left him and finally moved on with her life. Ryan relocated to the same city as Laurie in order to be near his son and took great pride in his relationship with his son.

But achieving something so great as an Olympic medal made everything else seem mundane. Ryan looked at life and people differently as a retired elite athlete. He found it hard to relate to nonathletes (and even to athletes who did not devote themselves entirely to their sport). At the end of our first interview, Ryan told me that he had decided about 10 minutes into the conversation that the interview could continue because I had met some "standard" he had set. Winning a medal and retiring soon after had affected him significantly. These experiences brought out his innate competitive nature as well as a judgmental side that he struggled with regularly. He said,

> I am transformed from my work as an athlete. How I look at life is different, like I realize I don't experience things the same way as other people, I feel more detached from other people just

because of how wound up I became or I made myself become. Yeah, I feel like I'm super, super competitive, and it's hard to turn that off. It's hard to have a normal conversation sometimes, because I'm just staring. I mean, you're a very warm, approachable person, but, like, if we hadn't connected right away, this interview would be over. For some reason, I'm just analyzing every word. Sometimes I'm not even listening to people . . . I think that my athletic career, my Olympic experience, my work over those years, really contributed to me just winding that up to such a high level. And with time, I think, you know, time heals that. It makes it better, and maybe it just takes more time for some people.

Soon after the Olympic Games, Ryan suffered a serious shoulder injury while rowing. Maybe he really had given it his all during his Olympic performance or maybe he didn't train properly after the Games, when he got back in a boat to row again. In any case, he ended up in the hospital with injuries to his hip and wrists and a shoulder that would never heal properly. He was grateful his body had held out until after the Games, but he felt significant discontentment with the fact that he would never be able to compete again.

Ryan spent much of his first year after the Olympics doing speaking engagements. He was repulsed by the idea of going back to banking and wanted to ride the "high" of his Olympic experience for as long as possible. When his body recovered (to the extent it was going to), he tried his hand at carpentry, tried to figure out a way to go back to rowing multiple times (despite the fact that his body would not cooperate), and tried a series of other types of work, all while still giving speeches about being a competitive athlete.

By 30, Ryan had to come to terms with the idea that he had to retire from sports to recalibrate his identity:

I wound myself up so tight with the Olympics that I went through some anxiety for a long time afterwards. I didn't really realize it because it was in my nature to be a little bit obsessive about things and about time, about results, and I always really took things hard. I started to feel shortness of breath and started to be so invested in these speeches I was giving, they had to be perfect and I could be so hard on myself. It's been tough just trying to take a breath and be around nonathletic regular people. It's been difficult, you know a little bit of depression at times and even now just trying to manage my finances and create the financial freedom that I thought I would have. But mostly it's working through the pain alone. In retirement, you alone work through the pain.

When I interviewed Ryan, he was in his mid-40s. He was equally proud of his son's academic performance and still beamed with pride over his Olympic medal. He brought evidence of both to our final interview. He was disappointed that he hadn't achieved financial freedom by that point in his life, but he still took pride in working out and staying in shape. Exercising helped Ryan counteract the lows he regularly experienced and helped him feel exceptional again. His upper body was not at its strongest, but when he biked or ran among nonathletes, Ryan could always go farther, faster, and harder than anyone else.

It took some time for Ryan to adjust to being a retired Olympic athlete. Winning a medal was a major highlight. Stepping down from the podium and into the real world was no easy feat.

Like Luiz, Ryan was driven to push his body to its limits. Both athletes embodied traditional notions of masculinity, which value strength, stamina, and unwavering focus. And sports exemplify dominant cultural ideals of masculinity, which teach men to cherish winning and setting records for the sake of achievement.[3] Since ancient times, athletics have been used as a way to socialize men, teach them loyalty and mental toughness. But sports may not leave men suitably prepared for the aspects of life that fall outside competition and force. Ryan was still trying to figure that stuff out. Omar, who we meet next, was much farther along.

THE COLD STOPWATCH TELLS THE TRUTH

Omar, Runner

Omar could fit into any of three chapters within this book—he was an elite athlete, an academic, and served in a CEO-level position as the head of a university campus. But more so than his other roles, Omar's experience as an athlete left an indelible mark on his core identity. As a highly successful runner, Omar was never fazed by the media or cheering fans; his focus was on the stopwatch. Later in life, this acumen and experience as an athlete would serve him well; it kept him on the path of success and taught him the power of being resilient even in the face of defeat.

When Omar retired from running, he had more medals than several humans could wear around their necks. He had competed at the highest levels and represented his country at an Olympic Games in his early 20s.

When I interviewed him, Omar was working as the head of a university campus. Now in his 70s, he faced some pressures to think about retirement from his position at the university. At the time of our last interview, Omar had not made up his mind about whether he would seek reappointment in his current role. He identified as a retiree, among his many other titles, but decided that he had been through the experience of retiring multiple times and wasn't enthused about the idea of retiring again. His wife, Amanda, wasn't keen on it either, primarily because the last time he retired, he had spent a great deal of time traveling away from home. Amanda worked full-time and had a great deal in common with Omar. They enjoyed being near each other, keeping healthy through regular exercise, and drinking a glass of wine together at the end of a full day of work.

Omar was well liked and respected for his work as an academic, athlete, and community leader. He was quick-witted, kind, and soft spoken, yet he could command any room. He was also delightfully dexterous. The second time we met, I dropped some papers, and Omar got down on one knee, gathering them up with one hand for me while he held some bags in the other. I remember thinking that it was not only kind of him to do so but also that his movements demonstrated great agility and strength. Although half his age, I could not have gathered those papers as gracefully as he did. Omar discussed physical pain at only one point in our conversation, and it was just to say that he had several surgeries early in his athletic retirement left him with recurrent joint pain. Other than this quick acknowledgment, he kept his pain to himself.

The Athlete Was Always in Him

Omar had always been adroit at sports and loved to run—it was *stopping* that he found hard. In his first race, Omar bolted out, over 100 meters ahead of anyone else, and he desperately wanted to keep going. He loved running and, at a very early age, he developed Olympic dreams. His initial running experience was telling of his work ethic, approach to life, and attitude toward retirement; Omar had natural talent, enthusiasm, and perseverance.

Omar's experience as an elite athlete was always with him, even when he wanted to leave it behind. At times in his life, Omar had resented being identified as an athlete. He tried moving on and embracing other professional identities, but Omar often was recognized on the street for his days as an athlete. He had achieved a level of fame that had made him a celebrity in his day, and as much as that could prove to be an annoyance, the taste of stardom left him craving the spotlight later in life. Even if it wasn't intentional, Omar constantly had an impatient sense of how much he could accomplish in a short time frame. He craved the rush of energy and immediate positive feedback that he had grown accustomed to when he ran.

Just as he was independent and resilient, Omar was also compassionate and developed a larger picture of the world when accompanying his father on work trips. At times, Omar's family would relocate temporarily to experience a new city or town. He first discovered his endurance as a runner when his family moved to Jamaica for his father's work. He explained,

> Our parents put me in high school for four months in Jamaica. I guess I hung out with my family sometimes while we were there, but mostly I remember being completely on my own. So, I started running, and I did that for four months, completely without any sense of training. I just ran all over the island. Then I went back to high school and a couple of months later I joined the high school track and field team. After two or three qualifying meets, I won the city championships. My track coach said, "You know you've got a lot of ability and a lot of natural talent. I wish I could help you, but I really don't know what you need to know about this sport. Why don't I call the track coach at the university, who happens to be the Olympic coach, to see whether he would be interested in taking you under his wing?"

Time and time again, Omar would prove himself to be a champion. He was practically unbeatable in national and international competitions all through his high school and college years. Unfortunately, he had a terrible Olympic performance. He had not given himself enough time to rest leading up to the Games and his execution suffered.

Finding Another Adrenaline Rush

At a press conference, approximately forty years after his Olympic Games, Omar was asked to comment on those Games. He explained that no one rehashes or laments their wins—it is the losses that haunt you forever. And when I interviewed him, about fifty years after his Olympic competition, Omar was an accomplished academic, a gracious, peaceful man, and a humanitarian, who nonetheless was haunted by his past mistakes. He was eager to learn from the past and driven to fight against social injustices. He wanted to create legacies.

When Omar returned home from the Olympics at 21, his international competitive sports career ended. He had major surgery on both of his legs, did some traveling, and then channeled his energy into human rights advocacy (including second-wave feminism and civil rights). This work gave him a rush, too. He explained,

> I had this terrible Olympics, but then I found other adrenaline. I went to India and then you know, I came back and became a controversial figure. I got the adrenaline a different way. Instead of opening the newspaper and seeing my name because I won a race, I would open the newspaper and I would see a write-up about something I did or wrote. So, I found some other ways to create that adrenaline. I gotta tell you, I'm still like that. I like to think that I learned a bit more with maturity; but there is a tremendous rush in being the center of attention and I've been very,

very lucky. And I worry . . . you know, will I ever be able to retire because I am addicted to work and although it's different for me now, there is still a great rush to being at the front of the room.

Omar genuinely wanted to make a positive difference in the world. A few years after retiring from running and finishing his undergraduate degree, he earned a master's degree and took up a career as a civil servant. Soon, he became aware that people were doing much more adventurous things in politics and decided to run for public office. Although he was not elected, during the process of running for office, one of his former professors came to him and asked for a favor—to fill a last-minute lecturer position. Omar stepped up to the task. This led to a university-level teaching appointment. Giving lectures, advancing his academic accomplishments, and engaging in research challenged Omar in a way that satisfied his desires to lead and be followed.

As a university professor, Omar's publication record was exceptionally competitive. He moved up through the ranks of the university system. He thrived on being engaged with work and remaining in the spotlight. Reflecting on his careers, Omar told me that he always maintained his athletic instincts. The core skill of being goal oriented always stuck with him. But in some ways, he also struggled with his identity as an athlete. As he explained,

There was a time when I was embarrassed about being an athlete. When people saw me only as an athlete. That would embarrass the hell out of me. It would upset me because people would attribute my other successes to being prominent in sport and to all of the evils of sport . . . Sport was seen as right wing, you know anti-intellectual, racist, sexist, culturist. And although I shared their critiques, I would argue that the sports world could be better. And so, I had a number of very painful, painful times when people who I was close to had no sympathy for me . . . Nowadays, people still come up to me and run into me and they treat me as if all I ever did in my life was what I did for six or eight years in the 1950s and 1960s. I thank them, but boy, oh boy, it can really hurt. Now I'm much more comfortable with my status. I see my trajectory as a runner who had an interest in politics, who had an interest in the arts, who has been an activist, and this is who I am. But boy, for a long time, I really had to struggle with that.

Multiple Retirements

When Omar retired from an administrative position at his university in his 60s, his retirement party included friends, family, academic colleagues, politicians, community organizers, athletes, and others who shared more than one of these roles. He had a feeling, even then, that he wasn't going to be able to truly leave the university behind.

After this, his second retirement, he traveled back to India. He struggled with being identified as an athlete and not wanting to be frozen in time, recognized only for his early life accomplishments in track and field. But that identity brought him praise that felt good to hear: "You know, I am both embarrassed and I love it because both times after I retired, I was in a restaurant in Delhi or Bombay, and someone came up to me, right out of the blue, and said, 'Aren't you [Omar]?' I mean, that kind of thing. It drives people crazy. And I am both embarrassed by it because they remember me as the artifact and only from this one point of time, but it's also it's a little bit of the drugs of celebrity, you know?"

When Omar returned from India, he spent a year working on a stack of unfinished writing projects and traveling for speaking engagements. Then he got a phone call from the president of a university, asking him to be the executive leader of an entire campus. The president phrased it as a favor, and it sounded similar to the one that initially got him into academia. Omar made the decision to return form retirement with his wife, Amanda, who was still working and who expressed her desire to see him feel fulfilled at the end of each day. Like others close to Omar, she could see that retirement didn't suit him well. Wearing a suit and being in a position of prominence was a good fit for his personality.

On his decision to work again, Omar said,

I looked at some of the men in my life and I realized, for me, there is a fear of retirement, the fear of not being part of the conversation, not being connected. I know some who have been perfectly happy to walk away and do other things, and some people feel very, very awkward about that. I would like to think that I, once I finally decided, you know, that I could leave the university and never come back. But I don't, I don't know how I'd actually do it. I asked a friend recently if I made a mistake coming back from retirement, and he said, "You are an idiot, ever since you took this job you are so much happier and so much more alert and alive."

As Omar reflected on work and retirement, he clearly articulated his interest in being productive and communicated a firm sense of his priorities in life. Amanda was the most important aspect of his life, following which he had a list of retirement projects that could be accomplished regardless of whether he was retired or working or some combination of the two. He credited Amanda with his happiness and for teaching him how to be healthy. He could push himself to the limit, and she helped him endure.

Omar led an exceptional life and was still building his legacy at the time we last met. He was also confident that work would not impede his ability to accomplish his remaining goals in life, and he was growing less afraid of retiring. He explained,

> I have always been able to find other stuff. I mean if I retire, if it's time, and my time is up, then that's that. I like people, I have a need for people. I have always been able to entertain myself, at least I think that's what I tell myself. I could certainly travel for two or three weeks and feel very comfortable and if I'm bored I would go find people or introduce myself and I have always been able to come up with projects. I usually have at least five projects. But I worry that there's still a lot of good I want to do and I see busy as good. If I am not busy, I'm going to be a wreck.

Omar achieved success in many different fields. Although he failed to earn an Olympic medal, his instinctual drive made him successful in just about everything he focused on. His resilience enabled him to overcome the letdown that often accompanies the transition from sport celebrity to ordinary person. And his perseverance allowed him to rechannel his energy toward causes larger than himself.

In spite of excelling in so many roles, Omar's story, like the others, is ongoing. He had much more he hoped to accomplish in his work and life. Being an elite athlete instilled a competitive drive in him that made it hard for him to be idle. His early experiences as a world-class runner and internationally recognized figure conditioned him to reject a retirement characterized by not working. Instead, he was destined to continually learn from past mistakes and rebound with larger ambitions.

RESILIENCE

It has been said that sport "is one of the few professions where a 27-year-old man can be referred to as a 'veteran' and a 35-year-old as an 'old man.' "[4] Elite athletes retire early after years of focusing on a single goal. In many ways, each of the athletes I interviewed did not lead ordinary young lives and yet, when they retired, they were expected to find ways to fit into the ordinary world.

The two hardest parts of retiring for these athletes included dealing with the physical pain of injuries they had endured while training, and dealing with the fear that they would never find work that was as exhilarating as their athletic careers. The difficulties of ending an athletic career have been previously described in some detail.[5] Sports psychology textbooks have started to acknowledge the challenges associated with retirement for elite athletes by including chapters with advice on career transitions. These suggestions tend to include finding social support, maintaining good physical health, and having a solid backup plan for what to do if and when a career in sports is off the table.[6]

As Allison's and Luiz's stories illustrate, however, these plans can be hard to execute. Both began their athletic careers when they were very young and were pushed to focus exclusively on their training. With little time to enjoy interests outside of their sport or spend with their families, they failed to develop strong social support networks or strategies regarding their next steps in life. Neither was prepared for the chronic pain they would endure after years of intense exertion and injuries.

Elite athletes know that an early retirement is all but inevitable; however, it can be extremely difficult for them to take time and mental energy away from training for a goal like the Olympic Games.[7] Enjoying a balanced life and fully preparing for what follows do not really have a place at the peak of a sports career.

Before working on this project, I would have thought that being in a team sport such as rowing or rhythmic gymnastics would have created a supportive network that would prove helpful in retirement. A big difference exists between excelling in an individual sport and excelling in a sport that requires coordination with a team. Evidence points to important subculture distinctions based on the type of sport from which an athlete retires.[8] But Ryan and Allison, who had each spent many years moving in unison with their teammates, felt desolate in their retirement. Neither one thought their transition was cushioned by having teammates to commiserate with or confide in. Instead, the fact that they had once been so closely surrounded by teammates and had been able to share their experiences made them feel all the more isolated in retirement.

Sure, a corporation might be interested in having them endorse a product from time to time, or opportunities for speaking engagements and coaching might arise, but outside these few prospects, much of the world has little regard for *former* athletes.

For elite athletes, retirement comes at a pivotal point in their lives. Many do not know what will come next, and it is not unusual for retirement to coincide with an elite athlete's first chance at living as an independent adult. The athletes I interviewed had grown accustomed to being in the spotlight, having their schedules planned out for them, and facing scrutiny. Their bodies were monitored by coaching staff, physicians, judges, and spectators. They fondly recalled the endorphins and adrenaline that made them feel so good. When they retired, each longed for a way to get back into the action and feel the excitement of excelling in their sport.

Even with so much in common, in their retirement, every one of these athletes took a different path. They all needed to earn money, but they worked in a range of different types of jobs, eventually finding ways to rechannel their energy by focusing on new goals. Omar was the only person in this chapter who competed at a time when

Olympians were required to be amateur athletes; perhaps his ability to successfully establish himself in other important roles throughout his life is owed partly to his opportunities for a more "normal" transition to adulthood.[9] He rechanneled his goals more times than any other retiree I interviewed and, in the process, probably created the biggest legacy of them all. Still, his recalibration took place only after phases of distress and disorientation.

Luiz and Ryan struggled as they transitioned away from being athletes and gave up selfish expectations that their own goals came before anyone else's needs. They both were driven to win, feared failure, and pushed themselves to their physical limits. Some would argue that their pursuit of athletic glory is a natural outcrop of the masculine hegemonic ideals that dominate elite sports. And according to these ideals, retirement is the only natural next step once the body declines.[10] If you can't be the best, get out.

Regardless of whether these athletes had a successful or disappointing Olympic performance, each one of them had a drive that made it tough to adapt to life in the real world. But it was many of those same qualities—their competitive instincts and determination—that helped them strive to find a new sense of purpose.

5

Late Retirement and Working in Place:
THE PROFESSORS

The path to becoming a professor is rather lengthy. Currently, in the United States, the average age when a person is granted tenure is 39 years old.[1] Until the 1900s, most countries did not set age limits to holding a university appointment. Then, in the early 1900s, mandatory retirement at 65 became the norm. The rationale was that it would allow universities to hire young faculty members as a means of entering into new research areas, circulating modern ideas, and removing older faculty who were deemed ineffective, costlier, or less productive. Then this standard reversed in some parts of the world and by the early 2000s, many universities abolished mandatory retirement for faculty. However, certain regions throughout Europe, Asia, and South America, continue to enforce a mandatory age when professors must retire.

The idea of mandatory retirement, in many ways, is an incompatible and contradictory concept to that of tenure, which generally is understood to mean a "job for life." When we consider their relatively late launch into academic careers, the idea of retiring a professor is somewhat strange. Those who have argued in favor of mandatory retirement for professors cite concerns that job security reduces incentives to work hard and commits universities to maintain fields of study or disciplines that might not remain relevant or in demand among students. Advocates of mandatory retirement have also explained that, without it, an enormous disconnect can be created by the large gap between the average age of university students and that of faculty members.[2]

This chapter focuses on the experiences of five professors I interviewed on multiple occasions. Each of these professors remained in a familiar setting by continuing their life's work in retirement. In essence they were "working in place." In gerontology, the term "aging in place" refers to living at home or in a familiar setting later in life rather than relocating to a health-care environment, such as an old-age home or long-term care facility.[3] In this book, working in place describes a work-lifestyle characterized by continuing to do the same type of work one has always done despite identifying as being retired. The professors in this chapter came from different disciplines, lived in various regions of the world, and had diverse work experiences within academia, but they each shared a common interest in finding ways to continue their life's work in their retirement.

I start with Sylvia, who struggled in her retirement, in part because she had never really taken time off work throughout her life. Then, there is Duncan, who was caught off guard by less-than-favorable circumstances that led to his retirement, but who found his way back to the university that had become his second home. Next, I introduce Tomas, who was hit with his university's mandatory retirement policy at age 65 and gracefully found a way to stay on. Grace had a strong work ethic that she found difficult to turn off, even when her husband who was also an academic wanted her to retire with him. Finally, there is David, who like the others, could not get his head around the concept of a traditional retirement and found his own way to retire while continuing to work.

LATE RETIREMENT

Sylvia, Professor of Anthropology

Sylvia was a warm and engaging woman with a keen sense of humor and a contagious laugh. She had an extensive list of hobbies that included knitting, needlepoint, sewing, reading, cooking, and traveling. She also had a serious side to her. She spent years focused on acquiring in-depth knowledge and writing on nuanced aspects of her subfield. She never married or had children and never had any major health problems. She never had any true interruptions to her prolific career. During her summers and sabbaticals, she conducted fieldwork around the world or focused on her academic writing.

When I interviewed Sylvia in the campus office she shared with another retired professor, Sylvia said it was probably fair to describe her summers and sabbaticals as "vacations," although she was always working. She clarified, "I've never really taken time off. Now that I'm retired, I realize that. All of a sudden, it's like: 'Wow, I really spent my whole life working!' I've always had a project. I mean, when I traveled it was mostly connected to a project. I didn't really like traveling any other way. I always loved my work and being able to travel for work. Anyway, I only recently realized this but, I've pretty much been continuously working my whole life!"

Work constituted the core of Sylvia's identity, but she had not always expected her life to turn out that way. When she graduated from college, her mother told her that the point of her education was to get a "Mrs.," not a necessarily a "B.A." And Sylvia *had* expected that she would get married and hoped that it would be to a man who traveled internationally for his work. She wanted to travel with him and learn about cultures far from the small town she grew up in.

She surprised herself by choosing to remain unmarried. This decision seemed both unique and lucky compared with her childhood friends who had married young and never pursued careers of their own. She told me, "I'm not sure if I was ever the kind of person who was going to have kids. I like them. I love my niece and nephews. . . . I think my dissertation was my first baby. My book was my second and maybe my first Ph.D. student was my third. Now I have lots of babies. You might even say I have some grandbabies." Sylvia considered her legacy to be the network of students she had fostered, her friends, treasured colleagues, family, and her work.

Making Room

Sylvia described her writings as genetic codes, which could be passed on and adapted through future generations of scholars. Her whole approach to academia was generative—including her decision to retire at 67, to make room for a younger faculty member. She knew it was difficult for her students to find academic appointments, and although her position would not make room for all the students on the job market, it would at least open up a new faculty position in her field.

Over the course of her career, Sylvia had remained at the same university but traveled around the world to collect data and attend international conferences. She accumulated a wealth of stories, and her work provided a sense of consistency in her life, as well as an important source of connection with people. Laughingly, Sylvia explained, "Work and my life outside of work are sometimes two completely different worlds. When I used to work from home, I could go days without talking with another person! Then sometimes, I'd come in to teach and I'd give my lecture and I'd realize it had been quite some time since I had spoken."

She distinguished herself as an expert, among the best in the world in her subfield. Her work had been exciting at times and slow paced at others, broad in scope and sometimes very nuanced. She was autonomous, though she often worked with members of local community organizations in order to conduct her research. However, she worried that they never really knew the full extent of her work. Sometimes this lack of understanding was the result of language barriers, but more often, it was because her purpose was to *observe them*; it wasn't about changing them or teaching them about her world. She explained that her work was both social and completely isolating at the same time. In some ways, her social network felt both large and small: "Because you travel around the world either for your research, or to present your work, you end up with friends from all over. On the one hand, you can make great travel plans. On the other hand, sometimes it means you don't have as many friends nearby."

Sylvia was independent in many ways. Yet she never described herself as alone in the world; she had a rich life and was fulfilled by her work. She admitted, however, that sometimes as a woman she felt a bit lonely at the university:

> I was one of several female faculty members in my department when I retired; but I think my experience was different, simply because there just weren't as many women when I started out. I'll tell you this much, I wasn't lonely but there were times when I felt alone as woman. I have my share of stories; they aren't all what is considered "good working conditions" these days . . . I had one colleague who told me his third kid was conceived while he was thinking about me!

She remembered, too, unwanted comments and actions from male colleagues. One of the first things her advisor told her when they met was that she reminded him of his last girlfriend. Another time, as she participated in a large panel presentation, a close male colleague sat next to her and put his hand on her leg just before she was to give her talk. She jokingly explained that this behavior was unlikely to have happened to a male colleague and suggested that it would be even less likely to be tolerated today. She laughed as she recalled, "I thought he'd try to keep it there during the whole talk!"

How Much Will I Need to Make Things Last?

Sylvia's experiences were also different from her male colleagues in that many of them had wives who had never worked, or they were able to time their retirement with their wives' retirements so that they could travel together. She lightheartedly questioned how much those wives enjoyed having their husbands around so much.

Being single made her retirement feel like a subtler change, but it amplified some of Sylvia's financial concerns. She was highly aware that her financial situation was not as comfortable as those of her friends. She estimated that her expenses were probably lower than what a couple might have, but she knew that retirement and scaling back her budget would feel less burdensome if she did not have to be entirely responsible for all expenses. She said,

Being a single woman, I realize that I would probably have a house that was paid off already if I had married. Each bill would probably feel like half the amount or less if I had a husband whose salary also contributed in. And when I get groceries, I'm used to buying the smallest packages, but I see that I could save more if I bought in bulk. One of the hardest parts of retirement is, "How much will I need to make things last?" You know, there's always that nagging in the back of your mind,

"What if I get really sick?" I mean I don't have that safety net that having a spouse provides.

Sylvia also wondered how much she would need to keep her stimulated in retirement. Before retiring, Sylvia had not spent a lot of time thinking about retirement. But when she did, she imagined that retirement would be a time to accomplish tasks that she had been putting off. Her thoughts about what her retirement would be like were as follows:

Oh, when I retire I'm going to do this, when I'm retired I'm going to do that. I'm going to do meals on wheels, I'm actually going to read my bank statements and take an interest in how I'm going to invest my money. I used to do needlepoint, I used to sew all my clothes, so I'm going to do that again. So, I had a hundred things. I've got lots of little projects. But the thing is, when you do have the time to do those things, they become instantly less interesting. When you have the time to do those things it's like, who cares about those things?

When she retired, Sylvia's department threw a luncheon for her that included mostly staff, colleagues in mid- or early-career stages, and a handful of old friends. She was most pleased by the students who attended and said kind words about her. But as she described the party, she commented on a different one she had attended because it was her cousin's son. This young man was a staff member at the university, and was moving on to another job at a rival university. Sylvia explained that he was half her age and had twice the number of people in attendance at his party. Elaborately crafted jokes were told through a slide show presentation set to music. Sylvia jealously noted that people were laughing and crying at his party. At her retirement party, there was not so much laughter and no one cried either. She felt undervalued, and the party actually made her question why she was retiring.

Immediately afterward, she suddenly felt lonely. She wondered whether she had overestimated her relationship with the university. Secretly, she wished someone would tell her, "Oh no you can't leave. We need you. You're not replaceable." At the very least, she imagined she would be thanked or acknowledged for leaving to open a coveted university position to a junior faculty member. Instead, it seemed like the relationship hadn't been reciprocal. She had demonstrated commitment and loyalty, and in return she got a token paperweight and a plaque, along with an emeritus office space and some menial campus privileges. In time, Sylvia came to realize that she did not need much by way of tangibles from the university to continue her work.

I Still Have Work to Do

Four years into her retirement, Sylvia had come to see this as a time to continue the projects that were most meaningful to her. Although she was no longer paid by the university, she worked on two book projects, served on the editorial review boards for a handful of academic journals, and wrote detailed letters of recommendation on behalf of students and faculty members around the world. She received her full pension benefits and was initially appreciative of the generous one-year financial package she received from the university when she retired, but she was disappointed to see that no new faculty position had opened up in the department. Other disciplines at the university were hiring, but her department remained one faculty member short.

Still, she was grateful to continue her work. It got her out of bed each morning (as it always had throughout her career). She appreciated being able to keep an office, even if it was shared, because having a familiar place to work was important to Sylvia. She compared herself with others who were no longer connected to the university and felt that they were missing out. She explained,

> When I think about some of my colleagues, I really feel sorry for them. My work hinges on my being affiliated with the university. I get to keep my e-mail and certain privileges that help me do my work. At one point, when I thought I would severe all my ties to the university, it was truly a dark moment. But luckily it was only a moment. The university is my home here. I don't take on any more students. I won't be asked to design any new courses. I'm technically retired, but I still have work to do.

IGNORING THE SIGNS

Duncan, Professor of Engineering

Like Sylvia, work was what got Duncan out of bed for most of his adult life. He also never married but struggled with his feelings of loneliness at the university in very different ways from Sylvia. When I first met Duncan over coffee, he explained,

> Retirement has always been very perplexing. Very, very perplexing. It's not something that I've looked forward to. It's not something that I planned for. It's not something where I've got someone I can talk to, to give me advice, to say, "You know, I did it this way and this didn't work." So, I had to approach it, I guess, on an individual basis. I don't have a life partner or whatever you want to call that so what I'm saying is that I had to approach retirement on my own. I think it is very different when you have a wife and can plan things out together. Things are set up to cater to couples. Alone, it is a different experience.

Duncan's parents had both been day laborers. His father had been an alcoholic and his mother worked until the day she died. His working-class upbringing set him apart him from his colleagues; nonetheless he felt at home at work. Duncan described academia as a solitary way of life and perhaps in light of this, he personified his work, loving it as if it were a person. He said,

One thing I like about academia is that we are all unique. There is actually nothing routine about our work and that really is something that is probably unique from a lot of other professions. I'm not sure, but I think that if you are a businessman the deals may change but structurally you're doing the same thing year after year. But teaching, and teaching new ideas and trying to reach different kinds of students requires adaptation. . . . Students have very different learning styles now. And, of course, our research projects go through cycles and sometimes you change them completely. My work experiences have been dynamic. What's been consistent is that I've always loved my work.

Duncan resented that he had been pushed into retirement in his late 70s. Over the years, he intentionally passed up generous, incentivized retirement packages. Duncan felt that no one had believed him or paid attention when he said he had no interest in retiring. For years, he would hear hints that it was time to "make room" for new faculty. He even received a prestigious university award that he knew was meant to signal that it was time for him to retire.

He acknowledged that he channeled resentment about retiring into his work and chose to ignore those signals to retire for about a decade:

I guess some of the feelings that I had were that for many, many years when you are a junior person people don't really listen to you that often. And, as you age and you get closer to retirement, people stop listening to you as well. It's like you no longer have a voice. You just get pushed to the side. It is downright insulting. I was insulted left and right. It was like people just didn't see me anymore . . . Suddenly you no longer seem vital. I found that a little perplexing because I still have something to offer.

After more than four decades of working at least five days every week at the same university, Duncan finally reached a point at which the dynamics within his department became intolerable. His voice was not being heard. He had been cast aside and felt that the insults were no longer worth tolerating. Faculty meetings that were once lively places for program planning turned into bitter experiences in which old issues would resurface but he was never consulted to share his knowledge and perspective. New committees would form, and he was no longer asked to join. He once had a PhD student approach him about her thesis, which was very much in line with his research. In spite of his willingness to supervise her, he was greeted with distasteful, snide remarks about whether he would be around to see her all the way through her PhD. At that point in his career, Duncan abandoned the idea of supervising any additional students and instead allowed himself to slip into retirement.

You Are Replaceable

The last straw for Duncan came when his department had to move into a new building. He was allocated the smallest office—the only one without windows. At that point, he could no longer take the fact that younger colleagues, whose careers he had helped develop, had advanced well beyond him in the university system and were failing to look back at him. Duncan knew he still had important contributions to make, but his colleagues unfortunately failed to see this possibility.

No personal retirement parties were held for Duncan. His retirement was marked by filling out a few forms and attending the large group retirement ceremony his university held. Sitting with me in a cafeteria on his campus, Duncan showed me the Plexiglas plaque he had received at the ceremony and said, sadly,

> You basically stand and get your picture taken and then you have these awards ceremonies and you know, it's got to the point where, in the olden days, when you retired you would get a gold watch or some kind of symbolism, some symbol that you are valued. Now, like a metaphor reflecting how much less they value you—now you get a piece of Plexiglas. And the Plexiglas has an interchangeable piece of paper in it so that they can fill in your name. The Plexiglas thing is the same for twenty-five, thirty, and forty years of experience. The only difference between the Plexiglas panels is your name. There is no difference. You are replaceable, and there is really no distinction that, "Woohoo you made it through so many years and that's quite a contribution you made!" That was also pretty demoralizing, you know?

When I interviewed Duncan on another occasion, it was in his little, windowless office. At that point, he had been retired for four years. Duncan reflected on his initial retirement period. His office had remained empty for several months. He pondered about this difficult time,

> Those were summer months; no one was really around. I don't think anyone used the office. I was so insulted. And some of that time I actually thought they were going to ask me back. It's the voicelessness and the sense of no longer being needed and that my opinion is not as important as it was. Or maybe it never was

important. That's what got to me the most. But then I realized, "What am I going to do with myself? They are not missing me." I gave so much to this place. At the same time, my rock has been this place. However shitty my life is, this is always the place I come to and yet nobody else feels that but me. That's why I felt so disenfranchised and that's why I felt so cut out because of the love I had for this place. And then I remembered former colleagues who just disappeared. I knew a lot of people who were forced into retirement before I retired. They were very bitter very, very, very bitter. They wanted nothing to do with former colleagues. And that helped me realize that I had been on the campus longer than most faculty had even been alive and for sure longer than any of the students.

Immediately following Duncan's retirement, he slept more than he wanted. He was not moving around much and had been unaccustomed to spending his days around his house. He was bitter that he had to leave the university he had devoted so much of his life to. Duncan found himself slipping into a deep depression. He was angry with the heads of his department until he came to the realization that there was no single person to blame for his retirement. And no one was missing him. The university carried on just fine without him. But, the university had always been like home to him. So, before the end of that summer, Duncan decided that he wanted to use the office without any windows.

He had always planned to leave a will stating that whatever money remained after he died would be left to the university, but instead he decided to make formal arrangements to leave his estate to the university that summer. Within a short time after these arrangements were made, he took the status of emeritus professor and was granted unrestricted and exclusive use of the office with no windows.

Four years into his retirement, Duncan admitted that he only used his office about half the time that he had expected to. But he valued the sense of continuity that came from having an office on campus. Occasionally, a student would stop by, but it was usually just someone looking for directions. Duncan explained,

> Obviously, I am not here for financial rewards. I am here because I enjoy being here. I enjoy being here more than I enjoy sitting at home by myself. I would probably enjoy being here even if there were someone else in my house because I get to talk to you right now and because being here, I feel like I am still relevant. There's no five o'clock clocking out for me; there never has been. I don't really look at the clock so much. I have never clocked in or out, you know?

Duncan rarely kept track of the time he spent working. But he was uniquely connected to his work. He *lived* for his work. He thought that his colleagues would miss him when he retired; he hoped the university would fall apart without him. Instead it was quite the opposite: *he* pined for the university. During the brief summer that the university was not a part of his life, he longed for that critical piece of his identity. Only when Duncan was able to reestablish a place for himself in the office with no windows did he find contentment in his retirement by working in place.

THE TONE WAS SET EARLY

Tomas, Professor of Musicology

I interviewed Tomas during the afternoon session of an academic conference in Europe; he was in his 70s at the time. As we walked to a coffee shop, he almost fell as a young student passed quickly in front of us. But Tomas smoothed his suit, realigned his posture, and maintained his graceful gait. A few minutes later, he explained in some detail how this brief encounter exemplified his responses to challenges throughout his life. He might have used a walking stick and moved at a slower pace relative to the young students, but he did not let external forces interrupt his pace or intentions.

Tomas's entry into academia was a smooth one. As a child, Tomas had excelled as a musician and though his mother fostered his musical education, his parents had made it clear that he should become a professional of some sort. So, Tomas entered the field of musicology: "I owe my advancements to my mum. Once I was in college, I liked it so much that I couldn't think of anything else to do. So, I went on to get a master's degree. After I got a master's degree I thought, 'That was so much fun, I think I'll stay here.' Then I got a PhD. And then with the PhD, I thought, 'Oh no, what to do now?' And then I was hired on as faculty."

Although his pathway to becoming a professor was a direct upward progression, he faced several obstacles early in his career. His mother died when he was in his early 20s. Then, in his mid-20s, Tomas's first wife died in childbirth after they had been married for only a year. The baby also did not survive. Tomas suffered deeply from the trauma of his loss, but persisted onward with his career as a professor. For several years following these tragic losses, he lived with his sister near the university. And in a short time, he moved up through the ranks of the university. In his late 40s, he remarried and, in his late 50s, he became the chair of his department.

As Tomas described moving up the ranks of academia, he fondly recalled his early days of lecturing to small groups of students. He clearly cared about his impact on students. His work brought meaning to his life, particularly when he was able to make a difference in his students' lives. He prepared his lectures with great detail. He took the time to listen to his students' questions and to engage with them. He contrasted his own experience as an educator with the current interests of junior faculty, lamenting their focus on publications and grants at the expense of providing a quality learning experience. With his second wife, Lucy, who had worked as a nurse in her earlier years, Tomas regularly hosted student dinners. Tomas and Lucy had no children of their own, and instead they created an environment that welcomed students who shared similar interests to their own. It was not unusual for them to have several students join them for Friday evening dinners or for Tomas and Lucy to accompany students to local musical performances.

Over time, Tomas became discouraged by how things had changed in academia. He observed that he had fewer opportunities to engage with students about shared cultural interests, and he was disappointed by shifts toward depersonalization within the university system. Tomas viewed one positive outcome of the vast growth in the higher education system—the demand it created for him to maintain a role, despite being retired.

A Mandatory Retirement

When Tomas turned 65, he was required by his university to retire. Tomas was given a date to clear out his office and accept his change in title. Just days before this date, a conference was held to honor Tomas's career. For two days, colleagues and students presented talks based on articles they had written, inspired by or related to Tomas's work. These writings would be compiled in a *Festschrift*—a formal, written commemoration of his life's work. There were also three retirement dinners to celebrate his career, but Tomas clarified, "I just didn't view it as a culmination of my career. I knew I had to retire. Retirement hasn't stopped me from what I've always enjoying doing. It just created new avenues for doing it."

Tomas never questioned his retirement. Retirement at 65 was a given part of the work–life cycle at the university. Nonetheless, he was surprised by his reaction to it. The year he retired was a difficult one in several ways. His sister died a few months after his retirement, and her death exacerbated his feelings of loss. During this time, Tomas described himself as depressed and lonely. He felt cast aside and abandoned. Yet, he viewed it as an important time for him to mourn and reconnect with other interests in his life. He began to play the violin again, after years of barely touching it. He spent more time going out to hear live music with Lucy. But he came to a point at which retirement felt like a void that he wanted to fill. He explained,

> I'm also a classically trained violinist. I played in Hungarian Orchestras. I played in orchestras and cafes in my youth. When my sister died, I finally started really playing again. There is much to commend the experience of truly immersing yourself in something. I had to adjust to retirement. I never anticipated the sense of loss retirement would engender. It is a loss, you know. I dealt with my losses by letting time pass, finding music again and figuring out what I needed to be doing. You see me now. I'm not slowed down all that much!

Approximately one year into Tomas's retirement, he had lunch with the head of the department he once ran. He learned that they had been unable to fill his position and, because of budgetary constraints, his courses remained untaught. By the end of the lunch, they agreed that it would make sense for Tomas to return to the university to instruct two courses, without paid compensation, in exchange for a small workspace and an "Emeritus Fellow" title. Tomas viewed his pension as compensation, although he was not required to do any work to receive it, and it was less than his full salary had been.

Retirement Is for Other People

When I first interviewed him, Tomas had been teaching again at the university for almost five years following his formal retirement. He attended conferences and occasionally gave invited seminar presentations. Tomas treasured this continued work. He could have resented doing the work without compensation or having been forced to retire at all. Instead, he described a sense of deep gratitude: "Were there not a need for me to contribute through my teaching, I would have been tossed out to sea. Even if it is a 'low tech' experience, I know I provide a meaningful experience for my students. And hell, it's why I wake up in the morning. Hell, I mean you know, I'm doing it for free, but it is incredibly meaningful to me. If it weren't, I would have stopped back when I retired."

Tomas contrasted himself with others he knew who also retired. He explained,

> I have colleagues who retired and it was as if they had dropped off the face of the earth. Never hear from them. I truly have no idea if they are still alive. If they are, you'd never know it. I love my wife. I live for her and I live for my work. They give me reason to keep living. I had a handful of friends who retired and most died right then, right around when they stopped. The others are on permanent holiday or else they twiddle their thumbs and, astonishingly, literally watch the TV all day. Without any exaggeration, they literally sit at home all day.

Tomas had no choice but to retire. Yet he made his retirement a comfortable experience by continuing to pursue the aspects of work he always enjoyed. He mentioned a few people he knew at other universities who had been given similar "Fellow" or "Emeritus" titles as they were "shuffled into retirement." He explained that for him and these other professors, retirement would not interfere with their personal interests. He said, "There are a group of us who are still at it. We really help make [these universities] this run. I have come to realize that retirement is for other people. Not me. Not people like me."

The idea of retiring and moving into another type of work in a different setting was unappealing to Tomas. He was not working for the compensation, but instead because teaching and working at the university gave him a sense of purpose and continuity. He was working in place. Mandatory retirement had almost shunted him, with its attempts to cast him off well before his expiry date. Perhaps if it had lasted more than a year or so, Tomas would have found another way to rechannel his energies. Just as likely, he may have deteriorated physically or mentally had he not found a way to reconnect with and serve at the university so quickly following his retirement.

DELAYED FULFILLMENT

Grace, Professor of Psychology

When Grace's husband retired, he wanted her to retire with him. But at that point, Grace's work was just starting to bring her a new level of fulfillment. She ended up gradually retiring later than her husband, but like Tomas, when she retired, she was not yet ready to end her career.

When we first met in a hotel lobby at an academic conference, Grace described herself as retired, but confessed that, in her heart, she was still devoted to her work. Grace and her parents had immigrated from Asia when she was 10 years old. Without much warning, she was tossed into a new culture with a new language, and her parents accepted no excuses for anything but success. They started a small business selling mostly candy, drinks, and cigarettes. Grace was expected to excel in school and to teach her parents English while also helping with the family store. Needless to say, she grew up with an incredibly strong work ethic but not much time to spare for friends or hobbies. Her only afterschool activities were helping at the store and completing her homework.

Once she learned English and proved that she was, in fact, *not* learning disabled as her first set of teachers suspected because of her lack of proficiency in English, she excelled in school. She immersed herself in learning. Being at school was a welcome break from working at her parents' store, the only time in her childhood that she could just be a kid. She said,

> At home my parents only spoke Korean. But in their store, they really needed to speak in English. So, I had to teach them. I guess that's how I became interested in teaching in the first place— early exposure! My parents were pretty traditional. There was no time for downtime. We never took holidays or traveled. My parents instilled the strong immigrant work ethic in me: I had to get the best grades, I always had to help with the store . . . No complaining, no excuses. My only breaks were when I was given time to do my homework.

Going away to college was an opportunity that was too good to pass up. However, her enrollment in college was the result of a series of unplanned events. When Grace was in high school, a teacher noted her exceptional intellectual ability and applied for a college scholarship on her behalf. At around this same time, Grace's mother suddenly passed away. This terrible event threw her life upside down, but it also created an opening to build a life for herself that was completely different from her parents' lives. Grace's father remarried quickly and with the help of his new wife's grown sons, he eventually turned his small store into a chain of stores. In the wake of the significant loss of her mother and in the shuffle of transitions at home with her father's new family and business ambitions, Grace welcomed the chance to focus almost exclusively on her studies and shut out the rest of the world.

Happiness

In college, Grace thrived. For the first time in her life she developed close friendships and enjoyed some activities outside of school. She explained, "The first time I ever took a 'vacation' was when I was in college. I learned what a 'break' was. I went hiking with some friends, that was it—just hiking in nature, but it was really eye-opening for me—realizing that, coming to understand that people associate taking time not to work with happiness."

After her college graduation, Grace went directly into a PhD program. And almost immediately after she finished her PhD, she married her husband, Matthew. As she reflected on this period in her life, Grace thought about how happiness had always been a confusing concept to her. She did not particularly *like* the concept of happiness and definitely did not feel that she had mastered it when I interviewed her in her early 70s. But, she explained that it was easier for her to associate happiness with retirement if she could separate each of these concepts from leisure or hobbies.

She described her happiest times in life as the first time she met Matthew, the birth of their son, Marc, and Matthew's retirement party. Matthew's retirement party had been a large get-together with lots of his friends and their wives. She saw it as a great commemoration of his career and recognition of his work. Grace also explained that it came at a point in her life when she was enjoying and thriving in her work. Although Matthew really wanted Grace to retire with him, his party actually gave her more time to keep working. In the wake of his retirement, Matthew kept busy by taking small trips and getting together with his old friends. His retirement was a great contrast to her own party, which occurred later and was much more subdued. But the time after his retirement was one of the first in her life that she was really free to focus on her interests, which of course were primarily work-related.

A Workaholic

As Grace spoke about whether she could be described as a "workaholic," she struggled with the fact that she felt uncomfortable with the idea of retiring and not working. With some sadness, she told me,

My son has often inferred that I personify my work. He once told me that I love my work more than I love him. He would complain that I didn't notice how messy our home was or that I didn't do things other mothers cared about—like decorate! But I don't think I was ever a workaholic. Obviously, someone else might have looked at me and said yes that I was a workaholic. I don't think I was because I've always had other things I had to do. Work was not my only purpose in life. I was devoted to my son. I guess it's just that my M.O. was to work anytime there was time for me to get work done. As soon as I put him to bed at night, I worked. I didn't take days off. Breaks were to catch up on writing. My son remembers one time, when he was young and I brought him in bathroom stall with me, you know because I needed him close. I got an idea for my project. So, I had to write it down. He remembers people yelling outside, "Are you ok in there?" But apparently, I couldn't even hear them because I was writing my ideas down and when we came out people were like "Why has she been in there so long?" So, I said, "Oh, he wasn't feeling well." And I don't think he's ever forgiven me for that. It made an impression on him and he sees it as that somehow that I was prioritizing work and he suffered. I don't know, I guess sometimes I just had a hard time turning it off.

Grace's husband, Matthew, was also a professor, but she described his approach to work as much more fluid and natural than hers. He had fewer work-related stressors, and he enjoyed what she perceived as a great deal of positive feedback about his work. Grace never explicitly said so, but it appeared that they had prioritized her husband's career in several ways. Early in her career, Grace accepted a lower paying position so that he could accept his "dream job." They had held the same credentials before they started as professors, but when they were launching their careers, she took the primary parenting duties and was not protected from additional administrative demands at work the way Matthew was.

At first, Grace had not paid much attention to differences between their pay gap or the fact that she was juggling multiple roles at the university while he was encouraged professionally to focus on his research. But when they started talking about retirement, she noted that his pension was significantly higher than her own, because of his years of higher earnings. She also reflected on the fact that his streamlined and focused career accrued numerous advantages over time that had propelled him into a steady upward career trajectory, while her trajectory felt much more turbulent.

Grace explained that it took her decades to get to the position that allowed her to focus on her research in the way that she wanted; there were just too many other demands on her time.

For years, it felt like she was barely keeping her head above water, trying to balance her son's needs with her teaching and administrative obligations. Then, when Grace was in her 40s, Matthew's mother died and his father moved in with them. Although her father-in-law was in relatively good health until he died, Grace's domestic duties increased during this period. She noted that it was not until her son became more independent and her father-in-law passed away that she could truly focus on her work. In her late 50s, she successfully acquired grant funding that propelled her career to a new level. The funding released her from certain teaching and administrative obligations that had been very time consuming, and at that point, she also saw her publication record increase.

Grace said, "I was always working and thinking about work, but I hadn't always channeled my energies effectively into my research. Over time, my work became gratifying. And then, when [Matthew] turned 65, he decided to retire. That was the year I turned 62, the age my father died."

Grace's father had worked until the day he died. He died of a heart attack, right there in one of his stores. He had taken very few days off work in his life. The only exceptions included the day he took off to marry his second wife and the day Grace got married. Even on the day of Grace's mother's funeral, the store was closed for just half the day. For Grace's parents, work was not something you took a break from. You worked to survive.

Falling Out of Sync

Her own work as an academic was quite different from the work her parents did, but Grace commented that she had inherited her father's drive to work hard and his need to feel like he was succeeding at work. Grace noted that academia was a strange combination of being stable and complacent, yet also dynamic and fiercely competitive. She viewed rejection as a common feature of academic life. Because career success came later in her life, Grace spent many years feeling uncertain about whether she was even doing the right kind of work. But she stayed with it because she wanted to keep her life and work schedule in sync with Matthew's.

Unfortunately, when Matthew was ready to retire, Grace wasn't. Her career was finally approaching the point at which she was feeling satisfied and rewarded by her work as opposed to frustrated and challenged. But Matthew had always been definitive when he made a decision and, because of a number of other previous retirements, Mathew's department had restructured. The concomitant increases in his administrative load eventually decreased his job satisfaction. He was tired of working and had a number of ideas about how he wanted to spend retirement, plans that obviously involved Grace.

Grace was able to convince Matthew that she was not ready to retire. Even though Matthew had tried to respect her decision to not retire, it was clear that he did not want her to wait too long. She said, "At one point, my husband complained about the quantity of e-mails I received; it made him feel less important. He said, 'Why am I so unpopular?' He was never all that bad about my putting off retirement, but I knew he wanted me to retire with him." She knew that she could not hold out working at the university much longer after he fully retired. She came to view each day that she held on to her office at the university as a sort of blessing.

When Grace turned 65, she decided to take a financial incentive package that allowed her to retire by gradually reducing her workload. She said, "In the end, I think it all balanced out. The first year I was supposed to do 75 percent and 50 percent the following year, but nothing really changed. Then the last year, I was supposed to work 25 percent of a full load, but I really had stopped my service and teaching almost completely by then. So, then I shifted to just doing research."

Grace was not so matter-of-fact as she explained how she felt about her transition to retirement. She had never been fond of the idea, and when she went from a 25 percent position to completely stopping, she feared having a void in her life. She suspected that unlike Matthew who seemed to enjoy filling his time with socializing and cooking, she would feel unsatisfied being fully retired. After Grace got a glimpse of a few of her other colleague's experiences, she was truly worried. She clarified,

When I think about people who have retired, I can't think of anyone except [Matthew] who enjoy being retired. I have no colleagues who retired in a way that I'd like to emulate. Anyone before me simply disappeared. I'm not big on retirement in general. Retirement is a depressing, boring concept. Except Matthew's party, I never enjoyed a retirement party. I once saw someone list speaking at another person's retirement party as a part of their annual service to the university. Can you imagine that? Imagine wanting to get credit for your "speech" at someone's retirement party.

My Experience Serves Me Well in My Retirement

Four years into her retirement, Grace told me that she had to give up her office, e-mail privileges, use of the university letterhead, and all formal connections to university, but she had figured out a way to make things work with the connections she had developed over her years. In her retirement, Grace was working in place. She continued writing and, with great enthusiasm, described in detail how continuing to work helped her maintain a strong semblance of consistency in her life.

She believed that the autonomous nature of her work was both a challenge and a blessing. It was a challenge because it meant that she alone had to make the decision about when and how she would retire. Matthew could exert his opinion and preference, but her university did not have mandatory retirement, and she had no boss who could force her to leave. As for a blessing, she said, "In some ways, I've been well prepared for retirement. I got to transition into it. And I've generally been a solitary worker, so I always found the inspiration for my work from within. Most of my career I worked from my home office and I've had to find ways to carry out my work and manage everything else. Luckily, my experience serves me well in my retirement."

Even though they lived in the same house and retired from the same profession, Grace's retirement was quite different from Matthew's. Their orientation to life and work were different but complementary. She did not resent Matthew for the way their career trajectories proceeded or for pressuring her to retire. She valued his role as her husband and the father of her son. Of her son, Grace said that he might always see her as a workaholic and less traditional mother, but she was proud of the way he turned out despite the fact that he was living far away from her. Grace said,

> So my son is now fairly grown up and independent and in China—that's just to defy me, I guess. And my husband and I have been together for forty-odd years. So, you know we have a very good working and marital relationship with lots of mutual tolerance and understanding. We'd like to be grandparents. But I know I set a model of work first in many ways. My son is very good at knowing what to get from each of his parents when he needs help. Yes, now that we are retired, we are probably the

most available to him that we've ever been. That said, right now my work is outweighing my life in the work-life balance equation more than I thought it would. But it's because I'm very interested and, at this point, kind of driven by my work.

Over time, Grace's career became more gratifying. Some of the opportunities to focus on research that had been afforded to her husband earlier in his career were not available to Grace until she neared a traditional retirement age either because of family obligations or nonresearch-related professional obligations. Then her decision to retire seemed to be largely influenced by her husband's desire to have her retire with him. But the strong work ethic that Grace inherited from her parents motivated Grace to continue working and contributing to her field of research well into her retirement.

MOST PEOPLE COULDN'T HANDLE AN ACADEMIC'S SCHEDULE

David, Professor of Health Sciences

At 74 years old, David was tall and handsome, with dark skin and dark features. He also came across as intimidating, competitive, and abrasive, but he had a disarming smile and clearly enjoyed a good laugh.

David described his upbringing in brief terms, only detailing that he had loving parents and was one of eight siblings. He also mentioned that his dark complexion exposed him to racism at an early age. His own family was smaller compared with the one he'd grown up in. David had five children between his wife Ellen and his ex-wife, Monique, and had seven grandchildren. He was good at compartmentalizing but admitted to having a hard time balancing his commitments between work and family.

In recalling some of the challenges he faced with Monique, David revealed that academia was more than just a job to him. He said,

> I remember my first wife kind of just didn't get it. I think it was when I got tenure, or something, and she said, 'Well, that is great. Now we can have a really good life!' I said, 'No, it's just the start of hard work.' Because she wasn't in academia, she couldn't understand what I was talking about. So, I think if you are married to a non-professional, our work seems crazy and if you think about it, it is. We spend all this time and money chasing grants. . . . The chances of making any real money are almost nothing.

According to David, most people couldn't handle the flexible schedule of academia (especially not people accustomed to working for someone else). As a professor at a top research university, David was expected to constantly discover, constantly publish. There were no excuses for interruptions in a publication record. He explained that "most people would probably do no work if no one were looking over their shoulder. Well, as an academic, we are always thinking about work. Your best ideas can come at any time, and you really can't afford to disengage for an extended period of time. New ideas develop quickly. Plus, you never know when someone will shine the spotlight on you."

Work-Life Balance

David hadn't spent much time thinking about retirement. Most of his adulthood had been spent focused on work and trying to spend time with his family. David took his first academic position in his

20s, and then, a few years later, he and Monique packed up their two children and moved abroad so that David could accept a position at a more prestigious university. Sadly, the strain of living in a different culture with no extended family support was too stressful for Monique and their marriage.

About three years after he and Monique divorced, David married Ellen, who had been a graduate student at the university where David taught. She never continued into academia, but she regularly edited his work and was a sounding board for many of his most important ideas. She was also a wonderful mother to their children. He explained that he had found a "soulmate" in Ellen. He told me, "We like solving puzzles, and, to me, life is a puzzle, and much of my research is about thinking through these epidemiological puzzles. She truly gets it. . . . I am really happy if I can solve the puzzle. And if I can get the puzzle published, even better!"

By the time he was in his 50s, his younger set of children were still under 10 years old, but his older children were in their late 20s and early 30s. During this time, David's workweek was filled with his research, teaching and administrative work; his weekends were filled with children. David's older children were "just not academically inclined." Reflecting on their lives, he explained how different his preferences and priorities were from theirs. David *always* thought about his work. He never failed to bring an academic journal article to read or review anytime there was the potential for spare time—on plane rides, to his kids' activities, to doctors' appointments, or anywhere really, just in case someone else was late for meeting.

David said, "It's very interesting to peer into their world and how different their world is from mine. On a Sunday, I think nothing of working on my laptop while I'm sitting with my younger kids watching TV. I bring my work to their soccer games. Thinking about work off the clock is just not part of their life. I probably never turn off the clock. If I go out with my wife in the evening, she drives the babysitter home, and I do some work again. I've always done that sort of thing."

Retirement Is a Hard One to Get Your Head Around

David started to think about retirement only because other people mentioned it. But he wasn't pressured to make any changes in his work situation, and he wondered why anyone in academia would *ever* retire. To him, there was no reason to give up any aspect of his work. His research and writing were a part of who he was. His teaching kept him connected with students and helped him identify who would make the best research assistants. David admitted, "Retirement is a hard one to get your head around. Tenure means a job for life, we give up a lot striving for that in the very beginning . . . looking back, I could have made so much more money if I had channeled my energy elsewhere. But, after all these years, the idea of leaving—it is really hard. With a job like this, what would it say about my life, if I was no longer doing this job?"

By his 60s, David had acquired several bank accounts and pension plans. When David turned 70, he started drawing his pension and considering himself retired. Up until our last interview, David had no plans to leave the university or to change his schedule in any way. In his own way, he was working in place. David admitted that sometimes he felt more tired than he once had, but he said,

My research is fulfilling, which means that I tolerate a very demanding day and try to remember or learn to take breaks. When I look back at the papers I wrote twenty years ago and the papers I'm writing now, they are much, much better now. Infinitely better, you know? There is a certain maturity, there is a certain amount of wholeness to my work now. When I started out, I would just focus on quantity. All the stuff came pouring out of me, but there was no context to it the way my work now has. My work now is very important. It has an advocacy piece. It has impact. I see now more clearly than I ever understood early on, and I articulate it better now too.

WORKING IN PLACE

The idea of "aging in place" has caught on, and organizations such as the World Health Organization have promoted the idea of having people remain in their homes and within the community for as long as possible, which they believe is better for individuals and hospital systems. Policy makers around the world have taken up this idea, too.[4]

Within the field of environmental gerontology, the dynamic relationship between a person's competence and their physical home environment has been applied to illustrate how changes within the home, such as removing rugs or other obstacles, can enhance independence among older adults.[5] This concept, often referred to as "person–environment fit", suggests that both personal and structural factors affect our ability to age in a comfortable and familiar environment.[6] The experiences of the academics whose stories are shared in this chapter illustrate the importance of considering other aspects of the environment when thinking about retirement and aging beyond the home.

The professors I interviewed made it clear that being able to carry on with their life's work was important to their sense of identity and well-being. In their retirement, each continued the same career they had throughout their life. Following the concept of "aging in place," I theorize this adaptation among extremely work-focused individuals as "working in place." I believe that for many whose work is intimately intertwined with their sense of self, this ability to work in place can be as important in maintaining happiness, stability, and mental acuity as being able to age in place.

Intuitively, it makes sense that the stronger the connection between personal identity and work identity, the more likely an individual is to seek postretirement employment. Yet little has been said about people who do the same work in their retirement as they did before they retired. Blended work is a term that has been used to describe work that can be performed in any of several types of locations, including the home, coffee shops, or more traditional office environments.[7] This way of thinking about work has been promoted as an alternative to retirement because it can be used to encourage mature adults to continue to work in ways that accommodate less desirable environmental constraints.

Despite the different ways each of the professors in this chapter retired, they found the idea of quitting their life's work objectionable. Sylvia retired to make room for a younger academic in her subfield; Duncan retired because of what he perceived to be untenable departmental dynamics; Tomas faced mandatory retirement at age 65; Grace retired gradually because of pressures to time her retirement with her husband's; and David self-identified as retired, but only because he started to draw on his pension. Each found a way to continue working because their work gave their life meaning. Because they had some flexibility in how, when, and where their work was accomplished, they were able to continue their work. Several saw the work they were doing in retirement as the most gratifying and meaningful work of their career.

Every one of the professors could have stopped work entirely, but without ties to compensation and in distinct ways, they each exerted a strong preference to continue their research by working in place. For them, retirement represented not a departure but rather a continuation of achieving their life goals. They continued in place by literally working in a similar environment, but also by carrying on with similar projects and work-related goals that had motivated them throughout their careers. Grace worked from her home office, much as she had throughout her career; the other professors were able to maintain or negotiate the privilege of having an office on their university campus.

Robert Atchley's articulation of continuity theory suggests that when adjusting to later-life transitions, people try to preserve and maintain existing structures from their lives. In this way, they maintain internal structures, like coping mechanisms or personality. So, if a person always had a tendency toward depression, they would react to retirement with depressive symptoms. Likewise, someone who adjusted well to earlier life transitions also would likely adjust well to retirement. Atchley has suggested that people have a tendency to maintain the external structures that speak to their preferences for continuity in multiple avenues of life, including social interactions and physical environment. So, a person who has always been social likely will continue to find ways to socialize in retirement, even if they move far away from old friends or are living in an entirely new environment.[8]

Continuity theory is often presented in opposition to the largely disputed disengagement theory, which characterizes older adulthood as a process of mutual disengagement between individuals and society. In contrast, continuity theory emphasizes humans' ability to adapt to circumstances and suggests that, instead of retreating or ceasing to do the things we have always enjoyed—whether it is socializing or working—we will find ways to continue to engage if it is our nature to engage. It is a parsimonious way of thinking about how our past and previous patterns of behavior help us adapt to structural changes, such as the socially imposed construct of retirement. The professors in this chapter, and Robert the academic physician from chapter 2, found ways to avoid disengagement or to selectively disengage areas that were unrelated to their primary ambitions. Full disengagement with work would have been commensurate with ruination. Their appropriate later-life trajectory was to continue their life's work.

It is possible that each of these professors would have succeeded in other types of employment in their retirement. They were all highly educated and skilled, with a wealth of work experience. Many recognized that their work was highly specialized and that they were making their most important academic contributions past the traditional retirement age. They all believed that they still had valuable contributions to make through their work.

Of course, not all retired professors continue to teach like Tomas or to write or to edit for journals like Sylvia. Grace's husband embraced retirement and seemed to enjoy his experience. Not all universities offer a staged retirement like Grace's or provide the option to draw a pension and keep working like David. Duncan's donation to the university was also quite distinct. This desire to continue to work beyond a specific chronological age or milestone set by an institution, however, seems to be gaining momentum.

The meaning people ascribe to their work also plays an important role in shaping postretirement employment experiences. Working in place can be a way for people with strong work identities to cope with the pressure to succumb to age-related incentives and retire. The professors interviewed in this chapter drew on the skillsets they had developed throughout their adult lives to shape a productive and engaging retirement. Some would argue that they were being used by their universities. Others might say that they were consuming valuable resources at their university or double-dipping by earning a salary and drawing a public pension. But each of these retirees was attempting to make the most of a system that shuttled them into retirement based largely on their chronological age, without regard for their abilities, talents, experience, or interests.

6

Undefined Retirement and the
Retirement Mystique: **THE HOMEMAKERS**

Homemakers are a rarely acclaimed, often-overlooked group of "nonworkers" who primarily are responsible for domestic duties, such as housekeeping and taking care of children, spouses, or other family members. In many ways, a homemaker's work is never done. The minute the laundry is finished, a new load must be prepared. Meals that can take hours to prepare are consumed in minutes; then it is time to do the dishes and restock the groceries. Children who need help putting on their socks also need help with their shoes. And once out in the neighborhood, an endless list of school and community efforts exist because of the work of these homemakers. Important and endless though it may be, the homemaker's work garners little respect.[1]

The idea of a "retired homemaker" will addle those who subscribe to the traditional idea that retirement begins at the end of a career of paid work. Being a homemaker is not typically considered a career, in part because it is not typically considered skilled or paid work. Homemakers may receive training and have access to discretionary bank accounts, but, by and large, they receive no certifications or direct compensation. And with regard to retirement, they are entitled to only minimal pension benefits, if any, depending on where they live.

Contemporary social surveys often exclude "homemaker" from the list of work status options. When it is included, "homemaker" is a notably distinct option from "worker" or "retiree." These distinctions have implications that potentially stigmatize the classification of homemakers by limiting the value associated with their contributions.

Although unconventional, this chapter focuses on the experiences of four women who were homemakers and self-identified as retired at the time I interviewed them. These women lacked any form of traditional status markers for their transition. In various ways, they struggled with conventional mores regarding domestic femininity and the traditional classifications of their time.

This chapter starts with Betty, who married and became a mother at nearly the same time she entered adulthood. Betty came to identify as retired when her husband did, and this shift not only changed her relationship with her husband but gave her a new basis for thinking about aging. Next, there is Theresa, who struggled in her role as a mother and wife but came to embrace her title as a retiree. Margaret's transition to retirement was influenced by her earlier transition into widowhood. Finally, we turn to Amna, who worked enthusiastically for decades as a community volunteer and came to view retirement as an opportunity to renegotiate her position in the household.

It could be argued that each of these women was simply misguided in identifying as "retired." Instead, we could claim that they ought to have identified as an "empty nester," "divorcee," "widow," or "volunteer." But as we have seen throughout this book, the construction of retirement identity can be contextualized, varied, and subjective. In many ways, these women found contentment in wearing the title of retiree, demonstrating both the persistence of the term and support for flexible understandings of what it actually means.

UNDEFINED RETIREMENT

Betty, Homemaker

When I first interviewed Betty, she half-jokingly told me that until very recently people often thought she was much younger than she actually was. She said, "It's only very recently now that I get away with the senior discount. Joe at the Dollar Store used to give me a hell of a time about it, saying 'Oh, let me see your I.D. young lady,' and whatnot. I like him."

Betty had come to enjoy her senior discount and retired status, but only after an intense period of anxiety and depression as she transitioned out of the multiple roles that defined her adulthood. In essence, Betty fulfilled many of the traditional duties of a homemaker since she was a child. Betty had grown up caring for her mother and younger siblings, and then in her early adulthood, she focused on raising her own children and taking care of her own household. When she finally had time to come up for air between caring for five sons, she focused on being a supportive wife. Her husband of just over fifty years, Stewart, was the breadwinner. Betty was always the homemaker.

Stewart sold insurance for a large company until he was pressured into taking his pension and retired at age 62. During my second interview with Betty, in a coffee shop about two blocks from the home she had lived in for half a century, Betty described the hectic schedule she maintained for most of her adult life. By the time she was 25, Betty had five young boys in the house. Raising them was a full-time job—and a welcome relief from caring for her mother, who had been ill since Betty was 11 years old.

The oldest daughter in a household of seven children, Betty had been "mothering" since middle school. Betty's father was an alcoholic and was inconsistently attentive to his children. He had strict ideas about "women's roles," and so it made sense for Betty to drop out of school at 12 to manage her mother's illness, care for her siblings, and manage the household. When Betty left home at 17, her younger sister, Elaine, was 14. She, too, dropped out of school to take Betty's place.

As Betty described her sister's accomplishments, it was clear that Betty still had mixed feelings about leaving home and having her sister fill her place. Betty spoke like a mother as she described Elaine. She was proud of Elaine's accomplishments despite the challenges they faced in their childhood. Betty said of Elaine, "She's retired now, too, after so many years of working hard to get her teaching certificate. I was so proud of her when she finally did it—the only one of us sisters who actually went back to school. She actually did it. Even though things were sort of stacked against us in that way. No one minded whether we went to school or not."

70,000 Hours of Motherhood

Betty loved being a mother and easily befriended the mothers of her son's friends. Being in her mid-20s with five young boys sounded daunting to me, but Betty recalled those years fondly: "When my boys were little, I was so happy. When they were babies, I made a room that was just for my boys [and me]. My husband usually had to get up early and it was important the he was well rested. It was almost like he was in a different world from ours. Sometimes my husband traveled for work. I was always in charge of the boys and the house. That was my job. I loved being the center of my boys' world."

At one point in a conversation about her sons, Betty mentioned that she had heard about Malcolm Gladwell's book, *Outliers*.[2] She was interested in his idea that being naturally talented was not enough to be truly successful; a person needed practice. Gladwell suggested that a person needs to practice around 10,000 hours to master a given skill, and Betty claimed that she had accumulated well over that amount of time raising her boys. And she was right: together, on the back of a napkin, we calculated that she had spent at least 70,000 hours devoted almost exclusively to honing her natural talent as a mother and homemaker.

Although she never clocked in, Betty never took a day off either—for at least two decades. The bulk of her life was consumed by making sure the grocery shopping was done, dinner was made, and her boys were fed. She ensured that they completed their homework and that they got to school and sports on time. She laughed especially hard when she thought about keeping five active boys fed. They were perpetually hungry! Jokingly, she described how she would feed them and then, one by one, they would request more food all day long.

Betty loved being a mother. She had a capacious heart. Though she put in long hours, in retrospect her time as a young mother was ephemeral. She explained,

> I was never bored. I look back now and feel like it would be really tiring to live my life then. Sometimes I miss when they were boys. You know, you never get to go back. In a way, it's like losing a person—you know, when your kids grow up. You know, it's almost like you lose them because you never get to go back and have them little like that again. I mean, because you never get to have them be 7 years old again. Once they grow up, especially boys, they grow so much. They need so much when they are little, you know? Like shoes always need to be tied, scarfs on, faces wiped. And then it's like one day you're left wondering, "What happened? Where did my little boy go?"

She spoke about the loss of her sense of purpose as a mother. Betty found it difficult to adjust to not having set tasks to accomplish for her sons. When her youngest left home, Betty felt a profound sense of loss. She experienced an unwelcome downsizing in her life's work. Talking with me, Betty agreed that her experience could be described as "empty-nest syndrome."[3] But she also viewed her feelings about retirement as distinct from the fact that all her sons had left home. She knew that, at some point, at least one of them would return home. She joked that the funny thing about raising children is that "the better the job you do, the more likely you are to lose your job."

I Retired When He Did

When I asked Betty why she identified as "retired" and how her life changed once she retired, her first response was to say,

> I think I identify with being retired because my husband is. His work has always been important. I worked around him when our boys were little, making sure to do what I could, though it really wasn't much, to help him stay on his path with work. I made things work. I made sure the boys were taken care of. Sure, it was hard work. I'd loved it. When they left home, it was hard for me. But it was when my husband retired, that I started identifying as retired.

The insurance company Stewart had worked for most of his life pushed him into retirement. He worried about money, and Betty was upset about the way they retired him. She explained that the human resources (HR) department at his office called him in one day and simply handed him a sheet of paper that explained the benefits he would be given for retiring. Betty perceived the process as cold, impersonal, and unexpected. He had been such a loyal worker.

She remembered asking her husband whether there had been any conversations about retiring before that meeting:

> Well, I asked him, "Were there any warnings this was coming? Did you ask them questions? Was there any reason for this?" He had no warnings, no one to talk with, there was no chit-chat or blah, blah, blah, that was it. He got some papers and he retired quietly. You'd have thought after all those years he would've looked beyond the papers and asked some questions. I was really quite disturbed by the fact that there was no sort of personal engagement by the HR people. I don't know how these things work, but it was not what I expected. I was expecting a sort of human personal touch because that to me was what I thought HR was for. I have friends who did that kind of work. All in all, I was probably more upset about it than he was.

When Stewart retired, he did not mope around the house harboring resentment against his company. He worried about money, yes, but he accepted his situation. Retirement triggered a big change in his routine of forty-some odd years, but he seemed to thrive on spending time with their sons and grandchildren. He enjoyed fixing things and messing things up around the house; he golfed and planned little excursions with Betty. He even started coming to the community center to join Betty in some of her regular exercise classes.

In retrospect, Betty realized she should have felt lucky. At the time, however, she resented his retirement. She felt confused and thrown off guard. *Her* routine had been interrupted by his perpetual presence. It was a big, abrupt change after decades of taking care of everything around the house and coordinating all the activities. Having Stewart home seemed to diminish her role. Betty experienced Stewart's retirement as a status change for her and a loss; it marked the end of her role as the homemaker.

Within the first month of his retirement, Betty threw Stewart a party. She thought he deserved this tribute to his career and recalled that he had a great time. But Betty was anxious. She worried about money and how they would get by on his pension. They could always move and downsize, but she wanted to have space for her grandchildren to come over and stay with them. She wanted to continue to buy things for her grandchildren without contemplating how it might eat into their savings. She had a modest lifestyle for the most part, but she had grown accustomed to her way of life. Retirement raised fears that they might outlive their money.

Perceptions About Aging

Betty's parents both died young. When we met, she had already lived well past the age they had lived to and, despite being the oldest, had already outlived three of her siblings. Betty had a sense that she was going to be around for a while longer. Yet she also feared that Stewart's retirement had indubitably pushed her into retirement and "aged" her sooner than she would have liked.

Betty saw herself in stark contrast to her mother. Being retired brought up fears about becoming inactive and physically weak. She explained,

> Growing up, I never saw my mother cooking or even standing in the kitchen. She was always in pain. From the time I can remember, it was so hard for her to get out of bed. She could barely walk and her hands were shaky. She trembled and she

could barely open her hands. I know my boys wouldn't think about me like that. I know they would remember me being in the kitchen. I was always on the move. Retiring made me worry that they'd start seeing me differently or remembering me differently.

Betty described herself as "young at heart." She took good care of herself and worried about being perceived as old. Throughout her life, she had grown accustomed to receiving attention, particularly from men, like Joe from the Dollar Store, for her beauty and for keeping herself in good shape. She had no problem identifying as retired or receiving the senior discount at the dollar store, but she struggled with the idea of being viewed as undesirable. As signs of aging became more visible, she worried about becoming invisible.

Betty assured me that she still received attention from men, but she feared that sometimes it was out of concern or pity: "In my day, I got my share of attention. Men would usually hold the door for me because I always took time to make myself presentable. I had a nice figure. Now, I know I'm in better shape than most my age, you can see that. Most my age don't even go to the community center." Nonetheless, she lamented that the reason men now held the door for her had changed.

Once Betty and Stewart settled into their retirement, she made a conscious effort not to focus on her aging self, but instead to compare herself with others she knew who were the same age. Retirement seemed to enlarge their social circle, because Stewart started making new friends, too. She told me, "I'm enjoying things now. Many of our friends are retired, and there are lots of social activities available to me now." For the first time in their lives, they were forming friendships that were not based on their children. Being retired gave Betty a new basis for thinking about aging.

LIFE WAS NO CUP OF TEA

Theresa, Homemaker

Like Betty, Theresa married young and became a mother as she entered adulthood, but notable differences in their experiences as homemakers led to differences in their experiences as retirees.

Theresa and I first met at the community center near her apartment. She had recently developed diabetes, and her doctor suggested regular exercise. Theresa had a small circle of friends she had known since her 40s, after her divorce, but none were into exercising. So, in her mid-50s, Theresa began walking on her own to the community center to see what sorts of activities were available. At first, Theresa considered the walk her major exercise for the day. She would walk there, sit in the reception area until she regained her energy, and then walk back home. Eventually, she joined a few activities offered at the center that would allow her to do some movement and talk with other retirees, if she was in a talking mood.

Our next interviews took place at a coffee shop, where we talked about her early life. Theresa's life hadn't been a cup of tea. She lacked happy childhood memories, struggled in her role as a mother, and had few close friends in the first half of her adult life. Her strongest connections were with the friends she developed after going through a divorce. Now, through the community center with the other retirees, she was making some newer acquaintances.

When she was a child, Theresa's parents both worked all day and sometimes had to take on evening shifts at their jobs. They were immigrants who fled abysmal conditions only to start a new life in menial factory jobs that left little time for them to spend with their children. Theresa and her brother's daily routine included walking to school alone, returning from school to idle away time in the neighborhood, and then hoping there was something to eat and a parent around for dinner in the one bedroom apartment they grew up in. They usually put themselves to bed, sharing a bed until they were early adolescents, when their parents added another mattress to the kids' shared bedroom.

Theresa's parents normally made sure there was food around, but that was about it. She referred to herself and her brother as "latch-key kids." It wasn't unusual to be a latchkey kid in their neighborhood; the kids all played unsupervised. She said, "Parents are so much more involved now. It's like you all have to be involved with everything. I didn't grow up like that. So, I never saw it as my job to be around all the time."

Theresa struggled with being a young mother. She had three children, each born within two years of one another. A few months after her third child was born, she had to be checked in to the hospital. At the time, she was diagnosed with "neurasthenia" and "exhaustion." Eventually, she would be diagnosed with "severe agitation" and treated with electroshock therapy (ECT).[4] She preferred to think of these as a "series of episodes of nervous breakdowns."

Theresa explained with some humor,

> Back then, I was a big mystery that no one wanted to deal with. These days, they'd use a million clinical terms for me, probably postpartum depression would be a big one they'd use. There are tons of pills now to deal with these sorts of issues. I was overwhelmed with motherhood and being a wife. I think I just needed a wife, too! The expectations of me as a mother and homemaker were so different from what I'd grown up with. They are also really different from what is expected now. I was in a truly unhappy marriage and it took me a long time to realize I had options.

Questioning Her Role

Neil, her husband until they divorced when Theresa was in her 40s, was credited for taking care of their children during the relatively brief phases of time when she was dealing with her anxiety-related health issues and was unavailable to them. She would have many less than generous things to say about Neil, but was unwaveringly grateful for his being grounded during the time her children were young. Outside of when Theresa was dealing with one of her "episodes," she was in charge of all the domestic tasks.

Once her children were in their teenage years, Theresa began to question her situation:

> At one point, I found myself wondering, "Why do I have to be the one who does the laundry?" This was literally after I had been doing the laundry for all five of us for well over ten years, but all of a sudden one day I questioned it. And I questioned why I couldn't be the one who went to the office. The truth is, I probably wouldn't have fared well in an office. But, I went through this phase of questioning things: "Why ECT? Was that the only way to deal with me?" Now, mind you, this was the 1970s, and I was in my 40s, so some part of questioning everything and feeling like my life was over was par for the course.

In the coffee shop with me, Theresa described recent trips to the grocery store where she would find herself irritated with working mothers who were so busy multitasking "with their phones, in their suits, with their children." She resented them for not realizing how lucky they were to enjoy it all. She lamented that now, it was normal for a woman to have an interesting career, and not dreaded factory work like her mother. She was jealous of young women who were encouraged to find work they loved. Theresa felt that she had never quite been content with the social norms of her time. She viewed herself as someone who absconded her duties and who never had as many opportunities as women today.

Throughout our interviews, I could see that Theresa deeply regretted what she perceived as her shortcomings as a mother and wife. At one point, she described a marital rating scale that had been used to give husbands feedback about their wives; she wished she could have scored better on that scale, she reflected, but she just didn't have it in her.[5]

His Work Was Always the Most Important

Giving up the title of homemaker was all too easy for Theresa; the title had only reminded her how she had failed in that role. She knew it hadn't been in the cards for her to have a career, but Theresa was jealous of her husband in many ways. She explained,

> His work was always the most important thing. He brought in the paycheck, so who was I to complain. I did, I complained my share, but I knew that I wasn't supposed to. There were just so many times when I thought that I would like to have meetings scheduled for me and to have to travel to different places. I saw how excited he'd get about his work. Sometimes I felt like he had it all right in front of him. He never once considered that I didn't want to be the one who took care of and managed everything for our children.

Theresa resented her role as a homemaker and was saddened that her husband got accolades for being the breadwinner and wonderful father, the man who stepped in when she had another "episode." Theresa could hardly remember her mother giving advice, but she did remember one warning her mother gave—that a woman should never compete with her husband. Her mother never encouraged her to work and never taught her how to find a job or how to be a homemaker, but according to her mother: "A wife should support her husband, regardless of what he did at work and she should not want to do what he did." In retrospect, Theresa was fairly convinced that she'd failed on all counts.

Although she never shared pictures or memorabilia with me, Theresa shared information about her husband and marriage that she had withheld from her children entirely. She told me that despite Neil's impeccable external image, he had been unfaithful to her from the start:

> There were so many times that I was so unhappy over the years. For one, I was always stuck with the laundry and never got excuses to go out. I mean, during the day, yes, but if the kids were sick, any time day or night—that was on me, because I was the mother. There were times that he went out, and I would hear about it, "He was out with so and so." Once my neighbor told me she saw him out with a lady friend, and I confronted him about it later. Of course, he brushed it off, turned it back around to me being paranoid, anxious, or what he said exactly I don't remember. I had no way to address things.

Until Neil died about 15 years after their divorce, and around the time Theresa turned 55, their children remained very close with him. Theresa's health was starting to decline, and it was only then that her children began coming around to pay more attention to her. Theresa's diabetes triggered concerns about her health, but she was equally worried about injuring the fragile relationship she recently reestablished with her children. She thought they would not react well if she shared unpleasant information about Neil, so she kept this knowledge of his affairs to herself and tended to walk on eggshells around her children.

Freedom 55

When I asked Theresa why she identified as retired and how her life changed once she retired, she explained that she had been charmed by a series of commercials that repeatedly used the words "freedom 55." All her life, she had longed to be free. She wanted freedom from "neurasthenia," "exhaustion," "severe agitation," or whatever her condition was called. She longed to escape the confines of being a mother and homemaker. She never had a retirement party, but she decided to start calling herself retired when she turned 55.

Though her use of the term "retiree" coincided with Neil's death, she made no mention of this connection. The first time she remembered using the term was on forms she filled out while she was shopping. Then, she recalled some government paperwork in which she selected the term to describe herself. Later, she began verbally identifying as a retiree when she started coming to the community center where she exercised. And she came to enjoy how being retired opened up a range of possibilities for who she could be and what she could do.

Like her divorce, her transition to retirement was associated with modest financial support. But unlike her divorce from Neil, the transition to retirement required little effort or compromise to her schedule or sense of purpose.

At one point, I mentioned to Theresa that some people don't consider it possible for a homemaker to be "retired." At first she laughed, thinking that I meant that a homemaker's work was never done, and she assured me that she couldn't *wait* to be done with the role of homemaker. I went on to explain that, in my job, some people define retirement as leaving paid work and might simply exclude homemakers from their analyses because they couldn't calculate an income or quantify the numbers of hours a homemaker worked. Theresa's interest was piqued, and it was clear she was a bit disturbed by my comment: It hadn't occurred to her that she might not count as a retired person or that she might have taken liberties with the title.

Theresa viewed being retired as a socially acceptable title that was preferable to homemaker. Having struggled with conforming to rigid expectations for women as a young wife and mother, she was eager to adopt an ambiguous term. I tried to reassure her that she was not alone in adopting an unorthodox use of the term retiree, but it was clear that my comment had slightly dented the sense of freedom she associated with being retired.

THE HAPPY HOUSEWIFE HEROINE

Margaret, Former Secretary and Homemaker

Like Theresa, Margaret worried about whether she was living up to the standards she thought she needed to achieve as a mother and housewife. But while Theresa learned to establish distance between herself, her husband, and her children, Margaret found herself dealing with far too much distance when she became a widow.

Margaret and I first started talking about Betty Friedan because I had a copy of *The Fountain of Age* sticking out of my bag when we met for the second time.[6] Our conversation quickly shifted to *The Feminine Mystique*, and Margaret explained how much the notion of the "happy housewife heroine" resonated with her as she described it.[7] As a young girl, she aspired to fit the mold of an ideal housewife and mother. She went to college to get her "Mrs." When she was in college, she took classes in accounting because she *wanted* to be outnumbered by men—it would increase her odds of finding a smart husband.

But instead of finding a husband in college, Margaret ended up with a bachelor's degree. In her early 20s, she worked as a secretary in a small legal office for a few years and, when she met her husband, she left the paid workforce forever. When I met her at her small apartment with a lovely view of a lake, she smirked as she told me about how the legal office she worked in used to have an annual party. At this party, all the lawyers and staff were invited to attend and the married lawyers would typically attend without their wives. The party was a chance for the men to strategize about work, and it was also an opportunity for them to meet and "mingle with the secretaries."

Margaret did not meet her husband at one of these parties, but several of her friends were married off to lawyers because of those parties, only later to realize that they would never be invited again. Their husbands would continue to attend and "mingle with the secretaries."

Margaret ended up meeting her husband, Leo, at a non-work-related party and she quit working once they started dating seriously. She tried earnestly to devote her life to taking care of her two children, supporting her husband, and taking care of matters around the house. While their kids were growing up, they also had dogs and several other pets. At times, Margaret described her life as a housewife as idyllic. But, throughout her interviews with me, Margaret also admitted that she often felt like a failure and that she wasn't living up to the standards she thought she needed to achieve as a mother, wife, and homemaker. On many days, she was exhausted and yet still had not accomplished half of what she had set out to do in terms of cooking and cleaning.

Most days Margaret tried to wake up at least an hour before her children to make herself presentable and prepare breakfast. On a typical day when her kids were young, she would bring them to school, then take care of the laundry, clean, and get their lunch ready. Then it would be time to bring them home for lunch, return them to school, focus on whatever she had not gotten to before lunch, get groceries, and prepare dinner.

Margaret saw being a homemaker as her calling in life. She only questioned why she had not been able to do more. For instance, she described her interest in keeping her house clean as akin to a business owner who wanted to provide the highest quality environment. Margaret and Leo had a daughter and a son. She described her children's work ethic as foreign from her own, I noted some similarities as she told me how much pride they took in their work: "They are so good at their jobs. They, the both of them, they both work such long hours and are always thinking about work. They so rarely let go or take time for themselves. I don't know who they got that from, me or their father, but it is a very strong work ethic they both have."

Times Have Changed

Margaret repeatedly remarked how much times had changed since she had been a young woman. There were more options for women these days, different expectations, too. She worried that her daughter would never marry because she worked too hard; she worried how her daughter-in-law could manage things with her busy, full-time career and all the lessons and activities her grandchildren were enrolled in. Women had so many expectations to "do it all," but Margaret also thought some things were better now. She cited her impression that ideas about a woman's weight and body type were much more generous than they had been in her day, and they also had many more options when it came to premade dinners. Margaret explained,

In my day, we had to really watch it. You couldn't just get fat and expect everyone to accept you. People would notice, and they would comment that you were not taking care of things at home if you put on too much weight. It was a clear signal that you were depressed or unhappy in your marriage if you gained weight. Now it seems to be, we accept all body types. I was just reading a book to my granddaughter about all types of body shapes and sizes. I'll admit that I struggled to keep my weight down. But in my day, we didn't have the healthy quick options you have now. I was so thrilled when, you know the Swanson TV dinners, came out. They really weren't healthy though. Now we know!

Times had changed since Margaret had come of age. Although Margaret followed the mores of her time, her husband Leo, focused on his work as an accountant and bookkeeper. They converted their garage into an office so that he could consult with clients. During tax season, he would disappear into the garage for a few months each year. The garage was demarcated as Leo's workspace, and the home was hers.

In addition to making sure meals were served, whether they were Swanson's frozen dinners or made from scratch, Margaret was also in charge of all the children's lessons:

I was careful not to overschedule them and to find the balance that was right for each of my children. Of course, we paid for it based on the money he earned, but I was the one who decided that it would be spent on piano instead of shopping trips. Other women I knew did that. They chose not to put their kids in lessons because it meant extra time and was an additional expense. I did what I thought was right. I made those executive decisions and if you look at my children now you'll see that they were the right choices.

Margaret took great pride in how her children turned out. She showed me photos: her son, a lawyer with two children himself, had married a woman who looked strikingly similar to Margaret in her younger years. Margaret's daughter was heavyset and seemed to resemble Leo's side. Margaret also brought me pictures of herself as a young girl. Together, we looked at photos from her young life through her time as a young mother and homemaker, and all the way until Leo's accident and funeral.

You're Not There

Before we started talking about Margaret's entry into widowhood or retirement, she made a somewhat morbid statement about herself as a mother. She said, "I had this idea after they left home, that, if I had died before they became teenagers, before they moved on from needing me, I would have been remembered as the best mother ever. I wasn't exactly the picture of sanity then."

Once her children left home and started on their professional trajectories, they rarely called and did not visit much. She compared her children with some of her neighbors' and friends' children who were never to become professionals or as independent and successful as her own, but she noted that those children came around and visited their parents more often.

Even though the time when her children stopped needing her was painful, it brought her closer to Leo. As empty-nesters, they started going on evening walks together. These were among Margaret's favorite memories with Leo.

And then one day, Leo was in a car accident. He never had the chance to retire; she never had the chance to say goodbye. He died without seeing his children married; she lamented that she wasn't able to take care of him into old age. Margaret missed out on so many things she had expected they would do together.

The Role-less Role

As a homemaker without children or a husband at home, Margaret felt rudderless. When I interviewed her, Margaret had worn the title of widow for more than a decade. During that time, she had spent many days wondering what her life would have been like had Leo survived the car accident. Some days, she wished she had been in the car, too. But most days, she carried on, adjusting to grocery shopping and cooking for one. She tried to maintain the friendships she and Leo had developed together as a couple, and she cried as she realized that she had lost not only her best companion, but also the roles that had defined her.

One of the first major decisions she made after dealing with the seemingly endless paperwork that accompanied Leo's death was to sell their house. Margaret had been in charge of the home, but Leo had taken care of anything that related to the household expenses. When he died, Margaret was overwhelmed with grief as well as the bills, tasks, and expenses related to their home. Margaret wanted to make sure her children could take what they wanted and to keep anything that Leo would have wanted her to keep. In retrospect, she observed that getting organized to put the house up for sale brought her closer to her children. So, she took several years to actually sell her house.

But once she moved into her condo, Margaret started to see that she would be able to carry on. Moving gave her a new sense of direction. Having a smaller kitchen and eating space made her feel more comfortable on her own. Becoming a grandmother also brought her great strength, although she regretted that Leo didn't get to be a grandfather. Margaret started identifying as retired a few years after she moved into her condo and noticed that many of their old friends and people around her age identified that way. She also considered when Leo would have retired from his job and in her own way timed her retirement with his. Leo had set up some private pensions that were starting to kick in, so even the mail started refer-ring to her as a retiree. On occasion, she alternated between calling herself a grandmother and calling herself retired.

In her retirement, Margaret had expected that she and Leo would travel together and spend time with their grandchildren together, and she imagined she would take care of him as he aged. She hadn't thought much about her own aging or who would take care of her. When we talked, she still hadn't figured that out. Although things had turned out so differently things from the plans she and Leo had made, she felt well-prepared for retirement.

She explained, "[Leo] was always the one who planned the vaca-tions. Then he was always so excited to get back to work after vaca-tions. It was hard for him to take too much time off. I always loved going away. We never went too far and I loved the change of scen-ery. I realize now, coming to my condo was the right move for me. Being retired is good for me. Everyone doesn't need to know I am a widow. I carry around a lot with that title. Being retired, you can be anything."

GIVING IT HER ALL

Amna, Homemaker

In different ways, but much like Margaret, Amna's experience with autonomy and a flexible schedule throughout most of her adult-hood also helped her adapt to the role-less role of being retired.

Amna and I met first in the community center where she volun-teered. That was where she told me about how she left everything behind to move with her husband, Samir. Together they moved across the world so that he could pursue a career in engineering. Amna recalled that it took her decades to adjust to the initial shock of being away from her family, dealing with winter, and learning to speak English. She spoke several languages, but English, she said, was the hardest to learn.

Amna felt isolated when they initially moved. Her family did not approve of her marriage, and so she had severed all ties back home. As a young woman, she had hoped for a large family and struggled for many years to get pregnant, but she was never able to conceive. In her early 30s and well into her 40s, she had a strong sense that she was missing out by not becoming a mother.

It might have been easier for her to make friends or to practice speaking in English if she had children; she imagined that her life might have felt fuller and less lonesome. She described times when she had very little interaction with other people: "Sometimes I wasn't sure what was real life or my imagination. I'd be doing the grocery shopping, someone would say to me something, and I'd realize—I hadn't spoken in a long time. Then I'd know, I had been stuck in my head all day. None of those ideas floating in my head were real. My life is so much more full and interesting now."

Amna and Samir were able to buy a house with a nice garden, and Amna started doing volunteer work. Initially, the idea was that she would volunteer at the community center to learn English. She blushed as she described the courage it took for her to approach Linda, the center's coordinator, about becoming a volunteer. Amna had only the equivalent of an elementary school education behind her, but Linda was keen to have help and quickly recognized that Amna's fluency in multiple languages could be an asset once she got a better grasp of English. Linda was instrumental in helping Amna establish a life outside her home and forming the circle of friends who would be so meaningful in her retirement.

Despite all the hard work it took for Amna to learn English and the effort she put in to volunteering at the community center, her number one priority was always to be a good homemaker. When we met, I asked Amna to describe her primary life's work, and she told me that she was a homemaker. When I asked why that description resonated with her more than being a volunteer, she explained that, "My priority is to make sure things are comfortable at home. You see, I was made to be taking care of things at home. I'm very good with that. I enjoy the cooking and knowing that my husband is cared for. He takes care of me too. You see, at home is where I give my all. What I'm doing at the center is good. I am helping, and it has helped me in so many ways. But I cannot go live there. I cannot exist with that alone."

She Worked Around His Schedule

When Amna initially started volunteering, she was excited to tell Samir all the details of her day. She would even rehearse the conversation she planned to have with him about her day while the events of her day were still unfolding. But then, some nights, he would come home and not be an attentive listener. She contrasted those memories with his new status as a retiree,

> Sometimes I just wanted him to really listen to me. He would go through these long phases of being so busy. It was clear he wasn't listening. For example, I'd tell him a story about someone. I say their name ten times. Then, I'd mention the person I'd been talking about the next day and he'd have no idea who I was talking about, when I had just told him all about that person. Now that he's retired, he's around all the time. Now he's telling me the same stories over and over and over. It's not like he's having dementia, or maybe he is. But it's more like, he's in this phase where he wants some attention. And sometimes, I'm thinking, "Hey, I know that feeling. I remember wanting you to just stop

and take a few minutes with me or notice something I just said." It's so funny. Sometimes, I just want to say, "Enough with that story" and to tell him "Go away."

For at least four decades, Amna worked around Samir's schedule, making sure that breakfast and dinner were ready on time. If he didn't listen to her, she worked around that, too. Making friends with other women was very helpful to her sense of well-being, and her friends often found the things that Samir ignored highly interesting. Other than the constraints of Samir's schedule and the handful of hours she volunteered at the community center most weekdays, her schedule was flexible. Amna enjoyed the autonomy. It was also important to her that she keep her house tidy. They never had housekeepers or maids so all the cleaning fell to Amna. When the weather was nice, she enjoyed growing her own vegetables and taking care of her garden.

He Was in Heaven; She Needed Some Space

Amna started to consider herself retired the day after Samir's retirement party. Samir had been looking forward to retiring for a long time. It was planned several years in advance, on his own terms, so that the timing coincided with financial security. Right around the same time that Samir retired, Linda also retired from her position at the community center. Amna noticed that several ladies she had befriended while volunteering also had started to identify as retired.

When they retired, Samir was in heaven. He had no demands on himself anymore; the few he had could be placed on Amna. But at that point, Amna had experienced decades of being responsible for setting her own schedule. Having Samir home all the time was a major disruption to her daily routine. She had happily shared the house with him every morning, evening, and weekend, but having him around during the day on weekdays initially felt like an invasion of her personal space. At first, Samir wanted to have lunch together every day at a specific time. Amna found this disconcerting. For roughly four decades she had grown accustomed to eating her weekday lunch alone or with her friends on whatever schedule they agreed to.

Amna admired Samir, not just as a husband, but for the way he exerted confidence when he walked into a room. She saw him as a warm person that people wanted to be around. But when she had him around all day, she found him imposing, in a way that was less desirable.

Samir also meddled around the house. He took up carpentry and woodworking, and he would take up large swaths of the house with his projects, like rebuilding the bookshelves. He was not messy, but his projects created messes. Samir also had many ideas for activities that he wanted Amna to coordinate. Amna said that it wouldn't have been a problem, except that Samir never liked the way she coordinated things. He would pick an activity, have her do all the planning for it, and then he would change his mind and ask her to switch things around. He was never satisfied with her work.

Eventually, Amna realized it was easier to be the person who comes up with the idea than the one who has to carry it out. She grew tired of Samir's scrutiny and how their retirement was leaving her little time for the community center and her friends.

Amna regularly reminded herself of the many qualities she loved about Samir, among which was his generosity. She deeply appreciated that he was always ready to give more than he expected in return. She described numerous occasions throughout their marriage when he would carry things for her or move things around the house for her. Many times, Samir would arrange a weekend trip without expecting anything from her, except to stick to their routine when they returned from the trip. Throughout the year, he would buy her special gifts on ordinary days, not just holidays, so that she would not be expected to give him anything in return.

But when he retired, he stopped doing these sorts of things. Amna was happy to retire together, but things were not as good as they once were. She presumed, at first, that he stopped with the gifts and planning their trips was because he was trying to be careful with their money. But she noticed that some of his new hobbies and the activities he wanted them to do were quite costly. When Amna confronted Samir about their new lifestyle as retirees, she was relieved to encounter his generosity again. Samir wasn't fully aware of how things had changed and explained that he saw retirement as the time for them to do everything they had not yet done. He wanted her to be happy. Amna explained that she needed more space and to be able to continue her volunteer work and lunch with the ladies. So long as she would leave him a lunch, Samir agreed not to meddle with her schedule.

Amna was mindful to help Samir adjust to his new freedom without letting him impinge on her own. She recognized that she had the upper hand, in many ways, because he had to adapt to a lifestyle that she was quite accustomed to. Overall, retirement leveled out some of the differences between them. In some ways, retirement was a sort of promotion for her because she became the one who came up with the ideas and gained greater control of their schedule.

In contrast to her earlier days of going grocery shopping and realizing how socially disconnected she was, Amna described spending hours on end in her retirement, mindfully grocery shopping in different neighborhoods for specific ingredients. In her retirement, Amna was learning to enjoy Samir again and learning how to negotiate with him to carve out her own space.

THE RETIREMENT MYSTIQUE

In *The Feminine Mystique*, Betty Friedan illustrated how idealized images of domestic womanhood constrained women's capacities to demonstrate their intellectual potential and undermined their confidence.[8] Friedan brought light to "the problem that has no name" by describing the limited career options available to women in the middle of the past century and identifying the unhappiness associated with being a suburban housewife. Although being a homemaker likely limited many women in ways that disallowed them and society from realizing the benefits of their full potential, much can be learned from the experiences of women who use the title homemaker to describe the work they carried out throughout their adulthood.

The women whose experiences are shared in this chapter expressed varying degrees of frustration with their role as home-makers. Several aspired to be the "happy housewife heroine" and experienced disappointment when they were not able to live up to expectations of domestic perfection. Their dominant shared experience had to do with making the transition from homemaker to retiree. In examining the contrasts and similarities in their retirement experiences, we also can observe parallels between the cultural norms that suggest a woman's place is limited to the home and those that suggest a retiree should be defined as someone who no longer participates in the paid workforce.

The retirement mystique can best be described as the ever-evolving, dynamic, and complex social construct we associate with the end of one's career. A problem has emerged in which a contrast exists between contemporary manifestations of retirement and traditional ageist stereotypes that link one's ability to productively contribute to society with chronological age. Contemporary structural forces paternalistically provide retirees with a pension that is typically a fraction of a worker's salary. Like the "happy house-wife heroine," retirees are often exploited by advertisers looking to sell products. And similar to social expectations that limit home-makers from achieving their full potential, for some, retirement is a social construct that stifles later-life engagement, productivity, and fulfillment.

The shared identification as a retired individual held by each of the women in this chapter illustrate the universality and ambiguity of the term "retiree" as a marker of personal identity. Researchers may scoff at these homemakers' use of this term, but without doubt, variations in how the term "retirement" is operationalized are unlikely to dissipate in the near future. Instead, as the experiences of the people whose stories are shared in chapters 2 through 5 illustrate, it is more likely that retirement will take on an even wider range of definitions. In this way, contemporary manifestations of retirement as a varied and heterogeneous construct not only challenge idealized, traditional images of retirement that suggest a retiree's place is in the home but also offer hope that we can dispel ageist stereotypes about age and productivity.

In their retirement, each of the women I interviewed felt uninhibited by adopting the identity of "retiree." Feminist gerontology has suggested that, for some women, social awareness plays a pivotal role in the construction of individual identity. All the women in this chapter embraced their title as a retiree in bold ways that contravened traditional mores. They simultaneously used and ignored social cues when they became retirees. And their experiences demonstrated that retirement can be both a change in day-to-day schedules or much of the same; retirement is indeed an ambiguous term. As homemakers, these women had been accustomed to setting autonomous schedules, while also meeting the needs of their households, for decades. Their retirement, in some ways, presented a happier front relative to many of the other retirees in this book.

Being retired offered these homemakers with the opportunity to embrace a new title and a socially preferable status. In some cases, retirement offered them an egalitarianism that younger women knew, but that was available to these homemakers only in the later part of their lives.

Although they each felt insecurities about living up to expectations of domestic perfection, they were able to recognize the important contributions they had made to their family, community, or household throughout their adult lives. Notably, most of these women, with the exception of Theresa, seemed to recall their role as homemakers in favorable terms. As a homemaker, Theresa experienced what can be described as *role captivity*—simply put, she was in a social role that she would have preferred not to be in.[9] And when the opportunity to retire presented itself, Theresa eagerly shed other possible roles to be a retiree. Theresa defined herself as retired when she reached age 55, because she had associated that age with retirement and had longed for a way to describe herself without revealing much about herself. She liked retirement's association with freedom, and the ambiguity of retirement allowed her to escape from her other roles, as a mother or wife, which she associated with shortcomings and regret.

Each of these woman ultimately enjoyed being retired. Betty and Amna both struggled with having their husbands around all day, but like Theresa, they came to find themselves to be well prepared for retirement. Theresa's discontentment with "retirement" was apparent only when I pointed out that her use of the term was unconventional. And Margaret's discontentment stemmed from her role-less-ness, but she was placated by prior experience with loss, which left her uniquely prepared for the challenges retirement presented.

On the whole, retirement for the women in this chapter was linked to their desire to broaden their identities and to find a more socially relevant title. Betty and Amna essentially identified as retired when their husbands retired. Without children or a husband to take care of, and exposure to lots of paperwork bearing the word "retirement," Margaret saw being retired as a fitting title and preferred it to being called a widow.[10] In some ways, for each of these women, their feelings about retirement contrasted with their earlier insecurities about meeting societal expectations. Retirement illustrated how they could make use of this social construct in ways that suited their needs.

Perhaps their relatively positive association with retirement had to do with the fact that these women experienced what bell hooks has described as being in the privileged position of being supported by someone else financially.[11] These homemakers were protected from the harsh experiences of having to work in lower paying jobs that many women of color, immigrants, and other women coming of age in the time of the happy housewife heroine had to endure. Some evidence suggests, however, that women who participate in the paid labor force fare more favorably relative to homemakers when it comes to measures of well-being, such as depressive symptoms, financial worries, and health.[12] Therefore, it would be unwise to assume that the experiences of the women in this chapter are generalizable or to suggest that the privilege of being financially provided for as a homemaker compensates for the limitations imposed by structural forces that have implied women should not work outside of the home.

Early research about retirement rarely included women; when it did, women were included only to better understand their husbands' experiences with retirement.[13] Focusing on this unlikely set of retirees illustrates how traditional definitions of retirement are becoming anachronistic. The reasons each woman identified as retired were not pellucid, and yet, like other more traditional retirees, they experienced a major transition as it related to their life's work. Their experiences mark the significance of retirement as both a context-driven, subjective status and an identity-shaping concept that reflects and defies social norms.

Furthermore, the experiences of the women in this chapter illustrate the persistence of retirement as a marker of personal identity despite variations in how it is operationalized.[14] These women could have chosen to identify as homemakers when I interviewed them, but with no preferable general term to describe themselves, they adopted a term that more commonly is used to describe the workforce transitions made by their spouses or people from their social networks. Being retired was a descriptor that resonated with them and, for the most part, they enjoyed being retired.

7

Conclusion

Given its dynamic history and popular appeal, retirement is full of potential. For some people, however, retirement is laden with discontentment. In chapter 1, I explained that the objective of this book was to better understand the perceptions and experiences of retirees whose departure from their life's work meant losing a fundamental component of their core personal identity. The narratives shared in this book illustrate that retirement can signify the end of a goal-oriented, purposeful life. Its expected quietude, freedom, and autonomy can be disorienting.

Each of the retirees whose stories are shared in this book internalized the notion that retirement meant an end to their life's work. Then when they retired, they experienced a tension between the freedom and autonomy associated with this phase of life and their desires to maintain structure, a sense of social connectedness, and personal fulfillment. Although it was clear that the disruption of retirement was not going to last long for several of the retirees, their overall experiences illustrate Freud's claim that a sense of discontentment can accompany attendance to civilization's rules and norms.

For people who can afford to retire and are in good health, a retirement that should be marked by enjoying life without the burdens of work can be a burden in itself—that is, the burden of life *without* work. Herein lies the irony of retirement's lack of boundaries and lauded freedoms, which can feel like a forced rupture from our core identity.

Ernest Hemingway wrote, "Retirement is the ugliest word in the language."[1] Despite the fact that some people despise the term "retirement" and believe that it lacks a clear and concise definition, many people do self-identify as retired. For many of the highly talented, dedicated retirees I interviewed, Hemingway's statement rang true. Their experiences drew a sharp contrast with portrayals of retirement that dominate popular culture. Rather than sun-dappled relaxation and leisure activities, the people I interviewed struggled in their initial transitions to retirement. They understood it to mean an end to their working lives, even though they still felt capable, engaged, and interested in working.

Their retirement experiences embody an important and less discussed aspect of the breakdown of social bonds between an individual and the community. Their experiences illustrate how retirement can lead, in essence, to what Émile Durkheim termed "anomie."[2] Retirement emerges as a situation in which society provides relatively no moral guidance and in which individuals lose their sense of identity. Ageist social norms that link age with decline and decreased capabilities, and that assume disengagement is mutually beneficial, can create conditions that have negative implications for individuals and society.

The desire to feel connected to a community and to have a social identity are fundamental to who we are as humans. For some people, the removal of a professional title, never mind a source of livelihood, social status, and moral guidance, can be akin to removing a protective shell. Therefore, it should not be surprising that retirement can be like losing one's compass.

In this concluding chapter, I begin by examining the unique Retirement Identities of those I interviewed. Following this,

I revisit the distinct shared traits of each group of retirees and discuss key themes from chapters 2 through 6 (Greedy Institutions, Fulfillment Employment, Resilience, Working in Place, and The Retirement Mystique). I then move to the alleged Joys of Being Retired and examine how, for example, a retirement party that was meant to celebrate the transition instead became a disquieting occasion marking the end of a productive life. I conclude by examining Somewhere Towards the End and the Beginning to suggest that, for some people, decoupling retirement from chronological age offers great value.

Retirement Identities

Each person I interviewed had a unique retirement identity, and yet each shared a common way of identifying themselves as "retired." Several succumbed to pressures to retire even as they held strong personal ambitions and goals for their life. Although some felt that they had been expected to retire, others willingly chose to retire. In contrast to workers who suffer poor health that renders retirement essential, the people I interviewed were in relatively good health and in relatively early stages of their retirement.[3] I cannot help but wonder whether the favorable health experienced by the retirees in this book actually enhanced their feelings of ennui and discontentment. Each of these characteristics—feeling that their time was up, holding ambitions, enjoying relatively good health, and being in relatively early stages of their retirement—combined to create a formula for discontentment.

The decisions to retire and when to retire are incredibly important and can be associated with a number of different push and pull factors.[4] Push factors include situations that cause a person to retire because of his or her own failing health or illness or because someone else requires caregiving, while pull factors can be described as reasons that entice someone into retiring. Examples of pull factors include the desire to pursue leisure activities or to make time to travel with a spouse. Each of these rationales for retiring can influence the extent to which people are able to feel in control of their retirement, the degree to which they are able to feel contentment, and the way they experience retirement.

The doctors in chapter 2 had traditional notions of retirement. With the exception of Robert, an academic doctor whose understanding of retirement was more in sync with the professors, the doctors identified a retiree as a person who terminates paid work after a long and stable career. The chief executive officers (CEOs) had held many different titles leading up to the culmination of their career and each came to embrace a retirement identity that involved reengaging in paid work. The elite athletes' identification with retirement was untraditional because they retired so early in the life course and were compelled to reenter the workforce in new roles largely because of financial urgency and the fact that they retired at an early stage in the life course. Although the career trajectory of the professors was fairly traditional leading up to their retirement, their identification as retirees who continued to perform the same work as they did before retiring (but without direct compensation) was a less-than-traditional type of retirement. And, in a similar vein, the homemakers continued to follow a schedule that was strikingly similar to the days before their self-defined retirement, though their life trajectories leading into retirement did not mirror traditional work experiences.

Each group of retirees in this book had a distinct career (or, in the case of the homemakers, a distinct sense of purpose) that dominated much of their adulthood. They also had a unique way of identifying as retired. In examining what retirement meant to each individual, it became evident that retirement was more than simply a term affiliated with receiving a pension. Retirement was understood as creatively negotiated and deeply personal, with a sense of purpose that suited each retiree and his or her circumstances.

Robert Atchley proposed a set of stages of retirement.[5] Initially, retirees experience an attendant planning and anticipatory state. Then, people enter the honeymoon stage, in which they tend to keep busy, lavishing in their newfound freedom to do all the things they never had time to do while working. Next, they enter the disenchantment stage, whereby disappointment sets in, which is followed by a reorientation stage that is characterized by an individual's development of more realistic expectations about what their daily routine of retirement will be like. This stage is followed by the stability stage during which people grow accustomed to their routine and master their retirement. And finally, they enter the termination stage, when retirement ends with the death of the individual or their return to paid work.

My interviewees were relatively early in their retirement trajectories, but by and large, most had skipped the honeymoon stage and were grappling with disenchantment. Several showed signs of moving toward reorientation: Some of the doctors were beginning to enter into new types of work or other creative endeavors, and many of the CEOs were beginning to explore new types of fulfillment employment. For the most part, the athletes were in the termination stage and had embarked on new types of work, though they continued to strongly identify as "retired"; the professors were stable in pursuing the work they had always done; and the homemakers were coming to embrace their newfound titles and developing a new a sense of themselves, while some were developing potentially stronger relationships with their life partners.

In identifying as retired, these retirees demonstrated an eagerness to seek out new titles, when old ones were removed or forced away from them or when they simply felt that it was time for replacement. Their stories illustrate how we struggle with who we are until we are able to adapt and make our new title align with our ambitions and sense of self. I observed support among these retirees for understanding retirement as a liminal or threshold state. They demonstrated that retirement can be a time in which an individual contemplates his or her next steps, while also considering whether the status of "retirement" will hold. When viewed as a time to reassess one's interests, options, and desires, retirement identities become flexible and yet manageable in ways that lend acceptance to existing between the lines of "the normal, day-to-day cultural and social states."[6] Although liminality implies ambiguity, viewing retirement as a liminal state opens up a broad range of ways to creatively and productively thrive at all stages of the life course.

As Donald Polkinghorne has explained, "the people we interview are always somewhere in the middle of their stories."[7] The retirement experiences of people whose narratives are shared in this book can also be described as being in the "involvement status" because the influence of their preretirement experiences continued to play a pivotal role in shaping perceptions of their daily experiences in retirement.[8] Perhaps, as time passes or as their health declines, some will find new paths and new ways of adjusting to being retired.

The Greedy Institution

Medicine may be the ultimate greedy institution.[9] It is all but required that doctors cultivate their work identity above all other identities, and they face constant pressure to be at the top of their game. They are, after all, responsible for taking care of people when they become ill and are at their most vulnerable. At the same time that doctors become vulnerable in their later years and are perceived to be less capable, they are expected to *know* that it is time to shut down their practice and retire.

The doctors I interviewed felt like renegades; they had abandoned their life's work, their patients, and the coveted title they had worked so long and hard to earn. Being a retired doctor was not as gratifying as being a working one. In their retirement, like elite athletes, they had to address withdrawal from the "highs" their work had brought them and find outlets for their continued interest in learning and contributing to society. Their dedication to medicine had been fostered by their intellect and personal inclinations toward helping others. But, the greedy institution of medicine selects individuals who possess these predispositions and then enculturates them to a strong, often single-minded dedication to work.

Needless to say, medicine is by no means the only greedy institution. As mentioned in chapter 1, many of the other professionals faced extremely demanding work schedules that often dominated other spheres of their life, including the CEOs and professors. The journey it takes to become a professional can span a long portion of the life course, whether through medical specialty programs, graduate programs in business administration that CEOs pursue along their career path, or graduate and postdoctoral work that are features of the academic work trajectory. Once in the role, being a professional implies a willingness to work at odd and extended hours, long past the times when other workers have clocked out. As people invest more time and energy into professionalization and specialization, it is no surprise that their personal identity becomes intricately connected with their professional identity. Once indoctrinated into their professional roles and exposed to their work culture, professionals will cede more of their time and loyalty to the greedy institutions.

Professionals are expected to be sharp, committed, and to act in a "professional" manner. This implies thinking about the consequences of work at all times and exhibiting competence and poise in situations that relate to human vulnerabilities, desires, or impulses to act in "unprofessional" ways. Under all circumstances, professionals are expected to consider the consequences of their actions and interactions with others, including patients, staff, students, or supervisees. They are accountable and must consider the effects of their position of power; failure to do so can affect others as well as their career.

Like the professionals I interviewed in medicine, business, and academia, the elite athletics also were expected to follow a code of ethics, to self-sacrifice, and to exhibit faultless dedication. Although homemakers are not professionals by definition, the institution they serve is among the oldest and most revered, and in many ways, it also is greedy. Raising children requires giving every aspect of one's self, starting at birth, when an infant demands full attention and knows no time boundaries. Like an on-call doctor, a mother who is fully devoted to caring for an infant may be woken up in the middle of the night and be expected to jump into her role as care provider. Rarely can anyone take over a mother's shift. Even without children, the expectations associated with being in charge of the household require intense obligation. After all, the homemaker literally lives at work.

The people I interviewed worked in a range of greedy institutions: from medicine to the top of the corporate ladder, to the world of elite sports, to the ivory tower, and to the institution of marriage and family. Like Emil, the surgeon who described retirement as akin to becoming a renegade, every person whose story is shared in this book demonstrated a deep sense of commitment and loyalty to his or her life's work. They all identified with their work role; several personified their work and described missing their work as if it were a person when they retired. Each felt an implied, suggested, or required sense of duty to retire from that role when they were no longer at the top of their game, could be replaced, or were no longer needed. Often, however, the only signal that such a moment had arrived was an arbitrary birthday. For someone who has given their all to a greedy institution, this departure can be anything but associated with contentment.

Fulfillment Employment

Most of the CEOs entered into retirement with favorable expectations; some had planned ahead and expected that they would have a refined retirement in which they would finally enjoy the fruits of their labor. Yet because their sense of enjoyment and satisfaction in life had been so connected to their work, they struggled to feel fulfilled without continued engagement in paid work. Many of them reentered the paid workforce to hold onto their core source of value and their primary means of contributing to society, ultimately finding a sense of personal fulfillment. In some ways, the professors and homemakers came to a similar conclusion in that their adjustment was ameliorated by a recognition that their fulfilling work need not end (even though a paycheck might).

Many of the CEOs felt pushed into retirement because of their age; some retired because of their own ageist assumptions, and others felt organizational pressure to stop working. We are a far cry from the time when young adults would wear powdered wigs to emulate the white hair (and wisdom) of their elders. Instead, dying our hair to conceal grays and undergoing medical procedures to produce a more youthful appearance are increasingly common practices around the world. In her writings, Susan Sontag developed the idea that society is particularly harsh in its evaluation of aging women.[10] Indeed,

Elizabeth, one of the CEOs I interviewed, considered dying her gray-ing hair as a requirement in her line of work. Similarly, some of the homemakers felt plagued by perceptions around aging that were closely associated with beauty and productive engagement with soci-ety. And age-related concerns about the perception of diminished capabilities and fears of invisibility extended to participants across all five groups of retirees, regardless of gender.

Despite their professional accomplishments, the experiences of the retirees in this book illustrate that negative perceptions of aging can foreshorten working lives. For the most part, the CEOs left near the peak of their careers. They chafed at a retirement enforced with blunt rules; yet to some degree, they also bought into stereotypes that insisted they had reached their expiry dates.

In societies that tend to favor speed, vitality, newness, and youth-ful images of beauty, advanced age is mistakenly associated with reduced productivity and a lowered ability to learn and adapt. All five groups of retirees questioned what it meant to be "productive" in their own way in retirement. As a whole, their stories underscore a desire for flexibility in the ways we think about productivity and success. But above all, their stories demonstrate the value of delink-ing chronological age from work-related norms about productivity.

Resilience

The elite athletes I interviewed made many sacrifices in pursuing their athletic careers. But these were not, on the whole, in the pursuit of money. They pushed their bodies to the limit, demon-strating incredible strength, endurance, and flexibility; their ability to focus even under intense scrutiny was commendable. And after this intense pressure to perform, they ended their athletic careers in what many would consider to be the prime of their life. In their retirement, they were pressed to adapt to the "real world" and to find a new way to earn money, because none—even those with Olympic medals—had achieved great wealth through their athletic career. For them, resilience was key.

Although these athletes experienced an "early" retirement, when compared with the rest of the individuals discussed in this book, they exemplify a form of anguish that can be associated with a retirement prompted by chronological age or physical decline. Their discontentment was in fact amplified because the actual *body* that had brought them to the pinnacles of success became "too old" for the challenge.

Athletes' careers are short, and even at the upper echelons of a big-money sport, a few years with enormous salaries often are not enough to sustain them financially forever. Some research acknowledges that athletes may experience a disappointing sense that earlier accomplishments are voided in retirement.[11] Other research suggests that retirement can be a positive experience—a rebirth of sorts—and that the initial stages of retirement can be a favorable time for the athlete to seek out new pursuits.[12] For the athletes I interviewed, retirement was a low point that quickly followed their athletic career highs.

After a lifetime pursuing one goal, retirement meant an abrupt shift out of the spotlight and into the world of nonathletes. This new world had few clear goals or markers of success and little acknowledgment that they had ever achieved something exceptional. Acknowledging retirement as a chance to adjust and adapt was a challenge to these athletes. Like some of the doctors and CEOs, athletes like Luiz grappled with a hope to retire at his "best," and once retired, he struggled with withdrawal from the excitement his career had brought him.

Another shared experience that the athletes encountered in retirement was a sense of disorientation in their day-to-day schedules. Much like the CEOs, their meetings, meals, routines, and itineraries had been carefully planned out for them, and after retirement, the freedom was quite shocking. Then, similar to the homemakers, the athletes experienced a retirement that was not traditional or even recognized as retirement. Unlike the professors and the homemakers, however, they could not, for the most part, continue their work in retirement. The athletes had to recalibrate their sense of self and strength to find a way to earn a living, all while giving up what had been, until the point of retiring, the most meaningful aspect of their life.

Working in Place

Much has been said about people who continue to work in their retirement, particularly those who find employment that bridges the gap between working full time and stopping work completely.[13] Less has been said, however, about retirees whose personal identities are so deeply intertwined with their work that they continue to focus on their preretirement work well into their retirement—a concept I've referred to as "working in place."

The professors I interviewed endured pressures to be the best throughout their careers, and held a steady focus on their work. Their careers rewarded focus and drive. So, although their devotion remained, they retired a bit later in the life course and without actually giving up what they valued most about their work. The professors had experienced years of working autonomously, in many ways, like the homemakers. Each had a great deal of practice in constructing their own schedule and designing curricula and research programs. Their professional accomplishments had, for the most part, reflected priorities and goals they had set for themselves within the structure of academia. Despite the challenges they faced in retirement, their earlier, consistent experience with independence and flexibility served them well.

In support of Robert Atchley's continuity theory, the professors were particularly adept at trying to preserve and maintain the existing structures they had created throughout their adulthood.[14] The external continuity they sought not only helped them cope with the identity ambiguity they experienced in retirement but also helped them address challenges associated with aging and social pressures to succumb to a more traditional life *after* work. Atchley suggested that a person can most efficiently adapt to retirement by maintaining a consistent set of personal goals, something the professors most certainly had. Their ability to do this was likely facilitated by their pension benefits, which brought a form of financial stability. Notably, the professors' pensions benefits required no obligations to engage in any work; nonetheless, they all chose to maintain consistency in their lifestyle by continuing to work. Like the CEOs, the professors' work brought them a sense of fulfillment, but in contrast, the professors gave less weight to their earnings. Retired CEOs were eager to reengage in paid work, whereas the professors tended to see retirement as a continuation of their life's work whether or not they received a paycheck for it. In some ways, their discontentment with retirement was akin to a writer averse to an editor trying to force a different structure on his or her book. These professors did not want to change their patterns or commitment to their work because they reached an arbitrary age or because society saw them as potentially less productive. As one of the professors, Tomas, put it, "Retirement is for other people."

In their own way, each of the people I interviewed found inner contentment from their continued engagement with work. Each demonstrated that retirement's challenges could be met by repurposing the personal resources they had developed throughout their careers. But none so clearly illustrated the benefits of external continuity as those who found ways to work in place.

The Retirement Mystique

Today's cohort of people approaching traditional retirement age includes, for the first time, large numbers of women with a wide range of work experiences. These women came of age as Betty Friedan's culture-shifting book *The Feminine Mystique* was circulating.[15] They witnessed massive shifts in cultural expectations regarding women's roles in the home and workplace. At the time the homemakers I interviewed were entering adulthood, roughly one-third of the paid workforce in countries such as the United States and Canada included women. Now, this rate has nearly doubled. When these women were getting married and most were becoming mothers, the leading paid occupations for women were secretaries, bookkeepers, and elementary school teachers. Women generally remain underpaid relative to men and underrepresented in high-status positions, but we now see a much broader range of paid and professional roles open to women, as well as a dramatic increase in the overall proportion of women who work outside the home. Such changing demographics render homemakers a distinct and diminishing subset of women.

Deborah van den Hoonaard has suggested that despite the resources professional women hold through their accumulated life experiences and interactions in the workforce, they are particularly susceptible to losing their sense of identity as they move into the diminished role of retiree. Some undergo "identity foreclosure" or the loss of personal and social identity as they relinquish professional titles and come to be viewed by society as both retired and old.[16] Other evidence suggests that women who participated in the paid labor force fare more favorably when it comes to adapting to retirement, relative to homemakers, underscoring the notion that social awareness plays a pivotal role in the construction of individual identity.[17] In many ways, however, for the women in this book, retirement offered an opportunity to take on a new title that was more socially preferable to being a homemaker.

The work a homemaker provides is low status in many societies and often is considered work that can be outsourced: housekeepers and nannies can be hired, prepared meals can be purchased, and clothes can be dropped off at the dry cleaners. A personal assistant can even be hired to coordinate these activities. Helen Ebaugh has distinguished role exits from stigmatized roles into more socially desirable roles as well as role exits from desirable roles into less appealing roles.[18] The women I interviewed seemed to exit the role captivity they experienced as homemakers and found that retirement provided the opportunity to shift into the potentially more socially desirable, albeit more ambiguous, role of retiree.

In contrast to the women and men featured in this book, the work the homemakers did in their preretirement years was dramatically different from the other interviewees. The reasons they did not enter the paid workforce were not obvious but generally could be explained by personal circumstances that either inhibited their career options early in life or allowed them the opportunity to choose to work in the home without pay, having been supported by their spouse. Theresa, for example, was envious of professional women and expressed her irritation with working mothers who were so busy multitasking that they failed to realize how lucky they were to be able to enjoy it all. Others relished the privilege of being able to focus on homemaking, and some feared that they were not living up to the expectations of being a homemaker.

Some of the initial discontentment these homemakers felt in retirement was notably comparable to other groups of retirees.

Their work as homemakers had been their duty, their passion, and their calling. In early retirement, they felt a sense of discontentment at the loss of a primary role. At the same time, they were, in many ways, distinctly prepared for the autonomy and freedom retirement represented. Several had to adjust to altered relationships with their spouse: Although their newfound time together often threatened their former sense of autonomy, it also shifted relationship dynamics in ways that required their husbands to make accommodations. For the most part, these women had relatively favorable perceptions about retirement.

The aging of the baby boomer generation means there is greater heterogeneity in the experience of being retired. It also means more women are approaching retirement and that we are able to observe great heterogeneity specifically in women's retirement experiences. This is a contrast to early conceptualizations of retirement that were based largely on men's experiences and to studies in which women were included only to provide a "wife's perspective."[19] Today, a growing body of literature on women's retirement experiences[20] is poised to multiply rapidly.

On the note of these women's retirement, three important points should be made. First, unlike women who participate in the paid workforce, homemakers are rarely eligible for their own public pension benefits, and in many parts of the world, they are eligible only for spousal benefits.[21] Second, even women who participate in the paid workforce are likely to have lower pensions compared with men, because these women are more likely to work part time, to experience career interruptions (often because of childbirth), and to end their careers earlier to slip into a caregiving role. And, third, in the cases in which they engaged in the same work as men, women are more likely to have earned a lower salary over their lifetime.[22]

The final point I want to reiterate here is that the social construct of retirement has become a mystique—one that embodies the contrast between contemporary manifestations of retirement and traditional ageist stereotypes. Paternalistic structural forces offer retirees a pension that is typically but a fraction of a worker's salary. And like Friedan's "happy housewife heroine"[23] retirees are often exploited by advertisers looking to sell products. Like the limiting expectations that suggested women's roles should be limited to the home, retirement can also be associated with expectations that can stifle later-life engagement, productivity, and fulfillment.

The Joys of Being Retired

Myriad contemporary understandings of retirement allow us to use it as an umbrella term, gathering many ways to retire. But umbrella terms have their faults: They can be ambiguous as well as reductive. They can conceal variation as easily as they can suggest it. In just fifty years or so, American understandings of retirement have generally shifted from associations with poverty, decline, and disengagement to wealth, pleasure, and leisure.[24] Yet we can be considered retired and also not working, working part time, working full time, volunteering, caring for grandchildren, or taking a break from working before reentering the workforce. We can be doing nothing *and* doing everything.[25]

The narratives in this book highlight the persistence of the term *retirement* even as it is deployed in ever-more divergent ways. Some of the people I interviewed continued to use the term retirement even after their experience proved different from its traditional meaning, and others used it without even realizing their usage was unconventional. They all agreed, however, that they were *supposed* to be enjoying retirement.

As introduced at the start of this book, the concept of the "third age" positions retirement as a phase in which people are freed from the constraints imposed by work and obligations to family.[26] This should be a time to enjoy life, to cross off items on a "bucket list," and to golf, travel, and develop new cultural and intellectual interests. This third age is a time for both reflecting on past accomplishments and a time for doing things before health declines and dependence sets in during the "fourth age." Yet for many of the people I interviewed, the third age was a time that was still dominated by career interests—their work would always be a part of who they are.

A key marker of the transition to the third age is the retirement party. This party (or set of parties) that marks the transition from work to leisure is a generally celebrated endeavor that often features big gestures of appreciation and acknowledgment as well as drinks, cake, and gifts. The traditional retirement party exemplifies the expected joys of retirement. In his book, *Breaking the Watch*, Joel Savishinsky questions how the retirement party ritual can affect people going through the important transition to retirement.[27] As I listened to people's descriptions of their retirement parties, I heard disappointment, regret, and sadness. Their parties marked the end of their professional journeys and exemplified a social-level recognition that they had passed their "expired-by" date.

The all-consuming nature of their work had prevented many of the people whose stories are shared in this book from cultivating other interests. They had taken deep pride and experienced great satisfaction from work-related achievements, such as moving up the career ladder, winning an Olympic medal, producing scholarly publications, or being "the best" at their jobs in various ways. When they reached retirement, they were less than satisfied. Developing an affinity for leisure and independence can take time; for some, it may be impossible.

In addition to Savishinsky's *Breaking the Watch*,[28] several other eloquently written books distinctly depict the experience of renewal and revival that so many baby boomers expect in retirement. For example, Robert Weiss's *The Experience of Retirement*,[29] Marc Freedman's *Prime Time*[30] and *The Big Shift*,[31] Sara Lawrence Lightfoot's *The Third Chapter*,[32] Nancy Schlossberg's *Revitalizing Retirement: Reshaping Your Identity, Relationships, and Purpose*,[33] Chris Farrell's *Unretirement*,[34] and Phyllis Moen's *Encore Adulthood*[35] each, in a unique way, share the experiences of people embracing new possibilities as they strive to achieve their full potential in retirement. These books illuminate the expected joys of retirement and celebrate it as a time during which traditional career norms, rules, and rituals become less restrictive and work-related goals shift to goals of generativity.

The possibility remains that the individuals whose stories are shared in this book will eventually embrace the full potential and expected joys of retirement. Because this book focuses primarily on the challenges encountered before achieving this retirement potential, it is noteworthy to conclude by considering how society and institutions can aid in reducing the discontentment associated with this early retirement stage.

Somewhere Towards the End and the Beginning

In the past hundred years, life expectancy has increased at a greater rate than in the previous *two thousand* years. Now that we are living longer, healthier, and wealthier, retirement is a significant and often long phase of life. This book was intended not to propose or endorse specific alternative policies or pension incentive schemes, but to share the ways limited, traditional understandings of retirement can create feelings of discontentment. The flexibility and lack of structure inherent in "retirement" make it a difficult concept for some people to embrace. It is also important to remember that certain rigid aspects of pension plans, such as strict rules about age eligibility, essentially validate ageist stereotypes, particularly for people who are not yet ready to stop working.

Comparative analyses of national labor market exits have demonstrated that social policy regimes influence retirement timing.[36] A critical point following these links between age-incentivized policies and retirement timing is that often people must retire because of their own health issues or because they must care for someone else. Put simply, people who retire before the age of full-benefit eligibility will incur financial penalties for the rest of their lives by virtue of the fact that their benefits will be lower because they retired "early." And, as evidence here suggests, for some people, no age is old enough to retire. For both sets of people, the relationships among age, work, and retirement is complex.

By confronting ageist assumptions about retirement timing, some of the challenges embedded in the transition to retirement can be ameliorated. As people become more experienced in, more committed to, and potentially more valuable to their work, there need not be a push toward the exit. Let those who want or need to retire do so. For those who are still interested in and able to continue working, institutions should be pushed to find ways of offering options that allow the institutions and society to benefit from their experience. The point is not to say that doctors who are unfit to serve patients ought to continue practicing medicine. And it is important not to overlook the point that some types of work are less physically demanding and better suited to rewarding experience. Still, it is time that institutions and policy makers wake up to the fact that an increasingly large proportion of highly skilled individuals are approaching an age traditionally associated with stopping work, yet they still have quite a lot to offer and are potentially still interested in contributing. Recall that at the genesis of pension income systems, on average, people were meant to die before or right around the standard retirement age. Being respectful means removing assumptions that advanced age is equivalent to decreased productivity and effectiveness. After all, when Walter, the rural doctor in chapter 2, finally retired, it took two new doctors to fill his place.

Instead of assuming that people can't wait to stop working as they near the traditional retirement age, consider that some people may not want to stop working; others may want flexible work conditions. Regardless, all individuals should be part of the decision-making process regarding how they retire. Olivia Mitchell has explained that as the workforce ages, unresolved tensions emerge between governments who want to defer retirement and workers and employers who want to encourage early retirement.[37] Rules and social norms that link age with retirement deter both the personal and the public good. As a society, we are failing people who have the ability and desire to continue working by insisting that retirement is tied to age and that, in essence, workers come with an expiration date.

Notably, although many anecdotes suggest that the biggest regrets people report when they are faced with their own imminent death is that they worked too hard, I question whether the set of people I interviewed for this book would agree. I suspect that most would *not* regret having worked so hard. Instead, they may very well regret having retired too soon. Their regrets might be embedded in the ways that society let them go and fostered the sentiment that they should relinquish their life's work before they were entirely ready.

By including atypical participants who retired well under traditional retirement age (the elite athletes) and those who transitioned out of unpaid work experience (the homemakers), this book demonstrates that retirement is a subjective developmental transition with which a range of people identify. Use of the term *retirement* is persistent but not simplistic. Retirement is a complex personal transition and social phenomenon that for some ought to be decoupled from chronological age and traditional meanings that link it with the end of working life. Policies and benefits that mandate or create incentives to retire at a specific age are convenient but flawed.

The true challenge for aging societies is not that the proportion of older adults is increasing, but rather how age influences economic and social life.[38] Just as there are many ways to be productive, there are also many possible ways to be retired. The narratives in this book point to how we might better exploit retirement's ambiguity, and these narratives serve as a warning for people with a strong work identity that the phenomenon of retirement *is* ambiguous. These narratives should also be used to encourage employers and institutions to abandon ageist and anachronistic age-graded assumptions about productivity, vitality, and potential contributions.

Freidan wrote that "the only way for a woman, as for a man, to find herself, to know herself as a person, is by creative work of her own."[39] The experiences of the people I interviewed suggest that retirement can be a time to creatively recalibrate a sense of one's "life's work." It is perhaps best to let the individual discover his or her own best time to pursue this work.

Like a traveler who does not speak the language, the retiree can feel rudderless. Freedom and uncertainty greet them both. The maps are incomplete, the guideposts are often unintelligible. Let the narratives shared in this book warn us that it is best to allow the retiree to choose whether and how to engage with this exciting and unnerving new landscape.

Appendix A
Methodological Overview

The purpose of this book was to discover the social meaning of retirement as it pertains to people whose preretirement work was paramount to their sense of identity. Guided by the methodological approach of narrative gerontology, I used qualitative interviews to elicit the "big story" surrounding each person's transition into retirement.[1] I conducted multiple interviews with five doctors, five chief executive officers (CEOs), four athletes, five professors, and four homemakers, each of whom self-identified as retired. The participants featured in this book were drawn from one of a set of larger retirement studies I conducted over a five-year period.

In what follows, I detail my methodology, beginning with a quick note on qualitative inquiry that includes descriptions of both narrative gerontology and the life course perspective. Next, I explain my data collection method, including the general protocols I used across all of these semistructured interviews. I also discuss my analytic process, reflecting on my role as an interviewer and as a researcher. I close with additional details about the five larger retirement studies that I led between 2012 and 2016, which formed the basis from which the participants in this book were drawn.

METHODOLOGY

Qualitative research is an interpretative, naturalistic approach to understanding the meaning people bring to understanding different phenomena,[2] beginning with the assumption that this meaning matters. In his book, *Qualitative Inquiry and Research Design*, John Creswell outlines the close connection between researchers' worldviews and the methods they select to assemble and analyze their data.[3] In my case, that guiding worldview is constructivism, which asserts that individuals' perceptions of their experiences are constructed out of their reflections on those experiences. The approach includes an implicit assumption of multiple, subjective realities. It allows for unresolved contradiction within and across data. Given that my research goal was to shed light on the way retirement can be perceived by certain people, rather than to make broad, sweeping generalizations about retirees (or, for that matter, retirement), a narrative approach provided an ideal framework for collecting, analyzing, and interpreting lived experience.[4]

Narrative Gerontology

The field of gerontology places significance on the phenomena of later-life transitions. Kate de Medeiros' book, *Narrative Gerontology in Research and Practice*, provided the primary guidepost for the narrative approach I followed in this book. Narrative gerontology encourages the researcher to listen to people's stories, engage with them on multiple occasions, and discuss substantive issues directly with them.[5]

As Brian de Vries writes, "sometimes a story is more than a story."[6] Thus, in narrative gerontology, life stories are understood not as exact replicas of events that have transpired, but as narratives that weave together perceptions and interpretations of the individual's experience.

James Birren has referred to narrative gerontology as the ultimate "insider's view" into later-life human development.[7] It is an intuitive approach that assumes the primary way humans make meaning of experiences, relationships, phenomena, and life transitions, like retirement, is by sharing stories rather than discrete facts.[8] Such narratives are clearly shaped by cultural expectations and social norms; here, perceptions about retirement are formed by age-related retirement incentives, professional norms, and concepts like work–life balance.

Narrative gerontology also provided a basis for asking participants to share photos and objects that held meaning to them as a way to enhance my understanding of their lives.[9] Finally, it encouraged me to examine overlapping themes across participants and even professional subgroups to gain further insights about each participant's experiences with retirement.

The Life Course Perspective

The life course perspective has been used to suggest that people process normative expectations of age in the context of their own circumstances.[10] It has, at times, been referred to as a vanguard gerontological theory.[11] According to this perspective, life stories are a way that people describe what they think is most meaningful about their own lives.[12] The life course perspective posits that early experiences may affect life course trajectories and later-life transitions. The key interconnected principles of the life course perspective include developmental timing, historical time and place, human agency, and linked lives.[13] With regard to developmental timing, the life course perspective suggests that aging, developmental changes, and decisions people make are continuous processes shaped by an individual's changing personal history as well as social circumstances and historical factors. This means that work experiences earlier in life, as well as patterns that emerge after a person entered into work, influence retirement perceptions and experiences. Developmental timing matters because humans develop in biologically, socially, and psychologically meaningful ways over the life course, and the impact of a transition depends, in part, on one's expectations of the "appropriate" timing of those transitions.

A second principle, historical time and place, states that expectations emerge not only out of individual experience but also out of a person's interactions with broad economic and cultural expectations that reflect the historical time and place in which they occur.

Notwithstanding the importance of sociohistorical factors, people retain a level of human agency—a third principle recognized in life course research—that allows them to make choices that adapt to or react against their context. For example, research on the human agency principle suggests that women are more likely than men to forgo paid employment at various stages in the life course to raise children or to be a caregiver.

And, finally, a fourth principle looks at how the degree to which lives are linked (say, through marriage, social networks, or family relations) can influence a person's experiences and transitions into and out of each stage of the life course. Each of these four principles are interrelated so that we can come to understand the importance of later life transitions or outcomes as influenced by cumulative life experiences and as actively constructed phenomena.[14]

DATA COLLECTION METHODS

My primary method of data collection was in-depth, semistructured interviews, following a narrative approach that allowed participants to situate their responses within the context they believed to be most appropriate to their story.

Participant Recruitment

My first step was to identify the types of participants who would help me address my questions about the experience of retiring from work that was closely intertwined with personal identity. The two primary characteristics that formed the basis of my inclusion criteria were people who (1) self-identified as retired for approximately four years or longer and (2) had previously worked full-time as a doctor, a CEO, an elite athlete who had represented their country at an Olympic Games, a professor, or a homemaker. For practical purposes, I restricted my search to those who had oral fluency in English; this way, they would be telling their stories in familiar terms and I would sidestep the additional layer of interpretation (and the possibility of misinterpretation) that comes with translation. I initially recruited participants through professional contacts affiliated with relevant professional or social organizations. These contacts made potential interviewees aware of my research interest and helped them get in touch with me. Once I had a chance to ensure that they met my eligibility criteria and after obtaining their informed consent, we set up a time for an interview. Additional participants were recruited through snowball sampling, whereby participants I had interviewed previously passed my contact information to a peer.[15]

The final set of people whose stories are shared in this book was drawn from a larger sample of more than 100 interviews in five larger retirement studies I undertook. The names of all participants (and spouses or children) are pseudonyms, and I have changed identifying characteristics to protect the confidentiality of all individuals (as promised in the informed consent process).[16]

Interview Style and Setting

My interviews had a conversational style that featured the questions listed in Appendix B, Interview Guide. The order of the questions varied across participants; for some, certain questions were addressed during the first interview, whereas for others, I did not address these questions until the third interview. Although I had a fair number of questions and probes, my goal was always to speak as little as possible. I invited participants to share their stories in ways that drew from their earlier life experiences while focusing on their perceptions about retirement.

Each initial interview was conducted in-person either in my office, the participant's office, or at a place of their convenience. Some interviews took place in a coffee shop, hotel lobby, golf club, or similar semipublic setting. The majority of my interviews took place in Canada; some took place in the United States and Europe. Most follow-up interviews took place in similar settings to the initial interview and, on occasion, some were held at the participant's home, a park, or, in a few cases, via online video chat. Each interview was audio recorded and transcribed verbatim. Also, I took notes during each interview and immediately afterward used these notes to flesh out my records.

Interview Guide

My interview guide was informed by the life course theoretical perspective.[17] In keeping with traditional methods employed within narrative gerontology, my primary objective in each interview was to hear each participant's story. I strove to listen to their work and retirement experience, hear about their trajectory into their line of work, learn how they balanced work and life throughout adulthood (in the case of the homemakers, identify how they balanced the needs of their family with other personal interests), examine their initial retirement transition, and understand their perceptions of retirement.

In trying to study each participant's initial transition to retirement, I inquired about their retirement party, a topic worth discussing in further detail. Erdman Palmore, Linda George, and Robert Atchley, each notable scholars of "retirement," aptly note that ceremonies or parties to mark retirement are relatively poorly understood for their personal and social meanings.[18] I was additionally inspired by Joel Savishinsky's work regarding the ritual of the retirement party.[19] Savishinsky has described retirement as a culturally meaningful event that marks the passage from work to a new and unknown stage of life, opening the door for further inquiry into this important transition. In addition, other scholars have remarked on the significance of retirement as a rite of passage, warning that societies that fail to provide appropriate retirement rites may open themselves up to discontentment among those who enter the liminal state that retirement can embody.[20]

In addition to asking participants to describe their retirement parties, I also asked them to show me something from their life that was meaningful to them. I asked them to share a memento that they felt was symbolic of their life's work and gave the following examples: a family photo, an award, or a retirement gift. In explaining the mementos they had chosen, my participants provided broad reflections on the context of their retirement. Often, they took a narrative "detour" that was, nonetheless, instructive for my understanding of their experience. The mementos, in effect, helped participants step into narrative rather than a recitation of facts and dates.

Supplementary Research on Participants

Some of my participants were what one might consider to be high-profile individuals, and thus, information about their work legacy or retirement experience was available on the Internet. In certain cases, I supplemented my interview data with such information so that I could gain a better understanding of the significance of a participant's work or retirement. For example, I was able to obtain media perspectives of certain CEOs' work and retirement stories from news articles. I watched the athletes' performances and obtained information about their Olympic performances and other athletic competitions online. I also read online reviews of several doctors and professors I interviewed; and, in some cases, read articles they published.

ANALYSIS OF THE DATA

My analytic process followed a method often invoked in narrative gerontology and by story analysts from a range of disciplines.[21] I listened to the audio recordings of my interviews, and after the files were transcribed, I spent a good deal of time reviewing my notes and reading each transcript. After I familiarized myself with the interviews, I applied analytic techniques as described in Kate de Medeiros' *Narrative Gerontology*,[22] as well as a set of coding techniques developed by Matthew Miles and Michael Huberman[23] and described by Johnny Saldaña in his book *The Coding Manual for Qualitative Researchers*.[24]

I coded each transcript beginning with an open-ended code sheet in which I created initial (first-level) codes that corresponded to responses to questions I had asked each participant over the course of approximately three interviews. Next, I created timelines that described each participant's career trajectory: their entry into their life's work, major life events (such as moving away from their parents, starting college or university, marriages, having children, starting professional careers, marital affairs, divorces, remarriage, career changes, having children move out of the house, changes in health, having grandchildren, and experiencing the death of a partner or friend), and other significant developments in their retirement transition. Figure A.1 presents a simplified example based on a participant whose story was not shared in this book, which gives a basic sense of my process as I homed in on participants' stories.[25]

Then I conducted a second round of coding in which I created categories that corresponded to groups of codes among participants within each type of work and that later revealed relevant themes. For example, a set of codes emerged that described being a doctor as someone who shares a strong sense of *camaraderie* with other doctors, a shared sense that you are *always working* and always *needing to be the best*, and retirement as *giving up something very important* and *potentially letting others down.* These led to a category that included terms like "alliance" and "disappointment" and that I ultimately combined to form the theme "Renegade Retirement."

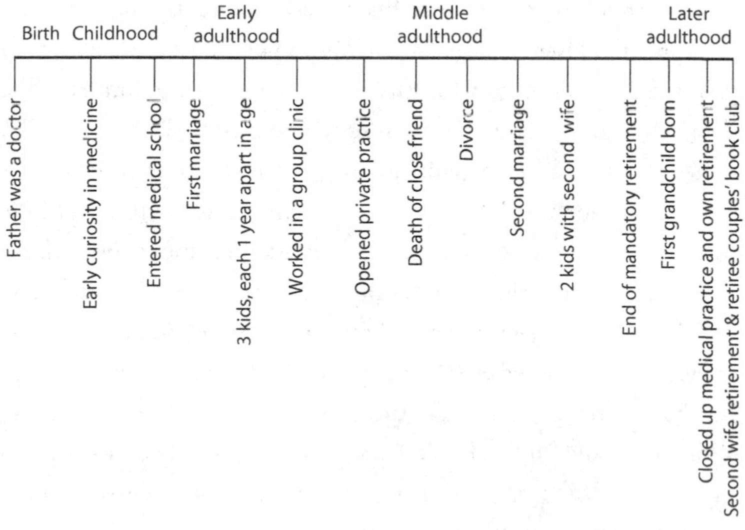

FIGURE A.1 Example of a Career Trajectory Timeline

The patterns that emerged from my analysis were based firmly in the descriptions provided by participants. Most of the time, the analysis followed a chronological order and was centered around the participant's retirement experience. My goal was to weave relationships between their work experiences and retirement transitions with things they shared about their life outside of work. Whenever possible, I included quotes and then reworked each story in a way that aimed to respect the confidentiality of each participant.

Finally, I searched across the five work types to identify commonalities and differences. Each participant had a distinct experience, yet they shared the sentiment that retirement was a disappointment. These participants' experiences contrasted sharply with media portrayals of retirement as the epitome of contentment.

REFLECTIONS AS THE INTERVIEWER

The information presented in this book is inherently subject to my interpretation; therefore, it is important to be transparent about my positioning and potential bias, as well as how they can influence the data I collected, analyzed, and presented in this book.

Qualitative research requires that the researcher consider his or her "positionality."[26] I have spent an inordinate amount of time thinking about retirement, but my perceptions about the concept of retirement are influenced by my position in the life course and my personal connection to my father's retirement. In my interviews, I rarely shared details about my life; still, I must be mindful that my professional title and physical traits were not hidden. When I worked on this book, I was in my mid- to late-30s, a point in life when the prospect of my own retirement seemed distant. I was several decades younger than most of the people I interviewed for this book, with the exception of the athletes, some of whom were close in age with me and one was almost two decades younger than me.

Because interviews are a form of discourse and necessarily imply interaction, these facets of my experience and position are relevant. As Brian de Vries explains, "something that is spoken or heard affects both speaker and listener."[27] Just as I was cognizant of the differences between my stage in life and those of my interviewees, I also had to be mindful of my earlier exposure to retirement and how it inspired me to undertake this project. As I described in the preface, I closed my father's medical practice after he was diagnosed with dementia and was unable to process his own retirement. Because he could not fully understand the implications of what was happening, it is very likely that his retirement left a deeper impression on me than it might have otherwise. His retirement predisposed me to see retirement as a significant and challenging life transition.

After my initial set of interviews, I did not seek out people to reinterview who had easy retirement experiences. Instead, I chose to dig deeper into the experiences of those who struggled, those who experienced a sense of discontentment. In reflecting on this practice, I am mindful of Laura Carstensen's socioemotional selectivity theory, which suggests that as a person's time horizon shrinks, he or she tends to emotionally invest in more favorable and meaningful goals and activities.[28] Carstensen's work on the positivity effect suggests that my interests in and perceptions of participants' retirement may be more negatively biased than if I were more experienced or facing a shorter time horizon. In trying to access the thoughts and feelings of participants, or in trying to put myself in their shoes, at many times, I had to be mindful of my ability and desire to participate in the paid workforce. In particular, when I interviewed the homemakers, I was highly aware that I came of age in an era when public perceptions about homemaking as a vocation had shifted dramatically from the time each of the women I interviewed had come of age.

It is also important to point out that the men and women who shared their stories with me enjoyed relatively good health at the point I interviewed them. In addition, I focused heavily on participants' relatively early experiences with retirement. Thus, my data in this book capture a snapshot of their retirement perceptions, which may have enhanced their feelings of discontentment. Both socio-emotional selectivity theory and the positivity effect suggest that these negative reactions may fade over time. Perhaps as they grapple with declining health or face their mortality, they might become less focused on career and more inclined to view life without work as a favorable stage. As Robert Atkinson has pointed out, the interviewer never quite knows how the story will end.[29]

Another concern is that the questions I asked may have served as a limiting factor, restricting the range of responses participants shared, and additionally participants may be selective about what they choose to share, either implicitly or explicitly.[30] For example, recall bias, in which a participant's recollections of earlier events are colored by inaccuracy or incompleteness, is a concern often mentioned in retrospective research on health and aging. In addition, social desirability bias, that is, the idea that people react differently because they know their story is being recorded, might cause the participant to select and focus on what they believe is most compelling.[31] The rapport between the participant and the interviewer also matters. In reviewing my notes, for example, I observed that in a few interviews, it took until the second or third interview for participants to candidly discuss what might be considered more personal matters. And although participants were willing to disclose and discuss personal information (such as their extramarital affairs, faking interest in a partner to preserve stability at home to focus on their work ambitions, or career terminations that were publicly presented as retirements), it is possible that participants were inhibited in other ways because of their concerns about my inability to relate to their situations or how I might judge their responses.

One last note on the subjectivity of interview data: My sample was made up of people who were willing to engage and share their stories. Each individual was socially connected with professional or community organizations, making them inherently different from more isolated, marginalized, or less socially connected people.[32]

In many ways, I see each of these concerns as a part of the beauty of narrative research; we hear what participants opt to tell us from those who are willing to talk. I only hope that what transpired is meaningful to others in ways that help the reader inspired to adopt a retirement strategy that might avoid some of the feelings of discontentment shared throughout this book.

THE FIVE LARGER STUDIES

To provide further context to my methodology, I also share additional details about the five larger studies I led between 2012 and 2016. These studies formed the initial pool from which I recruited individuals for this book project.

The Retired Doctors

In 2014, I began interviewing retired doctors in conjunction with a project focused on working doctors' perceptions about retirement.[33] With the help of professionals affiliated with medical organizations and associations in Canada, the United Kingdom, and the United States, I recruited retired men and women from a range of medical specialties and geographic settings. After our interviews, the doctors I interviewed passed on my contact information to other retired doctors. In total, I met with twenty-one retired doctors who had practiced in a total of five different countries: Australia, Canada, England, France, and the United States. In this larger sample, the average age of participants was 65 years old at the time of our first interview. Participants had been retired for approximately four years, and eleven of the people I interviewed were women.

The Retired CEOs

In early 2015, I was contacted by a retired CEO who had heard me give a talk on working doctors' aversion to retirement. I subsequently connected with a network of people affiliated with organizations that created social networking opportunities for retired CEOs. These contacts helped me connect with men and women who had worked as a CEO in the health-care sector by making announcements at events, using word of mouth, and providing potential participants with information about my study. In total, I conducted interviews with twenty-six retired health-care CEOs who had work experience in nine different countries: Australia, Canada, England, Germany, Ireland, Kuwait, Qatar, the United States, and United Arab Emirates. The majority resided in Canada at the time of their interview. The average age was 68 years old at the time of our first interview. Participants had identified as retired for four years or longer, and seven of the initial participants were women.

The Retired Elite Athletes

I began to study retired elite athletes after the 2015 Pan American Games in Toronto, Canada. I connected with experts in the field of sports and recreation to identify a set of organizations working with retired athletes. In consultation with these experts, I decided to focus on people who had represented their country in an Olympic Games and had been retired four years or more (to maximize the possibility that participants had actually ended their athletic careers). These experts helped me recruit through announcements at international sport summits and through communication with coaches or managers from a set of Olympic sport organizations. In total, twenty-four retired elite athletes completed an initial interview with me. These participants represented one of twelve countries at an Olympic Games: Argentina, Australia, Brazil, Canada, Denmark, France, Great Britain, Kenya, Japan, Poland, Russia, and the United States. They had each competed in one of twelve different sports: artistic gymnastics, diving, football, hockey, judo, kayaking, rowing, rhythmic gymnastics, running, skiing, speed skating, and swimming. In the study sample, the average age of participants was 46 years old at the time of my interview; and twelve were women.

The Retired Professors

Beginning in the spring of 2015, I interviewed retired professors recruited in conjunction with workshop announcements, conferences, and continuous learning opportunities affiliated with academic organizations. In total, I conducted interviews with twenty-five retired professors who had worked in ten different academic fields or disciplines: anthropology, biology, business, engineering, English literature, geography, health sciences, musicology, political science, and sociology. Participants resided in eight countries: Australia, Canada, Columbia, France, Germany, Great Britain, Spain, and the United States. The average age of participants was 76 years old at the time of my interview. Participants self-identified as retired for four years or longer, and fifteen of the original participants were women.

The Retired Homemakers

Between 2012 and 2013, I recruited self-identified homemakers who were over 50 years old through a set of community organizations, senior centers, and targeted social organizations. I determined eligibility by inviting each woman to choose from a limited set of work status categories (working, retired, or "other"; unemployed, disabled, or volunteer worker) and to describe their prior work. My original set of retired homemakers included eighteen women who all resided in Toronto, Canada, at the time I interviewed them. Five of these women were born in a country other than Canada, and their average age was 71 years old. Although I did not include gender as an eligibility requirement, this group was entirely composed of women.[34]

Appendix B
Interview Guide

THE RETIREMENT PROJECT, MICHELLE PANNOR SILVER,
PRINCIPAL INVESTIGATOR

I typically started interviews by thanking the participant and saying something similar to the following: "My goal is to listen as much as possible. I want to hear your story. I have a few questions that I may ask to guide the conversation, which you may or may not want to answer—that is up to you. I want to remind you that we can stop at any time."

The following questions reflect the types of issues I raised (questions that I asked only of the homemakers are bracketed); typically, I addressed these questions over the course of three interviews:

1. Tell me your story from the earliest days that you can remember so that I can understand your trajectory from your life's work into retirement.

2. How did your path lead to where you are now? How did you first realize you wanted to be a _____? [How did your path in life lead to becoming a homemaker?] What role, if any, did your parents or the family you grew up in play in influencing the type of work you did?

3. How did you balance work and life outside of work? [How did you balance your duties at home and outside interests?] If you have family, can you tell me about your family? How did you meet your spouse or life partner? How many children or grandchildren do you have? Can you tell me about your relationship with your spouse, partner, or children (if relevant)?

4. Did you have any gaps in your career? Or were you not working for any periods of time for health or other reasons? Did you travel much or take vacations throughout your life? [Did you have any health issues or other types of issues that interfered with your work at home?]

5. Have you had interruptions in your marriage or relationship with your partner?

6. Tell me more about your work. What was your typical work schedule like? What was the most rewarding aspect of your work? What strategies did you use to do well in your work? What was the hardest thing about your work?

7. Tell me about your transition to retirement. When did you retire? Why did you retire at that time? [What marked your transition to retirement? Why do you identify as being retired?] How did you plan your retirement?

8. Please tell me about your retirement party. What was it like? Did you enjoy it?

9. Tell me about the time after your retirement party. How did your life change in the time after your retirement party? [How did your life change once you retired?]

10. Can you show me something that is meaningful to you that can help me appreciate your work, your life outside of work, or your retirement? (It can be anything: a memento, a picture, an award, or even a photo on your phone of something along these lines.)

11. Tell me more about what retirement means to you. What are your perceptions of retirement? Have your perceptions of retirement changed now that you are retired?

12. Tell me about your typical schedule now that you are retired.

13. Is there anything else that you can share with me that seems relevant to understanding your work, family, or retirement experience?

14. Are there any questions you thought that I was going to ask you about retirement or thoughts on retirement that we haven't covered?

Acknowledgments

I am grateful to each of the participants who generously shared their time and stories with me, and to Eric Schwartz, who demonstrated true professionalism and encouragement at every stage of this process. Thank you to the anonymous reviewers; I am most grateful for their insight, support, and constructive feedback. Support from the Connaught Fund, the Mitacs Accelerate program, the University of Toronto Department of Medicine, and the University of Toronto Scarborough Campus Research Competitiveness Fund made projects relevant to this book possible.

I want to thank the following people for providing me with invaluable support at various career stages and/or for their contributions to this book at various stages along its journey: Lydia Sequeira, Letta Page, Anita Silver, Katie Dainty, Laurie Morrison, Clare Mitchell, Gillian Hawker, Frank Markel, Wendy Nelson, Mark Hundert, Victor Marshall, Bruce Kidd, Pedro Guedes, Scott McRoberts, Rhonda Cockerill, Adelstein Brown, Holly Wardlow, Paul Kingston, Michael Lambek, Patricia Landolt, Sarah Burns, Danielle Raimo, Mary Ann Mason, Kerwin Charles, C. Cybele Raver, Kathleen Cagney, Ariel Kalil, Robert Michaels, Linda Waite, Genaro Padilla, Lowell Frye, Ben Kolstad, Marielle T. Poss, Justine Evans, Zachary Friedman, Lisa Hamm, Joanne L. Raymond. I am so grateful to the following people for their support and inspiration in my life: Sarah Accomazzo, Jim Sussman, Richard Silver, Mary Ann O'Shea, Cindy Silver, Jake Silver, Trisha Freeman, Jenny Wilkson, Sasha and Heather Ross, Ascia Eskin, Tracy Fleischman Morgenthau, and Anna Greenberg. I especially want to acknowledge and thank David Pannor and especially Jane Pannor, who did the lion's share of the work when it came to dealing with the final stages of our dad's life. And a special thank you to Clayton Childress for enlightening me about books, and to Catherine Porter and Jessica Schmiedchen for their alternative title suggestions.

I also want to express special gratitude to my mother, the wonderful Joyce Sussman, who continues to teach me to love unconditionally and who gives me the strength to keep growing; my father, Harry Pannor, who taught me to love learning and whose retirement experience inspired my fascination with the topic; and my mother-in-law, Anita Silver for her love and willingness to read and edit an early version of this manuscript.

Finally, I want to acknowledge the eternal loves of my life Dan, Hannah, and Gabriel.

Notes

1. INTRODUCTION

1. See Freud 2002.
2. See Atchley 1976, 275. Atchley's work is also discussed in Kohli and Rein 1991.
3. By 2030, all baby boomers within the United States will have crossed into the traditional retirement age. Baby boomers are the American generation born between 1946 and 1964. In the United States alone, more than 79 million people belong to the baby boomer generation. For more statistics related to the retiring U.S. baby boomers, see Cohn and Taylor 2010.
4. See World Bank Group 2016a.
5. The statistic of adding three months per year is based on life expectancy data between 1840 and 2007; see National Institute on Aging, National Institutes of Health, and U.S. Department of Health and Human Service 2011.
6. For a rich discussion of retirement as lifestyle option, see Jones, Leontowitsch, and Higgs 2010.
7. See Klein 1971.
8. Although disengagement theory is now considered a historically important but essentially rejected theory of aging, it helps paint a picture of society's initial conception of retirement. For more on disengagement theory, see Cumming and Henry 1961; Cumming 1964. And for critiques on disengagement theory, see Achenbaum and Bengtson 1994; Hochschild 1975; Bengtson et al. 2009.
9. For a thorough history of pensions and retirement income systems, see Thane 2006; Graebner 1980.

10. The first U.S. Social Security retirement checks received by workers who had turned 65 were delivered in 1940 (at that time, the average life expectancy for men in the United States was 58 years).

11. In the early 1900s, public awareness of the dismal living conditions of some older adults created pressures to expand the policies to offer additional protections against extreme poverty for those who had eligible work experience. In roughly concurrent trends, industrialization caused the rupture of extended family supports as individuals moved to cities, and mass production eliminated many of the jobs that had remained open to older members of society. Authors such as Burgess have argued that the status of older adults decreased as they retreated from the paid labor force and that the aged were less connected to the twin supports of work and family. See Burgess 1960.

12. See Graebner 1980; Cowgill and Holmes 1972.

13. See Organisation for Economic Co-operation and Development (OECD) 2016.

14. See Levine 1988.

15. See Atchley 1982. In addition, much has been written about mandatory retirement and its implications; for example, see Yearwood-Lee 2006.

16. See Freedman 2008; Graebner 1980.

17. See McDonald and Donahue 2011.

18. For more on blended work, see van Yperen, Rietzschel, and De Jonge 2014. For a discussion of blended work as it relates to retirement, see Dropkin et al. 2016.

19. For a comprehensive understanding of professions, professionalization, professional work, and the system of professions, see Abbott 2014.

20. Stryker and Burke 2000, 284–297; see also Mead 1934.

21. See, for example, McCall and Simmons 1978.

22. Abrams and Hogg 1988.

23. Stryker 1980; Stryker and Burke 2000.

24. See Burke 1980.

25. See Ekerdt 1986.

26. Ekerdt 1986, 239.

27. See, for example, Ekerdt 2009; Ekerdt and Deviney 1990.

28. See Schellenberg 1994.

29. When retirement is defined as exiting the paid workforce and receiving a public pension.

30. Throughout Europe and North America, the Great Recession of 2008 increased the average retirement age in these economically developed regions of the world, when many people discovered that the investment portfolios they created for their retirement had suddenly diminished.

31. As per World Bank data on "Total Population for Age 65 and Above"; see World Bank Group 2016b.

32. The "third age" describes a time in life when healthy retirees in economically prosperous regions of the world enjoy their freedom unconstrained by obligations related to raising children or advancing at work; it occurs before the "fourth age" when ill-health and physical decline set in; see Laslett 1991. For an eloquent articulation of the range of opportunities open to retirees in the "third age," see Gilleard and Higgs 2000.

33. See Katz 2006. He has also articulated relevant critiques of the concept of successful aging and the promotion of agelessness in consumer societies; for example, see Katz 2013, Katz and Laliberte-Rudman 2004.

34. In many parts of the world, pension system managers and policy makers now find themselves in quite a different position from when pension income systems were first instituted, as they press for higher initial ages of eligibility for full benefits. For example, in 1986, the U.S. Congress passed legislation shifting Social Security's full-benefit retirement age from 65 to 66 years old for people born between 1943 and 1954, and it will gradually rise to age 67 for individuals born in 1960 and later. Early retirement benefits are available at age 62, but if an individual initiates Social Security benefits before the full-benefit retirement age, he or she will receive that lower benefit for the rest of his or her life.

35. See, for example Dennis and Thomas 2007; Powell 2010; Rupp, Vodanovich, and Crede 2006.

36. Older workers tend to have more highly developed skills, lower rates of absenteeism, and lower rates of turnover. For more on this, see Staudinger et al. 2016. Employers generally consider older workers to be more motivated, as articulated in Stamov-Roßnagel and Hertel 2010; Calo, Patterson, and Decker 2013. Other studies considered older workers to be more reliable, accurate, and committed to their work; see van Dalen, Henkens, and Schippers 2010.

37. The approach I took was largely informed by Kate de Medeiros's (2013) eloquent description of narrative gerontology. For more about narrative

gerontology and the methods I applied for the book, please see Appendix A, Methodological Overview.

38. See Appendix A for more on the life-course theoretical perspective and Appendix B for the interview guide I followed.

39. See Savishinsky 2000.

2. RENEGADE RETIREMENT AND THE GREEDY INSTITUTION

1. For more about sleep deprivation among doctors, see Eddy 2005.

2. Although research is limited on mothers who are doctors, the literature suggests that in other professions like academia, women tend to be penalized professionally for having children or they wait to have their babies at opportune times professionally; see, for instance, Mason and Goulden 2002; Armenti 2004.

3. For most patients, regardless of age, gender, or illness, family doctors are often the primary point of contact into the health-care system. These generalists are tasked with the diagnosis and prioritization of multiple clinical concerns and thus with sharing a wide scope of practice; see for example, Phillips and Haynes 2001.

4. Lewis Coser (1974) used the term "greedy institutions" to describe certain institutions that require total commitment from their members. These institutions enable the prioritization of institutional demands over participation in other nonwork spheres.

5. See for example, Shanafelt et al. 2013.

6. This point was articulated in Silver and Williams 2016.

7. Among the individuals who I interviewed, academic doctors seemed to have the most challenging transition to retirement. Doctors who go into academic medicine not only run a clinical practice and provide specialized care for patients but also are responsible for educating future doctors and conducting the research from which key medical decisions are made. These additional pressures, particularly the pressure to publish their research, can pose an additional barrier to retirement, creating additional layers of work identity that overshadow life outside of work; see Onyura 2015; Silver, Pang, and Williams 2015.

8. In Chapter 5, I describe in detail the concept of working in place—that is, experiencing retirement as less of a departure and more of a continuity with earlier professional aspirations.

9. See Miles 2004.

3. REFINED RETIREMENT AND FULFILLMENT EMPLOYMENT

1. See Katz 2006. Katz also has articulated concerns about what it means to age successfully and the implications of cultural imagery regarding mature adulthood in several of his other works, including Katz 2013; Katz and Marshall 2003.

2. Macro- and micro-level social processes have transformed what once was a status unavailable to the majority of older workers into a highly anticipated and often eagerly awaited stage of the life course. As the means of production shifted away from agriculture and the scale of enterprises grew, bureaucratic standardization of job entries and exits became a key component of labor force management; see Hardy 2011; Sass 2006.

3. See Rowe and Kahn 1987, 1997, and 1998.

4. For an engaging book on productive aging, see Morrow-Howell, Hinterlong, and Sherraden 2001. In specific, see the chapter written by Moody titled "Productive Aging and the Ideology of Old Age."

5. See Sonnenfeld 1991.

6. Although there is a larger body of research on forced retirement on athletes, as discussed in Chapter 4, evidence suggests that there are numerous negative implications associated with a forced retirement; for example, see Ebbinghaus and Radl, 2015; Szinovacz and Davey 2005; Wang, Henkens, and van Solinge 2011.

7. See Parsons 1942.

8. A well-cited example being Feldman 1994.

9. See Shultz 2003; Cahill, Giandrea, and Quinn 2015.

10. Previous research suggested that women found retirement less stressful because of weaker attachments in the paid labor force; see Tibbitts 1954.

11. See Catalyst Knowledge Centre 2017.

12. Along with wealth management strategies, these retreats sometimes included yoga, meditation, or other activities.

13. A vast array of literature is available on people from all income groups who derive a great deal of fulfillment from each of these; see, for instance, O'Brien 1981; Kremer 1985.

14. While Rowe and Kahn 1987, 1997, and 1998 are credited with coining the term "successful aging," Butler and Gleason (1985) can be credited with developing the concept of "productive aging." Butler and Brody (1995) initiated discussions about both concepts in an integrated way that have been continued in many academic discussions.

15. See, for instance, Anderson et al. 2014. For a discussion on volunteer work leading to longer lives, see Musick, Herzog, and House 1999.

16. During the "third age," people can enjoy a lifestyle that is not career dominated yet not isolated from the rest of society before the "fourth age" when dependency and decrepitude set in. Peter Laslett first articulated the "third age" in 1989; the concept was further elaborated upon by Chris Gilleard and Paul Higgs in several works; see Laslett 1989; Gilleard and Higgs 2002.

17. For a rich descriptive of the departure styles of CEOs and implications for retirement adjustment, see Sonnenfeld 1991.

18. See, for example, Martin, Nishikawa, and Williams 2009; Elmuti et al. 2003; Muller-Kahle and Schiehll 2013. Although not focused on women CEOs, a highly publicized study found that the inclusion of women on boards of directors had an influence on stock performance; see Adams and Ferreira 2009.

19. See Moen 2016.

4. EARLY RETIREMENT AND RESILIENCE

1. One of many well-told stories of incredible athletes whose careers were foreshortened by injury is that of Travis Roy, who was left paralyzed from the neck down eleven seconds into his first college hockey game; see Roy and Swift 1998. Much of the current research on osteoporosis and sarcopenia suggests that men and women achieve peak bone and muscle mass in their late 20s and early 30s, thus helping to explain why on average elite athletic careers end around this age; see Heaney et al. 2000.

2. See, for instance, Phoenix and Sparkes 2008; Ronkainen, Ryba, and Nesti 2013.

3. For more on sports and masculinity, and the ways sports socialize men, see Kidd 2013.

4. See Messner 1992.

5. See Adler and Adler 1989; for a systematic review of research on athletes' retirement see Park, Lavallee, and Tod 2013.

6. Numerous studies have been conducted to examine athletes' career transitions out of sport. See Park, Lavalee, & Tod, 2013; Baillie and Danish 1992; Wylleman, Alfermann, and Lavallee 2004; Crook and Robertson 1991. Recently, sports psychology textbooks have begun to include sections on

career transitions in sport. For examples, see Lavallee and Andersen 2000, 249–260; Wylleman et al. 2007, 233–247; Lavallee, Golby, and Lavallee 2002, 184–197.

7. Lavallee found that elite athletes tend to resist or be averse to career transition intervention programs because of the perception that it would be a distraction from their sport performance or signal a lack of focus on current goals; see Lavallee 2005.

8. See Park, Lavallee, and Tod 2013.

9. For more on the amateur athlete in relation to the Olympic Games, see Young 2008.

10. For more on the relationship among sports, masculinity, aging, and physical activity with age, see Tulle 2008; Vertinsky 2002; Phoenix, Faulkner, and Sparkes 2005.

5. LATE RETIREMENT AND WORKING IN PLACE

1. University contracts for faculty members tend to stipulate protection of a tenured professor's academic freedom by guaranteeing an indefinite appointment, which can be terminated only under extraordinary conditions; see European University Institute 2017.

2. Dr. Larry Summers, former president of Harvard University and director of the U.S. National Economic Council, among other prestigious titles, is of one of many scholars who have argued these and similar points; see for example, de Vise 2011.

3. Much has been written about aging in place; see, for example, Wiles et al. 2012;Dupuis-Blanchard, Neufeld, and Strang 2009.

4. The World Health Organization (2017) published a key strategy to facilitate the inclusion of older people to make our world more age-friendly.

5. For more on the concept of person-environment fit, see Lawton 1982, 33–59; 1990, 287–309.

6. This concept also suggests that broad policy decisions about health-care services and infrastructure, from the national level down to the regional level, directly affect the personal lives of older people, particularly as we become frail.

7. See van Yperen, Rietzschel, and De Jonge 2014; Dropkin et al. 2016.

8. For some of Atchley's relevant work see Atchley 1975, 1976, 1993, 1999.

6. UNDEFINED RETIREMENT AND THE RETIREMENT MYSTIQUE

1. Historically and most typically, homemakers are women; hence, I use the term "housewife" synonymously with homemaker. That said, it is possible for men to identify as a homemaker and evidence suggests that more men are entering into this role as the number of women who work full time increases; see, for example, Robertson and Verschelden 1993. For an in-depth study of homemakers, see Andre 1981.
2. See Gladwell 2008.
3. See Spence and Lonner 1971.
4. Electroconvulsive therapy (ECT) is also known as electroshock therapy or shock treatment. It involved a series of electrically induced shocks and is used as treatment for a psychiatric treatment for relief from a range of mental disorders, including major depression and anxiety.
5. Theresa was referring to the "Marital Rating Scale" which included a series of questions in checklist form about the duties a good wife or husband ought to complete developed by George W. Crane in 1939.
6. See Friedan 1993.
7. See Friedan 1963.
8. See Friedan 1963, 15–32.
9. Role captivity has been most notably used to describe the unwanted situation that caregivers find themselves in when they feel obligated to care for someone else and end up captive in that role; see Aneshensel, Pearlin, and Schuler 1993; Pearlin 2010.
10. Evidence suggests that Margaret is not alone in preferring not to identify as a widow. For eloquent and insightful work on widowhood, see van den Hoonaard 2006.
11. See hooks 2000.
12. See Silver 2010.
13. For evidence of the limited inclusion of wives in retirement studies, see Gratton and Haug 1983; Slevin and Wingrove 1995.
14. See Calasanti 2004; Price 2003.

7. CONCLUSION

1. As cited in Trafford 2004.
2. For a discussion of anomie and the cause and effects of weakening group ties on the individual, see Durkheim 1984, 1979. Note that

The Division of Labour in Society was originally published in 1893 and *Suicide* in 1897.

3. Much has been written on challenges associated with retirement for people in poor health; for examples, see McDonald and Donahue 2000; Disney, Emmerson, and Wakefield 2006; Markides 1993; Gallo et al. 2000.

4. Wang and Shi 2014; Shultz, Morton, and Weckerle 1998.

5. For some of Robert Atchely's prolific work on retirement and the stages of adjustment to retirement, see Atchley 1975, 1976, 1982.

6. See Turner 1979, 94.

7. See Polkinghorne 1988.

8. See Hershenson 2016.

9. As discussed at the end of Chapter 2, here I am referring to the concept of "greedy institutions," which suggests that some institutions require total commitment from their members, thus enabling the prioritization of work demands over participation in other nonwork spheres; see Coser 1974.

10. See Sontag 1972.

11. For more on the challenges associated with retirement from sport, see Tinley 2015; Kerr and Dacyshyn 2000.

12. For example, see Sinclair and Orlick 1993; Coakley 2015.

13. For more about continuing to work in retirement or "bridge employment," see, for example, Kim and Feldman 2000; Wang et al. 2008.

14. See Atchley 1989, 1993.

15. Betty Friedan's (1963) book challenged widely shared beliefs about women's roles, and was often claimed to have brought about a second wave of feminism.

16. See van den Hoonaard 1997.

17. Findings support the idea that participating in the paid labor force may have been a protective factor with regard to self-assessed well-being; see Silver 2010.

18. See Ebaugh 1988.

19. For further support of this point, see Price and Joo 2005; Szinovacz 2003; Moen and Roehling 2005.

20. See for example, van den Hoonaard 2015; Price 2003.

21. Exceptions include countries like Austria, Finland, France, Germany, Ireland, Italy, Luxembourg, and Portugal were pension benefits take into account the period of time in which a person is engaged in childcare; see Monticone 2008.

22. A broad perspective of the history of women's work is provided in Tilly and Scott 1987. For more on women's retirement, see Price and Nesteruk 2010; Loretto and Vickerstaff 2015.
23. See Friedan 1963, 15–32.
24. See Sargeant 2006; Ekerdt and Deviney 1990.
25. See Ekerdt 2010, Maestas 2010 has argued in favor of the term "unretirement", and McDonald and Donahue 2011 have suggested that retirement has been "lost".
26. See Laslett 1991. Christopher Gilleard and Paul Higgs (2000) eloquently articulate the range of opportunities open to retirees in the third age in their book.
27. See Savishinsky 2000.
28. See Savishinsky 2000.
29. See Weiss 2005.
30. See Freedman 2008.
31. See Freedman 2011.
32. See Lawrence-Lightfoot 2009.
33. See Schlossberg 2009.
34. See Farrell 2014.
35. See Moen 2016.
36. For more on this, see for example, Kohli et al. 1991.
37. See, for example, Lusardi and Mitchell 2007.
38. See Carney and Gray 2015 for a discussion on societal challenges surrounding retirement.
39. See Friedan 1963, 472.

APPENDIX A. METHODOLOGICAL OVERVIEW

1. de Medeiros (2013, 108) provides an indispensable description of narrative gerontology in her book. Other important work on narrative gerontology include Kenyon, Clark, and de Vries 2001; Birren et al. 1996.
2. See Denzin and Lincoln 2011.
3. See Creswell 2007.
4. Creswell 2007.
5. See Clandinin and Connelly 2000. They explain that participants are often actively involved in the process of learning about the phenomena or life experience being studied.

6. See de Vries 2015, 338.

7. See Birren et al. 1996.

8. In addition to the important work by de Medeiros, several authors have described storytelling and narratives as fundamental to our nature as humans; see Gold 2002; Gubrium and Holstein 1998; Holstein and Gubrium, 2011; McAdams 1993.

9. See de Medeiros 2005; Kenyon, Clark, and de Vries 2001. Both works have explained that narrative gerontology can be applied in a way that allows people to make connections between cultural artifacts and personal experiences.

10. See Elder 1994; Marshall and Mueller 2003; Ekerdt 2004; George 1993; Moen 1996, 2011.

11. For some of the prominent literature from authors who have referred to the life course perspective as a vanguard gerontological theory, see Alley et al. 2010; McDonald and Donahue 2011.

12. See Linde 1993; Chase 2003.

13. See Giele and Elder 1998.

14. Holstein and Gubrium 2000.

15. My recruitment procedures followed Patton 1990 and Creswell 2007.

16. I received ethical approval from the University of Toronto Research Ethics Board.

17. See Appendix B, Interview Guide for a detailed list of questions

18. See Atchley 1976, 1980; George 1980; Palmore, Fillenbaum, and George, 1984.

19. See Savishinsky 1995, 2000.

20. For example, Nancy Foner warns of inadequately marking this important transition; see Foner 1984; Myerhoff 1980.

21. This process can most essentially be described as collecting stories and then conducting an analysis of them; see de Medeiros 2013; Atkinson and Delamont 2006.

22. See de Medeiros 2013.

23. See Miles and Huberman 1994.

24. See Saldaña 2015.

25. See Riessman 2008.

26. See Finlay 2002.

27. See de Vries 2015, 338.

28. For more on socioemotional selectivity theory, see Carstensen 1992; Carstensen, Fung, and Charles, 2003; Carstensen, Isaacowitz, and Charles 1999.

29. See Atkinson 1995.
30. See, for example, the following, which outline important strengths as well as limitations in qualitative research to consider: Maxwell 2012; Lincoln and Guba 1985.
31. See Given 2008.
32. See, for instance, the following important works on retirement and isolation: Wenger et al. 1996; Nicholson 2012.
33. See the following for some of the work I have published on working doctors' perceptions about retirement: Silver 2016a; Silver and Easty 2017; Silver, Hamilton, Biswas, and Warrick 2016; Silver, Hamilton, Biswas, and Williams 2016; Silver, Pang, and Williams 2015; Silver and Williams 2016.
34. See Silver 2016b.

References

Abbott, Andrew. *The System of Professions: An Essay on the Division of Expert Labor.* Chicago: University of Chicago Press, 2014.

Abrams, Dominic, and Michael A. Hogg. *Social Identifications: A Social Psychology of Intergroup Relations and Group Processes.* London: Routledge, 1988.

Achenbaum, W. Andrew, and Vern L. Bengtson. "Re-engaging the Disengagement Theory of Aging: On the History and Assessment of Theory Development in Gerontology." *The Gerontologist* 34, no. 6 (1994): 756–763.

Adams, Renée B., and Daniel Ferreira. "Women in the Boardroom and Their Impact on Governance and Performance." *Journal of Financial Economics* 94, no. 2 (2009): 291–309.

Adler, Patricia A., and Peter Adler. "The Gloried Self: The Aggrandizement and the Constriction of Self." *Social Psychology Quarterly* 52, no. 4 (1989): 299–310.

Alley, Dawn E., Norella M. Putney, Melissa Rice, and Vern L. Bengtson. "The Increasing Use of Theory in Social Gerontology: 1990–2004." *Journals of Gerontology Series B: Psychological Sciences and Social Sciences* 65, no. 5 (2010): 583–590.

Anderson, Nicole D., Thecla Damianakis, Edeltraut Kröger, Laura M. Wagner, Deirdre R. Dawson, Malcolm A. Binns, Syrelle Bernstein, et al. "The Benefits Associated with Volunteering Among Seniors: A Critical Review and Recommendations for Future Research." *Psychological Bulletin* 140, no. 6 (2014): 1505–1533.

Andre, Rae. *Homemakers, the Forgotten Workers.* Chicago: University of Chicago Press, 1981.

Aneshensel, Carol S., Leonard I. Pearlin, and Roberleigh H. Schuler. "Stress, Role Captivity, and the Cessation of Caregiving." *Journal of Health and Social Behavior* 34, no. 1 (1993): 54–70.

Armenti, Carmen. "May Babies and Posttenure Babies: Maternal Decisions of Women Professors." *Review of Higher Education* 27, no. 2 (2004): 211–231.

Atchley, Robert C. "Adjustment to Loss of Job at Retirement." *International Journal of Aging and Human Development* 6, no. 1 (1975): 17–27.

——. *Continuity and Adaption in Aging: Creating Positive Experiences.* Baltimore, MD: John Hopkins University Press, 1999.

——. "Continuity Theory and the Evolution of Activity in Later Adulthood." In *Activity and Aging: Staying Involved in Later Life,* edited by John Robert Kelly, 5–16. Thousand Oaks, CA: Sage, 1993.

——. "A Continuity Theory of Normal Aging." *The Gerontologist* 29, no. 2 (1989): 183–190.

——. "Retirement as a Social Institution." *Annual Review of Sociology* 8, no. 1 (1982): 263–287.

——. *The Social Forces in Later Life: An Introduction to Social Gerontology.* Belmont, CA: Wadsworth, 1980.

——. *The Sociology of Retirement.* Cambridge, England: Halsted, 1976.

Atkinson, Paul, and Sara Delamont. "Rescuing Narrative from Qualitative Research." *Narrative Inquiry* 16, no. 1 (2006): 164–172.

Atkinson, Robert. *The Gift of Stories: Practical and Spiritual Applications of Autobiography, Life Stories, and Personal Mythmaking.* Westport, CT: Greenwood, 1995.

Baillie, Patrick, and Steven J. Danish. "Understanding the Career Transition of Athletes." *The Sport Psychologist* 6, no. 1 (1992): 77–98.

Bengtson, Vern L., Daphna Gans, Norella M. Putney, and Merril Silverstein. "Theories About Age and Aging." In *Handbook of Theories of Aging,* 2nd edition, edited by Vern Bengston et al., 3–23. New York: Springer, 2009.

Birren, James E., Gary M. Kenyon, Jan-Erik Ruth, Johannes J. F. Schroots, and Torbjorn Svensson. *Aging and Biography. Explorations in Adult Development.* New York: Springer, 1996.

Burgess, Ernest W. *Aging in Western Society.* Chicago: University of Chicago Press, 1960.

Burke, Peter J. "The Self: Measurement Requirements from an Interactionist Perspective." *Social Psychology Quarterly* 43, no. 1 (1980): 18–29.

Butler, Robert Neil, and Gleason, Herbert P. *Productive Aging.* New York: Springer, 1985.

Butler, Robert Neil, and Jacob A. Brody. *Delaying the Onset of Later-Life Dysfunction.* New York: Springer, 1995.

Cahill, Kevin, Michael D. Giandrea, and Joseph F. Quinn. "Retirement Patterns and the Macroeconomy, 1992–2010: The Prevalence and Determinants of Bridge Jobs, Phased Retirement, and Reentry Among Three Recent Cohorts of Older Americans." *The Gerontologist* 55, no. 3 (2015): 384–403.

Calasanti, Toni. "Feminist Gerontology and Old Men." *Journals of Gerontology Series B: Psychological Sciences and Social Sciences* 59, no. 6 (2004): S305–S314.

Calo, Thomas J., Meredith M. Patterson, and Wayne H. Decker. "Employee Perceptions of Older Workers' Motivation in Business, Academia, and Government." *International Journal of Business and Social Science* 4, no. 2 (2013): 1–10.

Carney, Gemma M., and Mia Gray. "Unmasking the 'Elderly Mystique': Why It Is Time to Make the Personal Political in Ageing Research." *Journal of Aging Studies* 35 (2015): 123–134.

Carstensen, Laura L. "Social and Emotional Patterns in Adulthood: Support for Socioemotional Selectivity Theory." *Psychology and Aging* 7, no. 3 (1992): 331–338.

Carstensen, Laura L., Helene H. Fung, and Susan T. Charles. "Socioemotional Selectivity Theory and the Regulation of Emotion in the Second Half of Life." *Motivation and Emotion* 27, no. 2 (2003): 103–123.

Carstensen, Laura L., Derek M. Isaacowitz, and Susan T. Charles. "Taking Time Seriously: A Theory of Socioemotional Selectivity." *American psychologist* 54, no.3 (1999): 165–181.

Catalyst Knowledge Centre. "Women CEOs of the S&P 500." *Catalyst Knowledge Centre.* 2017. http://catalyst.org/knowledge/women-ceos-fortune-1000.

Chase, Susan E. "Taking Narrative Seriously: Consequences for Method and Theory in Interview Studies." In *Turning Points in Qualitative Research: Tying Knots in a Handkerchief,* edited by Yvonna S. Lincoln and Norman K. Denzin, 273–298. Walnut Creek, CA: AltaMira, 2003.

Clandinin, D. Jean, and F. Michael Connelly. *Narrative Inquiry: Experience and Story in Qualitative Research.* San Francisco: Jossey-Bass, 2000.

Coakley, Jay. "Assessing the Sociology of Sport: On Cultural Sensibilities and the Great Sport Myth." *International Review for the Sociology of Sport* 50, no. 4–5 (2015): 402–406.

Cohn, D., and Paul Taylor. "Baby Boomers Approach 65–Glumly." *Pew Research Social and Demographic Trends.* Last modified December 20, 2010. http://www.pewsocialtrends.org/2010/12/20/baby-boomers-approach-65-glumly/.

Coser, Lewis. *Greedy Institutions: Patterns of Undivided Commitment.* New York: Free Press, 1974.

Cowgill, Donald Olen, and Lowell Don Holmes. *Aging and Modernization*. New York: Appleton-Century-Crofts and Fleschner, 1972.

Creswell, John W. *Qualitative Inquiry and Research Design: Choosing Among Five Approaches*. Thousand Oaks, CA: Sage, 2007.

Crook, Jan M., and Sharon E. Robertson. "Transitions Out of Elite Sport." *International Journal of Sport Psychology* 22, no. 2 (1991): 115–127.

Cumming, M. Elaine. "New Thoughts on the Theory of Disengagement." In *New Thoughts on Old Age*, edited by Robert Kastenbaum, 3–18. Berlin: Springer Berlin Heidelberg, 1964.

Cumming, Elaine, and William Earl Henry. *Growing Old: The Process of Disengagement*. New York: Basic Books, 1961.

de Medeiros, Kate. "The Complementary Self: Multiple Perspectives on the Aging Person." *Journal of Aging Studies* 19, no. 1 (2005): 1–13.

——. *Narrative Gerontology in Research and Practice*. New York: Springer, 2013.

de Vise, Daniel. "Larry Summers on Some of Higher Education's 'Bad Ideas.'" *Washington Post*. November 11, 2011. www.washingtonpost.com/blogs/college-inc/post/larry-summers-on-some-of-higher-educations-bad-ideas/2011/11/09/gIQAdFubCN_blog.html?utm_term=.387ffe673033.

de Vries, Brian. "Structuring the Insider's View: Narrative Gerontology in Research and Practice." *The Gerontologist* 55, no. 2 (2015): 337–338.

Dennis, Helen, and Kathryn Thomas. "Ageism in the Workplace." *Generations* 31, no. 1 (2007): 84–89.

Denzin, Norman K., and Yvonna S. Lincoln. *The Sage Handbook of Qualitative Research*. Los Angeles: Sage, 2011.

Disney, Richard, Carl Emmerson, and Matthew Wakefield. "Ill Health and Retirement in Britain: A Panel Data-Based Analysis." *Journal of Health Economics* 25, no. 4 (2006): 621–649.

Dropkin, Jonathan, Jacqueline Moline, Hyun Kim, and Judith E. Gold. "Blended Work as a Bridge Between Traditional Workplace Employment and Retirement: A Conceptual Review." *Work, Aging and Retirement* 2, no. 4 (2016): 373–383.

Dupuis-Blanchard, Suzanne, Anne Neufeld, and Vicki R. Strang. "The Significance of Social Engagement in Relocated Older Adults." *Qualitative Health Research* 19, no. 9 (2009): 1186–1195.

Durkheim, Émile. *The Division of Labour in Society*. Basingstoke, England: Macmillan, 1984.

——. *Suicide: A Study in Sociology*. New York: Free Press, 1979.

Ebaugh, Helen Rose Fuchs. *Becoming an Ex: The Process of Role Exit.* Chicago: University of Chicago Press, 1988.

Ebbinghaus, Bernhard, and Jonas Radl. "Pushed Out Prematurely? Comparing Objectively Forced Exits and Subjective Assessments of Involuntary Retirement Across Europe." *Research in Social Stratification and Mobility* 41 (2015): 115–130.

Eddy, Richard. "Sleep Deprivation Among Physicians." *British Columbia Medical Journal* 47, no. 4 (2005): 176–180.

Ekerdt, David J. "The Busy Ethic: Moral Continuity Between Work and Retirement." *The Gerontologist* 26, no. 3 (1986): 239–244.

——. "Born to Retire: The Foreshortened Life Course." *The Gerontologist* 44, no. 1 (2004): 3–9.

——. "Frontiers of Research on Work and Retirement." *Journals of Gerontology Series B: Psychological Sciences and Social Sciences* 65, no. 1 (2010): 69–80.

——. "Population Retirement Patterns." In *International Handbook of Population Aging*, edited by Peter Uhlenberg, 471–491. New York: Springer-Verlag, 2009.

Ekerdt, David J., and Stanley Deviney. "On Defining Persons as Retired." *Journal of Aging Studies* 4, no. 3 (1990): 211–229.

Elder Jr., Glen H. "Time, Human Agency, and Social Change: Perspectives on the Life Course." *Social Psychology Quarterly* 57, no. 1 (1994): 4–15.

Elmuti, Dean, Judith Lehman, Brandon Harmon, Xiaoyan Lu, Andrea Pape, Ren Zhang, and Terad Zimmerle. "Inequality Between Genders in the Executive Suite in Corporate America: Moral and Ethical Issues." *Equal Opportunities International* 22, no. 8 (2003): 1–19.

European University Institute. "USA, Academic Career Structure." *Academic Careers Observatory.* 2017. www.eui.eu/ProgrammesAndFellowships/AcademicCareers Observatory/AcademicCareersbyCountry/USA.aspx.

Farrell, Chris. *Unretirement: How Baby Boomers Are Changing the Way We Think About Work, Community, and the Good Life.* New York: Bloomsbury, 2014.

Feldman, Daniel. "The Decision to Retire Early: A Review and Conceptualization." *Academy of Management Review* 19, no. 2 (1994): 285–311.

Finlay, Linda. ""Outing" the Researcher: The Provenance, Process, and Practice of Reflexivity." *Qualitative Health Research* 12, no. 4 (2002): 531–545.

Foner, Nancy. *Ages in Conflict: A Cross-Cultural Perspective on Inequality Between Old and Young.* New York: Columbia University Press, 1984.

Freedman, Marc. *The Big Shift: Navigating the New Stage Beyond Midlife.* New York: Public Affairs, 2011.

——. *Prime Time: How Baby Boomers Will Revolutionize Retirement and Transform America.* New York: PublicAffairs, 2008.

Freud, Sigmund. *Civilization and Its Discontents.* London: Penguin UK, 2002.

Friedan, Betty. *The Feminine Mystique.* New York: Norton, 1963.

——. *Fountain of Age.* New York: Simon and Schuster, 1993.

Gallo, William T., Elizabeth H. Bradley, Michele Siegel, and Stanislav V. Kasl. "Health Effects of Involuntary Job Loss Among Older Workers: Findings from the Health and Retirement Survey." *Journals of Gerontology Series B: Psychological Sciences and Social Sciences* 55, no. 3 (2000): S131–S140.

George, Linda K. *Role Transitions in Later Life.* Monterey, CA: Brooks/Cole, 1980.

——. "Sociological Perspectives on Life Transitions." *Annual Review of Sociology* 19, no. 1 (1993): 353–373.

Giele, Janet Z., and Glen H. Elder, eds. *Methods of Life Course Research: Qualitative and Quantitative Approaches.* Thousand Oaks, CA: Sage, 1998.

Gilleard, Chris, and Paul Higgs. *Cultures of Ageing: Self, Citizen, and the Body.* Harlow, England: Pearson Education, 2000.

——. "The Third Age: Class, Cohort, or Generation." *Ageing and Society* 22, no. 3 (2002): 369–382.

Given, Lisa M., ed. *The Sage Encyclopedia of Qualitative Research Methods.* Thousand Oaks, CA: Sage, 2008.

Gladwell, Malcolm. *Outliers: The Story of Success.* London: Penguin Books, 2008.

Gold, Joseph. *The Story Species: Our Life-Literature Connection.* Markham, Toronto: Fitzhenry & Whiteside, 2002.

Graebner, William. *A History of Retirement: The Meaning and Function of an American Institution, 1885–1978.* New Haven, CT: Yale University Press, 1980.

Gratton, Brian, and Marie R. Haug. "Decision and Adaptation: Research on Female Retirement." *Research on Aging* 5, no. 1 (1983): 59–76.

Gubrium, Jaber F., and James A. Holstein. "Narrative Practice and the Coherence of Personal Stories." *Sociological Quarterly* 39, no. 1 (1998): 163–187.

Hardy, Melissa. "Rethinking Retirement." In *Handbook of Sociology of Aging*, edited by Richard A. Settersten, Jr., and Jacqueline L. Angel, 213–227. New York: Springer, 2011.

Heaney, R. P., S. Abrams, B. Dawson-Hughes, A. Looker, R. Marcus, V. Matkovic, and C. Weaver. "Peak Bone Mass." *Osteoporosis International* 11, no. 12 (2000): 985–1009.

Hershenson, David B. "Reconceptualizing Retirement: A Status-Based Approach." *Journal of Aging Studies* 38 (2016): 1–5.

Hochschild, Arlie Russell. "Disengagement Theory: A Critique and Proposal." *American Sociological Review* (1975): 553–569.

Holstein, James A., and Jaber F. Gubrium. *Constructing the Life Course*. Lanham, MD: Rowman & Littlefield, 2000.

Holstein, James A., and Jaber F. Gubrium, eds. *Varieties of Narrative Analysis*. Thousand Oaks, CA: Sage, 2011.

hooks, bell. *Feminist Theory: From Margin to Center*. Boston, MA: South End Press, 1984.

Jones, Ian Rees, Miranda Leontowitsch, and Paul Higgs. "The Experience of Retirement in Second Modernity: Generational Habitus Among Retired Senior Managers." *Sociology* 44, no. 1 (2010): 103–120.

Katz, Stephen. "Active and Successful Aging: Lifestyle as a Gerontological Idea." *Recherches sociologiques et anthropologiques* 44, no. 1 (2013): 33–49.

——. *Cultural Aging: Life Course, Lifestyle, and Senior Worlds*. Toronto: University of Toronto Press, 2006.

Katz, Stephen, and Debbie Laliberte-Rudman. "Exemplars of Retirement: Identity and Agency Between Lifestyle and Social Movement." In *Old Age and Agency*, edited by Emmanuelle Tulle, 45–65. New York: Nova Science, 2004.

Katz, Stephen, and Barbara Marshall. "New Sex for Old: Lifestyle, Consumerism, and the Ethics of Aging Well." *Marshall Journal of Aging Studies* 17, no. 1 (2003): 3–16.

Kenyon, Gary M., Phillip G. Clark, and Brian De Vries, eds. *Narrative Gerontology: Theory, Research, and Practice*. New York: Springer, 2001.

Kerr, Gretchen, and Anna Dacyshyn. "The Retirement Experiences of Elite, Female Gymnasts." *Journal of Applied Sport Psychology* 12, no. 2 (2000): 115–133.

Kidd, Bruce. "Sports and Masculinity." *Sport in Society* 16, no. 4 (2013): 553–564.

Kim, Seongsu, and Daniel C. Feldman. "Working in Retirement: The Antecedents of Bridge Employment and Its Consequences for Quality of Life in Retirement." *Academy of Management Journal* 43, no. 6 (2000): 1195–1210.

Klein, Ernest. *A Comprehensive Etymological Dictionary of the English Language*. Amsterdam: Elsevier Scientific, 1971.

Kohli, Martin, and Martin Rein. "The Changing Balance of Work and Retirement." In *Time for Retirement: Comparative Studies of Early Exit from the Labor Force*, edited by Martin Kohli, Martin Rein, Anne-Marie Guillemard, and Herman van Gunsteren, 1–35. Cambridge: Cambridge University Press, 1991.

Kohli, Martin, Martin Rein, Anne-Marie Guillemard, and Herman van Gunsteren, eds. *Time for Retirement: Comparative Studies of Early Exit from the Labor Force*. Cambridge: Cambridge University Press, 1991.

Kremer, Yael. "Predictors of Retirement Satisfaction: A Path Model." *International Journal of Aging and Human Development* 20, no. 2 (1985): 113–121.

Laslett, Peter. *A Fresh Map of Life: The Emergence of the Third Age.* Cambridge, MA: Harvard University Press, 1989

Lavallee, David. "The Effect of a Life Development Intervention on Sport Career Transition Adjustment." *The Sport Psychologist* 19, no. 2 (2005): 193–202.

Lavallee, David, and Mark B. Andersen. "Leaving Sport: Easier Career Transitions." In *Doing Sport Psychology*, edited by Mark B. Andersen, 249–260. Champaign, IL: Human Kinetics, 2000.

Lavallee, David, Jim Golby, and Ruth Lavallee. "Coping with Retirement from Professional Sport." In *Solutions in Sport Psychology*, edited by Ian M. Cockerill, 184–197. London: Thomson, 2002.

Lawrence-Lightfoot, Sara. *The Third Chapter: Passion, Risk, and Adventure in the 25 Years After 50.* New York: Sarah Crichton Books, 2009.

Lawton, Mortimer P. "Competence, Environmental Press, and the Adaption of Older People." In *Aging and the Environment: Theoretical Approaches*, edited by Mortimer P. Lawton, Paul G. Windley, and Thomas O Byerts, 33–59. New York: Springer, 1982.

——. "Knowledge Resources and Gaps in Housing for the Ages." In *Aging-in-Place: Supporting the Frail Elderly in Residential Environments*, edited by David Tilson, 287–309. Glenview, IL: Pearson Scott Foresman, 1990.

Levine, Martin Lyon. *Age Discrimination and the Mandatory Retirement Controversy.* Baltimore, MD: Johns Hopkins University Press, 1988.

Lincoln, Yvonna S., and Egon G. Guba. *Naturalistic Inquiry.* Vol. 75. Thousand Oaks, CA: Sage, 1985.

Linde, Charlotte. *Life Stories: The Creation of Coherence.* Oxford: Oxford University Press, 1993.

Loretto, Wendy, and Sarah Vickerstaff. "Gender, Age and Flexible Working in Later Life." *Work, Employment and Society* 29, no. 2 (2015): 233–249.

Lusardi, Annamaria, and Olivia S. Mitchell. "Baby Boomer Retirement Security: The Roles of Planning, Financial Literacy, and Housing Wealth." *Journal of Monetary Economics* 54, no. 1 (2007): 205–224.

Maestas, Nicole. "Back to Work Expectations and Realizations of Work After Retirement." *Journal of Human Resources* 45, no. 3 (2010): 718–748.

Markides, Kyriakos S. "Trends in Health of the Elderly in Western Societies." In *Age, Work and Social Security*, edited by Anthony Barnes Atkinson and Martin Rein, 3–16. New York: St. Martin's, 1993.

Marshall, Victor W., and Margaret M. Mueller. "Theoretical Roots of the Life-Course Perspective." In *Social Dynamics of the Life Course*, edited by Walter R. Heinz, 3–32. New York: Aldine de Gruyter, 2003.

Martin, Anna D., Takeshi Nishikawa, and Melissa A. Williams. "CEO Gender: Effects on Valuation and Risk." *Quarterly Journal of Finance and Accounting* 48, no. 3 (2009): 23–40.

Mason, Mary, and Marc Goulden. "Do Babies Matter?" *Academe* 88, no. 6 (2002): 21–27.

Maxwell, Joseph A. *Qualitative Research Design: An Interactive Approach.* Vol. 41. Thousand Oaks, CA: Sage, 2012.

McAdams, Dan P. *The Stories We Live By: Personal Myths and the Making of the Self.* New York: Guilford, 1993.

McCall, George J., and Jerry L. Simmons. *Identities and Interactions: An Examination of Human Associations in Everyday Life*, revised ed. New York: Free Press, 1978.

McDonald, Lynn, and Peter Donahue. "Poor Health and Retirement Income: The Canadian Case." *Ageing and Society* 20, no. 5 (2000): 493–522.

——. "Retirement Lost?" *Canadian Journal on Aging/La Revue canadienne du vieillissement* 30, no. 3 (2011): 401–422.

Mead, George Herbert. *Mind, Self and Society.* Vol. 111. Chicago: University of Chicago Press, 1934.

Messner, Michael A. *Power at Play: Sports and the Problem of Masculinity.* Boston: Beacon, 1992.

Miles, Matthew B., and A. Michael Huberman. *Qualitative Data Analysis: An Expanded Sourcebook.* Thousand Oaks, CA: Sage, 1994.

Miles, Steven. *The Hippocratic Oath and the Ethics of Medicine.* Oxford: Oxford University Press, 2004.

Moen, Phyllis. *Encore Adulthood: Boomers on the Edge of Risk, Renewal, and Purpose.* New York: Oxford University Press, 2016.

——. "A Life Course Approach to the Third Age." In *Gerontology in the Era of the Third Age: Implications and Next Steps*, edited by Dawn C. Carr and Kathrin Komp, 13–31. New York: Springer, 2011.

——. "A Life Course Perspective on Retirement, Gender, and Well-Being." *Journal of Occupational Health Psychology* 1, no. 2 (1996): 131–144.

Moen, Phyllis, and Patricia Roehling. *The Career Mystique: Cracks in the American Dream.* Lanham, MD: Rowman & Littlefield, 2005.

Monticone, Chiara, Anna Ruzik, and Justyna Skiba. "Women's Pension Rights and Survivors' Benefits: A Comparative Analysis of EU Member States and

Candidate Countries." *European Network of Economic Policy Research Institutes Research Report* No. 53. Brussels, Belgium: Centre for European Policy Studies, 2008.

Moody, Harry. "Productive Aging and the Ideology of Old Age." In *Productive Aging: Concepts and Challenges*, edited by Nancy Morrow-Howell, James Hinterlong, and Michael Sherraden, 185–196. Baltimore, MD: John Hopkins University Press, 2001.

Morrow–Howell, Nancy, James Hinterlong, and Michael Sherraden. *Productive Aging: Concepts and Challenges*. Baltimore, MD: John Hopkins University Press, 2001.

Muller-Kahle, Maureen, and Eduardo Schiehll. "Gaining the Ultimate Power Edge: Women in the Dual Role of CEO and Chair." *Leadership Quarterly* 24, no. 5 (2013): 666–679.

Musick, Marc A., Regula Herzog, and James S. House. "Volunteering and Mortality Among Older Adults: Findings from a National Sample." *Journals of Gerontology Series B, Psychological Sciences and Social Sciences* 54, no. 3 (1999): S173–S180.

Myerhoff, Barbara. *Number Our Days*. New York: Simon and Schuster, 1980.

National Institute on Aging, National Institutes of Health, and U.S. Department of Health and Human Service. "Global Health and Aging." *World Health Organization Report* (NIH Publication no. 11–7737). October 2011. http://www.who.int/ageing/publications/global_health.pdf.

Nicholson, Nicholas R. "A Review of Social Isolation: An Important but Underassessed Condition in Older Adults." *Journal of Primary Prevention* 33, no. 2–3 (2012): 137–152.

O'Brien, Gordon. "Leisure Attributes and Retirement Satisfaction." *Journal of Applied Psychology* 66, no. 3 (1981): 371–384.

Organisation for Economic Co-operation and Development. "Average Effective Age of Retirement in 1970–2014 in OECD Countries" *Ageing and Employment Policies—Statistics on Average Effective Age of Retirement*. Last modified 2017. http://www.oecd.org/.

——. "Labour Force Participation Rate." Last modified 2016. https://data.oecd.org/emp/labour-force-participation-rate.htm.

Onyura, Betty, John Bohnen, Don Wasylenki, Anna Jarvis, Barney Giblon, Robert Hyland, Ivan Silver, and Karen Leslie. "Reimagining the Self at Late-Career Transitions: How Identity Threat Influences Academic Physicians' Retirement Considerations." *Academic Medicine* 90, no. 6 (2015): 794–801.

Palmore, Erdman B., Gerda G. Fillenbaum, and Linda K. George. "Consequences of Retirement." *Journal of Gerontology* 39, no.1 (1984): 109–116.

Park, Sunghee, David Lavallee, and David Tod. "Athletes' Career Transition Out of Sport: A Systematic Review: 1." *International Review of Sport and Exercise Psychology* 6, no. 1 (2013): 22–53.

Parsons, Talcott. "Age and Sex in the Social Structure of the United States." *American Sociological Review* 7, no. 5 (1942): 604–616.

Patton, Michael Quinn. *Qualitative Evaluation and Research Methods.* Thousand Oaks, CA: Sage, 1990.

Pearlin, Leonard I. "The Life Course and the Stress Process: Some Conceptual Comparisons." *Journals of Gerontology Series B: Psychological Sciences and Social Sciences* 65, no. 2 (2010): 207–215.

Phillips, William, and Deborah Haynes. "The Domain of Family Practice: Scope, Role, and Function." *Family Medicine* 33, no. 4 (2001): 273–277.

Phoenix, Cassandra, and Andrew C. Sparkes. "Athletic Bodies and Aging in Context: The Narrative Construction of Experienced and Anticipated Selves in Time." *Journal of Aging Studies* 22, no. 3 (2008): 211–221.

Phoenix, Cassie, Guy Faulkner, and Andrew C. Sparkes. "Athletic Identity and Self-Ageing: The Dilemma of Exclusivity." *Psychology of Sport and Exercise* 6, no. 3 (2005): 335–347.

Polkinghorne, Donald E. *Narrative Knowing and the Human Sciences.* Albany: State University of New York Press, 1988.

Powell, Mebane. "Ageism and Abuse in the Workplace: A New Frontier." *Journal of Gerontological Social Work* 53, no. 7 (2010): 654–658.

Price, Christine A. "Professional Women's Retirement Adjustment: The Experience of Reestablishing Order." *Journal of Aging Studies* 17, no. 3 (2003): 341–355.

Price, Christine A., and Eunjee Joo. "Exploring the Relationship Between Marital Status and Women's Retirement Satisfaction." *International Journal of Aging and Human Development* 61, no. 1 (2005): 37–55.

Price, Christine A., and Olena Nesteruk. "Creating Retirement Paths: Examples from the Lives of Women." *Journal of Women and Aging* 22, no. 2 (2010): 136–149.

Riessman, Catherine Kohler. *Narrative Methods for the Human Sciences.* Thousand Oaks, CA: Sage, 2008.

Robertson, John M., and Cia Verschelden. "Voluntary Male Homemakers and Female Providers: Reported Experiences and Perceived Social Reactions." *Journal of Men's Studies* 1, no. 4 (1993): 383–402.

Ronkainen, Noora J., Tatiana V. Ryba, and Mark S. Nesti. " 'The Engine Just Started Coughing!'—Limits of Physical Performance, Aging and Career Continuity in Elite Endurance Sports." *Journal of Aging Studies* 27, no. 4 (2013): 387–397.

Rowe, John, and Robert Kahn. Human Aging: Usual and Successful. *Science* 237 (1987): 143–149.

Rowe, John, and Robert Kahn. Successful Aging. *The Gerontologist* 37 no. 4 (1997): 433–440.

Rowe, John, and Robert Kahn. *Successful Aging.* New York: Random House, 1998.

Roy, Travis, and E. M. Swift. *Eleven Seconds: A Story of Tragedy, Courage and Triumph.* New York: Warner Books, 1998.

Rupp, Deborah E., Stephen J. Vodanovich, and Marcus Crede. "Age Bias in the Workplace: The Impact of Ageism and Causal Attributions." *Journal of Applied Social Psychology* 36, no. 6 (2006): 1337–1364.

Saldaña, Johnny. *The Coding Manual for Qualitative Researchers.* Thousand Oaks, CA: Sage, 2015.

Sargeant, Malcolm. *Age Discrimination in Employment.* Hampshire, England: Gower Publishing, 2006.

Sass, Steven. "The Development of Employer Retirement Income Plans: From the Nineteenth Century to 1980." In *The Oxford Handbook of Pensions and Retirement Income*, edited by G. L. Clark, A. H. Munnell, and J. M. Orszag, 76–97. Oxford: Oxford University Press, 2006.

Savishinsky, Joel. *Breaking the Watch: The Meanings of Retirement in America.* New York: Cornell University Press, 2000.

——. "The Unbearable Lightness of Retirement: Ritual and Support in a Modem Life Passage." *Research on Aging* 17, no. 3 (1995): 243–259.

Schellenberg, Grant. *The Road to Retirement: Demographic and Economic Changes in the 90s.* Ottawa: Canadian Council on Social, 1994.

Schlossberg, Nancy K. *Revitalizing Retirement: Reshaping Your Identity, Relationships, and Purpose.* Washington, DC: American Psychological Association, 2009.

Shanafelt, Tait D., Sonja L. Boone, Lotte N. Dyrbye, Michael R. Oreskovich, Litjen Tan, Colin P. West, Daniel V. Satele, Jeff A. Sloan, and Wayne M. Sotile. "The Medical Marriage: A National Survey of the Spouses/Partners of US Physicians." *Mayo Clinic Proceedings* 88, no. 3 (2013): 216–225.

Shultz, Kenneth. "Bridge Employment: Work After Retirement." In *Retirement: Reasons, Processes, and Results,* edited by Gary A. Adams and Terry A. Beehr, 214–241. New York: Springer, 2003.

Shultz, Kenneth S., Kelly R. Morton, and Joelle R. Weckerle. "The Influence of Push and Pull Factors on Voluntary and Involuntary Early Retirees' Retirement Decision and Adjustment." *Journal of Vocational Behavior* 53, no. 1 (1998): 45–57.

Silver, Michelle Pannor. "Critical Reflection on Physician Retirement." *Canadian Family Physician* 62, no. 10 (2016b): 783–784.

——. "An Inquiry into Self-Identification with Retirement." *Journal of Women and Aging* 28, no. 6 (2016a): 477–488.

——. "Women's Retirement and Self-Assessed Well-Being: An Analysis of Three Measures of Well-Being Among Recent and Long-Term Retirees Relative to Homemakers." *Women and Health* 50, no. 1 (2010): 1–19.

Silver, Michelle Pannor, and Laura K. Easty. "Planning for Retirement from Medicine: A Mixed-Methods Study." *CMAJ Open* 5, no. 1 (2017): E123 129. doi:10.9778/cmajo.20160133

Silver, Michelle Pannor, Angela D. Hamilton, Aviroop Biswas, and Natalie Irene Warrick. "A Systematic Review of Physician Retirement Planning." *Human Resources for Health* 14, no. 67 (2016): 1–16.

Silver, Michelle Pannor, A. D. Hamilton, A. Biswas, and S. A. Williams. "Life After Medicine: A Systematic Review of Studies of Physicians' Adjustment to Retirement." *Archives Community Medicine and Public Health* 1, no. 1 (2016): 26–32.

Silver, Michelle Pannor, N. Celeste Pang, and Sarah A. Williams. " 'Why Give Up Something That Works So Well?' A Preliminary Investigation of Retirement Expectations Among Academic Physicians." *Educational Gerontology* 41, no. 5 (2015): 333–347.

Silver, Michelle Pannor, and Sarah A. Williams. "Reluctance to Retire: A Qualitative Study on Work Identity, Intergenerational Conflict, and Retirement in Academic Medicine." *The Gerontologist* 58, no. 2 (2018): 320–330.

Sinclair, Dana A., and Terry Orlick. "Positive Transitions from High-Performance Sport." *The Sport Psychologist* 7, no. 2 (1993): 138–150.

Slevin, Kathleen F., and C. Wingrove. "Women in Retirement: A Review and Critique of Empirical Research Since 1976." *Sociological Inquiry* 65, no. 1 (1995): 1–21.

Sonnenfeld, Jeffrey. *The Hero's Farewell: What Happens When CEOs Retire.* New York: Oxford University Press, 1991.

Sontag, Susan. "Double Standard of Aging." *The Saturday Review*, September 23, 1972, 29–38.

Spence, Donald, and Thomas Lonner. "The 'Empty Nest': A Transition Within Motherhood." *Family Coordinator* 20, no. 4 (1971): 369–375.

Stamov-Roßnagel, Christian, and Guido Hertel. "Older Workers' Motivation: Against the Myth of General Decline." *Management Decision* 48, no. 6 (2010): 894–906.

Staudinger, Ursula M., Ruth Finkelstein, Esteban Calvo, and Kavita Sivaramakrishnan. "A Global View on the Effects of Work on Health in Later Life." *The Gerontologist* 56, no. Suppl. 2 (2016): S281–S292.

Stryker, Sheldon. *Symbolic Interactionism: A Social Structural Version.* Menlo Park, CA: Benjamin/Cummings, 1980.

Stryker, Sheldon, and Peter J. Burke. "The Past, Present, and Future of an Identity Theory." *Social Psychology Quarterly* 63, no. 4 (2000): 284–297.

Szinovacz, Maximiliane E. "Contexts and Pathways: Retirement as Institution, Process, and Experience." In *Retirement: Reasons, Processes, and Results*, edited by Gary A. Adams and Terry A. Beehr, 6–52. New York: Springer, 2003.

Szinovacz, Maximiliane E., and Adam Davey. "Predictors of Perceptions of Involuntary Retirement." *The Gerontologist* 45, no. 1 (2005): 36–47.

Thane, Patricia. "The History of Retirement." *The Oxford Handbook of Pensions and Retirement Income*, edited by Gordon L. Clark, Alicia H. Munnell, and J. Michael Orszag, 33–51. Oxford: Oxford University Press, 2006.

Tibbitts, Clark. "Retirement Problems in American Society." *American Journal of Sociology* 59, no. 4 (1954): 301–308.

Tilly, Louise A., and Joan Wallach Scott. *Women, Work, and Family.* New York: Holt, Rinehart and Winston, 1987.

Tinley, Scott. *Racing the Sunset: How Athletes Survive, Thrive, or Fail in Life After Sport.* New York City: Skyhorse, 2015.

Trafford, Abigail. *My Time: Making the Most of the Rest of Your Life.* New York: Basic Books, 2004.

Tulle, Emmanuelle. "The Ageing Body and the Ontology of Ageing: Athletic Competence in Later Life." *Body and Society* 14, no. 3 (2008): 1–19.

Turner, Victor Witter. *Process, Performance, and Pilgrimage: A Study in Comparative Symbology.* Vol. 1. New Delhi: Concept Publishing, 1979.

van Dalen, Hendrik P., Kène Henkens, and Joop Schippers. "Productivity of Older Workers: Perceptions of Employers and Employees." *Population and Development Review* 36, no. 2 (2010): 309–330.

van den Hoonaard, Deborah Kestin. "Constructing the Boundaries of Retirement for Baby—Boomer Women: Like Turning Off the Tap, or Is It?" *Qualitative Sociology Review* 11, no. 3 (2015): 41–58.

——. "Identity Foreclosure: Women's Experiences of Widowhood as Expressed in Autobiographical Accounts." *Ageing and Society* 17, no. 5 (1997): 533–551.

——. *The Widowed Self: The Older Woman's Journey Through Widowhood.* Waterloo, ON: Wilfrid Laurier University Press, 2006.

van Yperen, Nico W., Eric F. Rietzschel, and Kiki M. M. De Jonge. "Blended Working: For Whom It May (Not) Work." *Plos One* 9, no. 7 (2014): e102921.

Vertinsky, Patricia. "Sporting Women in the Public Gaze: Shattering the Master Narrative of Aging Female Bodies." *Canadian Woman Studies* 21, no. 3 (2002): 58–63.

Wang, Mo, K. Henkens, and Hanna van Solinge. "Retirement Adjustment: A Review of Theoretical and Empirical Advancements." *American Psychologist* 66, no. 3 (2011): 204–213.

Wang, Mo, and Junqi Shi. "Psychological Research on Retirement." *Annual Review of Psychology* 65 (2014): 209–233.

Wang, Mo, Yujie Zhan, Songqi Liu, and Kenneth S. Shultz. "Antecedents of Bridge Employment: A Longitudinal Investigation." *Journal of Applied Psychology* 93, no. 4 (2008): 818–830.

Weiss, Robert Stuart. *The Experience of Retirement.* New York: Cornell University Press, 2005.

Wenger, G. Clare, Richard Davies, Said Shahtahmasebi, and Anne Scott. "Social Isolation and Loneliness in Old Age: Review and Model Refinement." *Ageing and Society* 16, no. 3 (1996): 333–358.

Wiles, Janine L., Annette Leibing, Nancy Guberman, Jeanne Reeve, and Ruth E S Allen. "The Meaning of 'Aging in Place' to Older People." *The Gerontologist* 52, no. 3 (2012): 357–366.

World Bank Group. "Life Expectancy at Birth, Male (Years)." *World Bank Data.* Last modified 2016a. http://data.worldbank.org/indicator/SP.DYN.LE00.MA.IN.

——. "Total Population for Age 65 and Above (Only 2005 and 2010) (In Number of People)." *World Bank Data.* Last modified 2016b. https://data.worldbank.org/indicator/SP.POP.65UP.TO.

World Health Organization. "Towards an Age-Friendly World." *Aging and Life-Course.* 2017. www.who.int./ageing/age-friendly-world/en.

Wylleman, Paul, Dortothee Alfermann, and David Lavallee. "Career Transitions in Sport: European Perspectives." *Psychology of Sport and Exercise* 5, no. 1 (2004): 7–20.

Wylleman, Paul, P. de Knop, Marie-Christine Verdet, and S. Cecic Erpic. "Parenting and Career Transitions of Elite Athletes." In *Social Psychology in Sports*, edited by Sophia Jowett and David Lavallee, 233–247. Champaign, IL: Human Kinetics, 2007.

Yearwood-Lee, Emily. *Mandatory Retirement.* Victoria: Legislative Library of British Columbia, 2006.

Young, David C. *A Brief History of the Olympic Games.* Malden, MA: Wiley, 2008.

Index

Page numbers in italics indicate figures.

allegiance to colleagues, 25–27

Allison (retired athlete), 16–17, 92; chronic pain of, 97; discontentment for, 96–97; financial planning for, 98; identity of, 100; at Olympic Games, 93, 94, 96; physical ailments for, 97, 98–99, 101; postretirement work for, 98, 100; retirement party for, 96; retirement planning for, 93, 95–96; retirement status of, 99–100, 101; retirement travel for, 96; sense of purpose for, 16, 93, 95, 96–97, 100; support network for, 124–125; training for, 93–95; unstructured schedule for, 98; working mother of, 98

Amna (retired homemaker), 164; family life of, 184–185; husband retirement for, 187–189; identification as retired for, 187–189; identity for, 186; routine of, 188; unstructured schedule for, 184, 187–189; volunteer work of, 185–186, 189

anomie, 196

Atchley, Robert, 2, 223; continuity theory of, 160, 207; on retirement stages, 199

athletes, 92. *See also* elite athletes

Atkinson, Robert, 228; on analytic process, 249*n21*

average retirement age, 2; life expectancy and, 10–11, *11*; for men, 10

baby boomer generation, 2, 12–13, 214, 239*n3*; women in retirement and, 210

Betty (retired homemaker), 18, 164; aging perceptions of, 170–171; early life of, 165–166, 170–171; empty-nest syndrome of, 168; financial worries of, 170; forced retirement of husband of, 168–169; identification as retired for, 165, 168–170; multiple roles for, 165; retirement of husband impacting, 169–170; role of women for, 165–166; social life of, 171; tasks of, 167–168; 10,000 thousand hour theory and, 167

Birren, James, on retirement, 6; on narrative gerontology, 219

Bismarck, Otto von, 5

blended work, 7; professors and, 17, 159; selection bias and, 8; work-related interest and, 8–9

Bob (retired CEO), 16, 58; discontentment of, 73–74; on firing, 71; identity of, 73; infidelity analogy for, 73; non-work interests of, 71–72; personal fulfillment for, 74; postretirement work for, 74; retirement parties for, 72; retirement planning for, 72; role theory and, 75; travel in retirement for, 72–73, 88; wounded vet analogy for, 70

Breaking the Watch (Savishinsky), 212

bridge employment, 75, 206

busy ethic, 10

calling, 9, 14–15, 180; 210

Canada, 231; Great Recession in, 241*n30*; interviews in, 222, 230, 232;

43–44; discontentment for, 42; domestic help outsourced by, 37–38; identity of, 36, 37–38, 39; infidelity and, 38, 39–40, 41, 43, 54; lifestyle of, 36; non-work interests for, 37, 42, 43–44; outsourcing domestic help for, 37–38; regrets in retirement for, 42; retirement activities for, 43; retirement party for, 40–41; retirement planning for, 35–36, 38–39, 41, 44; sleep anxiety for, 42; unstructured schedule of, 41–42, 43; as working mother, 36–37, 38, 39, 42, 43

widow, 164; Margaret as, 182–183, 184; Robert as a widower, 44

women, role of, 19, 82, 220; baby boomer generation and, 210; Betty on, 165–166; as CEOs, 75; cultural norms and, 190; as doctors during motherhood, 242n2; domestic duties for Grace and, 149–150; feminist revolution and, 79; fertility rates and, 13; financial planning and, 80, 132–133; happy housewife heroine concept and, 178–179, 190, 191, 193, 211; having it all and, 37; identity foreclosure and, 208; Margaret on changing, 180–181; outsourcing domestic help

and, 37–38, 78–79; paid laborers compared to homemakers for, 193, 208–209, 210, 243n10; pension income system and, 210; physical appearance and, 40, 78, 83, 170–171, 203–204; postpartum depression and, 173; professorship and gender tensions for, 131–132, 149–150, 154; retirement and, 75; retirement mystique and, 190, 208–211; Sontag on age and, 203; Theresa questioning, 174–175; wage gap and, 208, 210; work-life balance and, 77–79. See also homemakers; working mother

work identity: academic doctors and, 242n7; athletes and, 92; CEOs and, 16, 57; personal identity and, 75, 159; retirement and, 9, 14, 16

working in place, 242n8; for David, 157; for Grace, 152–154, 160; professors, 128, 158–161, 206–208; for Robert, 54–55; sense of purpose and, 145; for Tomas, 145

working mother: Allison having, 98; Elizabeth as, 58, 77–79, 81; Grace as, 148–149, 153–154; Wendy as, 36–37, 38, 39, 42, 43. See also homemakers

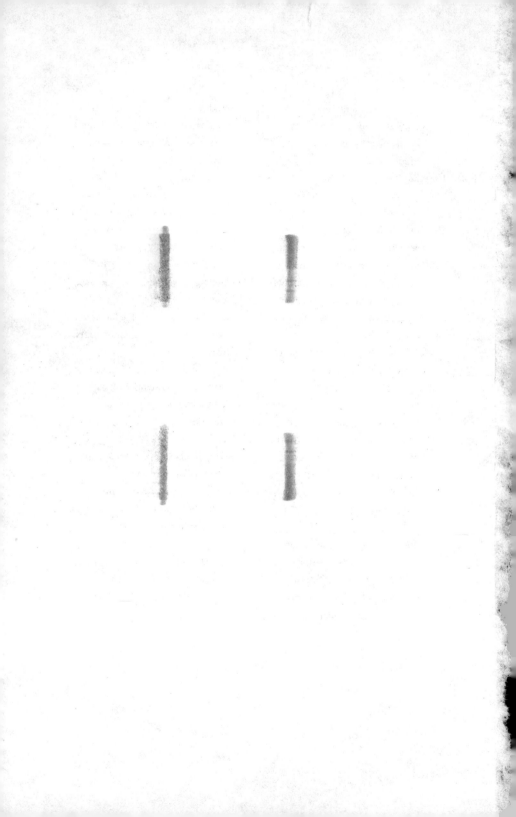